Praise for *My New Mac*

"Highly recommended for newbies and switchers."
—MACWORLD

"Wallace Wang has hit the nail on the head . . . some people just learn better and faster by doing projects rather than trying to stay awake doing tedious lessons."
—INFOWORLD

"Clearly written projects that will instantly net you more from your Mac."
—MAC.NZ

"Wang's book is a fine text, written with knowledge and wit."
—CERTFORUMS.CO.UK

"A 'must' for any brand new to the Mac system."
—THE MIDWEST BOOK REVIEW

Topazlabs.com

My New™ Mac
Snow Leopard Edition

54 Simple Projects to Get You Started

WALLACE WANG

7120
000 439-120 - 006908 · 789718 · 504990
-000439- 120120·006908 - 789718~
504990~

no starch press

MY NEW MAC, SNOW LEOPARD EDITION. Copyright © 2009 by Wallace Wang

13 12 11 10 09   2 3 4 5 6 7 8 9

ISBN-10: 1-59327-209-X

ISBN-13: 978-1-59327-209-8

Publisher: William Pollock

Production Editor: Magnolia Molcan

Cover and Interior Design: Octopod Studios

Developmental Editor: William Pollock

Technical Reviewer: Tyler Ortman

Copyeditor: Magnolia Molcan

Compositor: Riley Hoffman

Proofreader: Philip Dangler

Indexer: Karin Arrigoni

For information on book distributors or translations, please contact No Starch Press, Inc. directly:

No Starch Press, Inc.

555 De Haro Street, Suite 250, San Francisco, CA 94107

phone: 415.863.9900; fax: 415.863.9950; info@nostarch.com; http://www.nostarch.com/

The Library of Congress has cataloged the first edition as follows:

```
Wang, Wally.
  My new Mac : 52 simple projects to get you started / Wallace Wang.
      p. cm.
  Includes index.
  ISBN-13: 978-1-59327-164-0
  ISBN-10: 1-59327-164-6
  1. Mac OS.  2. Operating systems (Computers)  3. Macintosh (Computer)--Programming.  I. Title.
QA76.76.063W365173 2008
005.4'4682--dc22
                                    2008003640
```

Dedication

This book is dedicated to everyone who has ever felt frustrated when trying to use a computer. Welcome to the Macintosh. Though you may still run into problems no matter what type of computer you use, problems on a Macintosh will appear far less frequently than on any other type of computer. Get ready—you may soon experience trouble-free computing.

Acknowledgments

This book owes its life to Bill Pollock, the publisher at No Starch Press, who pretty much lets me write about anything I want, as long as he thinks there's a market for it. Thanks also go to Megan Dunchak and Magnolia Molcan for keeping this entire project together, Riley Hoffman for laying it out, and Rickford Grant and Tyler Ortman for making sure everything I wrote actually made sense and really worked.

Additional thanks also go to Jack Dunning at ComputorEdge Online (*http://www.computoredge.com/*) for giving me a weekly Macintosh column where I can spout off about anything I want, just as long as it's not advocating the overthrow of the government or using language unsuitable for children's eyes. And more thanks go to Monish Bhatia for giving me a chance to write Macintosh hardware and software reviews for MacNN (*http://www.macnn.com/*), one of the best little sites on the Internet for tracking the latest Apple news and rumors.

I'd also like to thank all the people I've met during my 17-year career as a stand-up comedian: Steve Schirripa (who appeared on HBO's hit show *The Sopranos*) and Don Learned for giving me my first break performing in Las Vegas at the Riviera Hotel & Casino, Russ Rivas, Dobie "The Uranus King" Maxwell, Doug James, Darrell Joyce, and Leo "The Man, the Myth, the Legend" Fontaine.

I'd also like to thank my former radio comedy co-hosts from the year we spent on 103.7 FreeFM in San Diego: Drizz, Rick Gene, Justin Davis, and Dane Henderson. We may not have always known what we were doing, but every night was a complete blast until the radio station switched to an all-music format and kicked us off the air.

Finally, I'd like to acknowledge my wife, Cassandra, my son, Jordan, and my three cats, Bo, Scraps, and Nuit, for putting up with all my time spent sitting in front of the computer instead of doing anything else. These three cats enjoy sleeping next to my Macintosh for the heat that it generates, so they're constantly hovering around my keyboard and getting in the way.

Brief Contents

Part 5: Maintaining Your Macintosh

Contents in Detail

Introduction

Most people don't care how their computer works; they just want to use it. Tell the average person how to give commands to his computer's operating system and his eyes will glaze over with boredom. But tell that same person how to have fun and do something useful with his computer and his eyes will light up immediately.

That's why this is a different kind of computer book. Instead of babbling about every possible feature and command and then hoping that you'll find an actual use for that information, this book teaches you how to do something fun and useful with your Macintosh right away.

With most computers, the biggest problem is just getting them to work. With a Macintosh, the biggest problem is figuring out all the different ways you can put your computer to work for you. People often use a Macintosh for years just to write letters or send email and then suddenly discover that they could have also been using that Macintosh to organize and edit photos, watch DVDs, or make their own audio CDs containing their favorite songs.

The whole purpose of this book is to teach you how to get the most out of your Macintosh without having to buy a single extra thing. If you already know how to use a different type of computer, you'll find that your Macintosh works in similar ways. If you're new to computers altogether, you'll find that the Macintosh can be a friendly, forgiving, and fun tool that will make you wonder why anybody in their right mind would ever want to use a different type of computer. No matter what your experience with computers may be, you'll soon learn that the Macintosh comes loaded with dozens of neat programs and tools for making your life easier. This book will show you how to use them.

This book won't just teach you how to use your Macintosh; it will teach you how to use your Macintosh to make your life easier without having to become a computer expert. After all, you probably bought a Macintosh because you wanted a computer that works for you, not the other way around.

Understanding Computer Terms

If you're already familiar with computers, you can skip this section. If you aren't comfortable using a computer, take the time to learn some common terms that you'll see in this book. Basically, using a computer involves the computer displaying information on the screen and waiting for you to select from a limited number of choices. Depending on your selection, the computer then displays new information and waits for you to choose another option.

To use a computer, you need to know how to decipher the options the computer displays and how to tell the computer what your selection is.

Telling the Computer What to Do

With a desktop Macintosh, you control the computer using a mouse. The two main functions of the mouse are:

▶ Pointing

▶ Clicking

Pointing simply means using the mouse to move the pointer on the screen. The two main purposes for pointing include:

▶ Choosing a command

▶ Selecting something, such as text or a picture that you want to modify

Once you point to something on the screen, the computer won't do anything until you click the mouse.

Pointing and clicking are the main ways to tell the computer what to do. However, there are five ways you can click the mouse:

▶ **Clicking**   This means pressing the mouse button once and releasing it. Clicking often selects a command or moves the cursor to a new location.

▶ **Double-clicking**   This means pressing the mouse button twice in rapid succession. Double-clicking is most often used to select a file and open it.

▶ **Dragging**   This means holding down the mouse button and moving the mouse. Dragging is often used to move items from one location to another or to select two or more items, such as several words in a paragraph.

▶ **Clicking and holding**   This means holding down the mouse button without moving it. Clicking and holding on an icon on the Dock displays a menu.

▶ **Right-clicking**   This means either holding down the CTRL key and clicking the left mouse button or clicking the right mouse button (on a mouse that has two buttons). Right-clicking typically displays a menu of additional commands from which you can choose.

With a laptop Macintosh, you control the computer using a trackpad. With older laptop models, you use a trackpad with a single button. With newer laptop models, the trackpad acts like a giant button and allows multitouch finger gestures. Table 1 lists ways of clicking, double-clicking, dragging, clicking and holding, and right-clicking with a mouse or a trackpad.

Table 1: Using a Mouse or Trackpad

Device	Click	Double-Click	Drag	Click and Hold	Right-Click
Standard two-button mouse	Press and release the left mouse button	Press and release the left mouse button twice in rapid succession	Hold down the left mouse button while moving the mouse	Hold down the left mouse button	Press and release the right mouse button
Trackpad with a button	Press and release the trackpad button	Press and release the trackpad button twice in rapid succession	Hold down the trackpad button while sliding your finger across the trackpad	Hold down the trackpad button	Hold down the CTRL key then press and release the trackpad button
Trackpad without a button	Press and release anywhere on the trackpad with one finger	Press and release anywhere on the trackpad with one finger twice in rapid succession	Press and hold down the trackpad with one finger while sliding that finger across the trackpad	Press and hold down the trackpad with one finger	Press and release anywhere on the trackpad with two fingers

Finding a Command

Your Macintosh displays lists of available commands in menus. The top of every Macintosh screen contains a *menu bar*, which organizes related commands into categories with names such as *File*, *Edit*, or *View*, as shown in Figure 1.

✳ **NOTE:** The menu bar always displays the name of the active program, which is the program that will accept input from the keyboard. The menu bar changes every time you switch to a different program, such as from iPhoto to the Safari web browser.

Before you use some pull-down menu commands, you may need to tell your Macintosh what

FIGURE 1: *The menu bar at the top of the screen lists related commands in pull-down menus.*

you want to modify by pointing to and selecting an item (such as dragging the mouse to select several words). After you've selected what to modify, you can choose a menu command.

As an alternative to pull-down menus, you can also use *pop-up menus*, which appear when you point at an item and right-click the mouse. Pop-up menus simply display the most common commands you might use on the selected item. So if you right-click a picture, you'll see a different pop-up menu than if you right-click a folder, as shown in Figure 2.

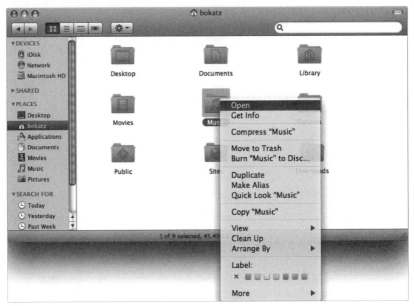

FIGURE 2: *Pop-up menus display a short list of commands to modify the item to which the mouse currently points.*

When you choose some menu commands, such as Cut, your Macintosh immediately obeys. However, some menu commands may require more information. For example, if you choose the Print command, your Macintosh has no idea which printer you want to use or how many pages you want to print. When the Macintosh needs more information after you choose a command, it displays a list of additional options in a small window called a *dialog*, as shown in Figure 3.

Dialogs often display one or more of the following options:

▶ **Radio button**   Lets you choose from one of out of many available options

▶ **Checkbox**   Lets you turn on (or off) certain options

▶ **Text box**   Lets you type information, such as a number

▶ **Pop-up menu**   Displays a list of valid options you can choose

▶ **Button**   Displays a command you can choose by clicking it

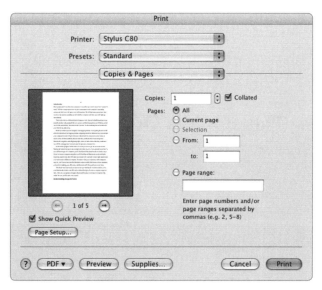

FIGURE 3: *A dialog provides additional options to define how your Macintosh should follow a menu command.*

Most dialogs also display at least two buttons. One button is labeled *Cancel* and appears white. The second is highlighted in blue and is the default button. It has a label specific to the dialog, such as *Print*, *OK*, or *Save*.

Clicking the Cancel button (or pressing the ESC key) makes the dialog go away and tells your Macintosh, "Oops, I changed my mind and I don't want you to do anything right now."

Clicking the blue default button (or pressing the RETURN key) tells your Macintosh, "See all the options I picked in the dialog? Use those options and obey my command."

Using the Keyboard

Most of the time, you'll use the mouse to control your Macintosh and use your keyboard to type numbers and letters. However, you can also use the keyboard to use pull-down menus. This can be handy in case your mouse isn't working or you don't want to take your fingers away from the keyboard.

To access the pull-down menus with the keyboard, follow these steps:

1. Press CTRL-F2. (Hold down the CTRL key, press the F2 key, and then let go of both keys). This highlights the Apple menu.
2. Press the left and right arrow keys to highlight a different menu title, such as File or Edit.
3. Press the down arrow key or press RETURN to view a pull-down menu.
4. Press the up and down arrow keys to highlight a command on a pull-down menu.

5. Press RETURN to choose a command (or press ESC to exit out of the pull-down menus without choosing anything).

Once you understand the basics for using the mouse and keyboard, you're ready to start using your Macintosh.

How This Book Is Organized

To help you get started doing something useful right away with your Macintosh, this book is divided into short projects that act like recipes in a cookbook. Each project states a common problem you may face when using a computer, explains how your Macintosh can help you solve that problem, and then lists all the steps you need to follow to solve that particular problem in a way that only a Macintosh can.

By teaching you how to do something fun and useful right away, using hands-on instructions, you'll learn how to achieve specific results with your Macintosh. Think of this book as a combination tutorial and reference guide. As a tutorial, this book can teach you how to use your Macintosh. As a reference guide, it can provide step-by-step instructions for helping you solve different problems using your Macintosh.

You don't have to follow this book in any specific order, just as you don't have to follow a cookbook in any specific order. Feel free to jump around—follow along with the projects that show you how to do something you find useful, and skip the projects that you don't care about. Nobody really needs to know everything about their computer to use it; you only need to know just enough to be productive. By following the projects in this book, you just may surprise yourself with how you can have fun while learning to use a computer all at the same time.

PART 1

Basic Training

<table>
<tr><td>

1

</td><td>

Turning Your Macintosh On and Off Manually or Automatically

</td></tr>
</table>

You'd think that turning on your Macintosh would be easy—and it is. To turn a Macintosh on, just press the power button, which is usually located on the front or back of your machine, depending on the type of Macintosh you have. Once you've pressed the power button, your Macintosh should start up. If there's anything wrong with the hardware in your computer, such as a defective memory chip, it won't start up and you'll probably need to take it to a repair shop. (Unless you're a hardware expert, you probably shouldn't try to fix your own Macintosh because you could damage something and void the warranty.)

When you're done using your Macintosh, you can turn it off. You can also schedule times for your Macintosh to turn itself off and on automatically.

Project goal: Learn how to turn your Macintosh on and off in different ways or automatically according to a fixed schedule.

What You'll Be Using

To turn a Macintosh on and off automatically, you'll need the following:

▶   The System Preferences program

Turning Your Macintosh Off the Normal Way

Most of the time, you'll turn your Macintosh on and off by following the instructions in this section. Here's how to turn your Macintosh off:

1. Click the Apple menu. A pull-down menu appears, as shown in Figure 1-1.

FIGURE 1-1: *The Apple menu contains the Shut Down command.*

2. Select **Shut Down**. A dialog appears, asking if you are sure you want to shut your computer down.
3. Click **Shut Down** (or **Cancel**).

∗ *NOTE:* **If you don't click Shut Down or Cancel, your Macintosh will shut down automatically after 60 seconds.**

You can also shut down the computer by pressing CTRL and pressing the eject key simultaneously or, if you have a laptop, you can also press the power button. This displays the dialog shown in Figure 1-2. Click **Shut Down** and your Macintosh should turn off.

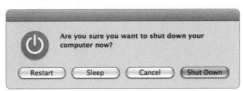

FIGURE 1-2: *A dialog gives you choices for shutting down your Macintosh.*

∗ *NOTE:* **Never turn off a desktop Macintosh by unplugging it. When you choose the Shut Down command, you give your computer time to close running programs and tidy up before it shuts down. If you suddenly cut the power, your Macintosh won't have time to tidy up before shutting down, which could keep it from working properly the next time you turn it on.**

Forcing Your Macintosh to Shut Down

The Macintosh is typically very reliable. However, things can go wrong that may cause your computer to "freeze up" and stop responding. If this happens, you may need to force the computer to shut down. Here are two ways to force your Macintosh to shut down:

▶ Hold down the power button for several seconds.

▶ Press COMMAND-CTRL-power (laptop models only).

Once your Macintosh shuts down, turn it back on again and hope that the problem has gone away. If not, you may need to pay a visit to an Apple store for help.

Restarting Your Macintosh

When your Mac isn't frozen but is just running slowly or acting strangely, and shutting down some programs to free up memory doesn't solve the problem, try a restart. A *restart* turns your machine off and then on again. (You may also need to restart after you install a new program.)

Here's how to restart your Macintosh:

1. Click the Apple menu. A pull-down menu appears.
2. Select **Restart**.

＊ *NOTE:* **You can also restart your Macintosh either by pressing the power button once or by pressing CTRL and the eject key. The eject key appears in the upper-right corner of the keyboard, above the DELETE key. The eject key displays a symbol of a triangle with a line underneath it (see Figure 1-3). When a dialog appears (see Figure 1-2), click Restart.**

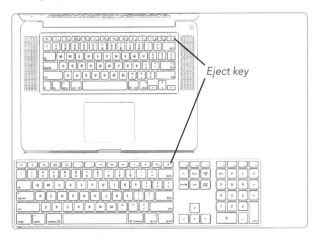

FIGURE 1-3: *The eject key is located above the* DELETE *key on your keyboard.*

Scheduling a Time to Turn Your Macintosh On or Off

When you turn on your Macintosh, you have to wait for it to start up before you can use it. You can save time by having it turn itself on automatically at a set time so that it will be waiting for you when you arrive at your desk, just like your morning coffee.

For example, you could schedule your Macintosh to turn itself on at 8:50 AM, just before you start work (or when you wake up), and then turn itself off at 5:10 PM, after you get done with work, or whenever you usually go to sleep. By scheduling your Macintosh to turn itself on and off, you won't have to worry about turning it on or off yourself.

Here's how to schedule a time to turn your Macintosh on and off:

1. Click the Apple menu and select **System Preferences**. A System Preferences window appears.
2. Click the **Energy Saver** icon under the Hardware category. An Energy Saver window appears, as shown in Figure 1-4.

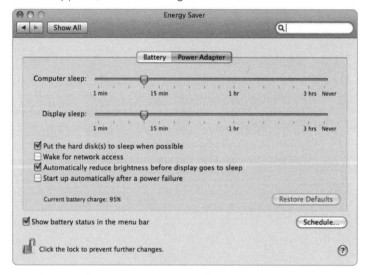

FIGURE 1-4: The Energy Saver window

3. Click the **Schedule** button in the bottom-right corner of the Energy Saver window. A sheet drops down and displays different time options, as shown in Figure 1-5.
4. Select the **Start up or wake** checkbox.
5. Click the pop-up menu next to the checkbox and choose an option such as Every Day or Monday, as shown in Figure 1-6.

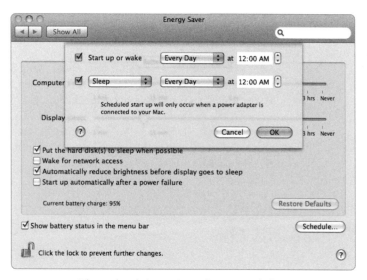

FIGURE 1-5: *The scheduling sheet lets you define a start up and shut down time.*

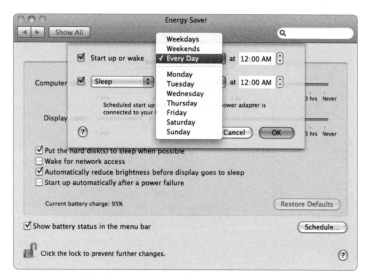

FIGURE 1-6: *The Start up or wake pop-up menu gives you a choice of days to start up your machine automatically.*

6. Click in the time text box and enter a time, or choose a preset time using the up and down arrows.
7. Select the second checkbox underneath the Start up or wake checkbox, click the pop-up menu, and choose **Shut Down**.

8.   Click the next pop-up menu and choose a day, such as Every Day or Friday.

9.   Click in the time text box and enter a time, or choose a preset time using the up and down arrows.

10.   Click **OK**. The Energy Saver window appears again.

11.   Click the close button of the System Preferences window, or select **System Preferences ▸ Quit System Preferences**.

✳ **NOTE:** If you're still working on your Macintosh when its scheduled shut down time arrives, a dialog asks whether you want to shut down or keep working. You can, of course, choose either option.

Starting Programs When Your Macintosh Turns On

In addition to turning your Macintosh on or off automatically, you can make your Macintosh automatically load your favorite programs when it turns on. Here's how:

1.   Right-click a program icon on the Dock (or point to a program icon on the Dock and hold down the left mouse button) to reveal a shortcut menu, as shown in Figure 1-7.

2.   Select **Options ▸ Open at Login**. Now this program will load automatically whether you turn your Macintosh on manually or schedule it to turn itself on automatically.

✳ **NOTE:** If you create additional accounts on your Macintosh (see Project 16), your programs won't load automatically until you log in to your account.

FIGURE 1-7: *The Open at Login command tells a program to start up when your Macintosh turns on.*

Now that you know how to turn a Macintosh on and off, you just have to figure out how to do something useful with it in the time between.

2 Learning to Use the Mouse

To control your Macintosh, you use the *mouse* (or *trackpad* if you have a laptop). Both the mouse and the trackpad control an arrow on your screen called a *pointer*. When you move the mouse or slide a fingertip across the trackpad, you move the pointer on the screen. The pointer lets you choose commands on menus, items in folders, the point where you want to start typing text in a document, and more. Think of the pointer as a virtual finger that tells your Macintosh what to select.

If you have a desktop Macintosh (such as an iMac), you'll be using a mouse called the *Mighty Mouse*, which has one button on each side and a scroll ball on top. If you use an older laptop Macintosh, you'll have a trackpad and a single trackpad button. If you have a newer laptop Macintosh, you'll just have a trackpad, which also works as a giant button. Figure 2-1 shows the Mighty Mouse and trackpad.

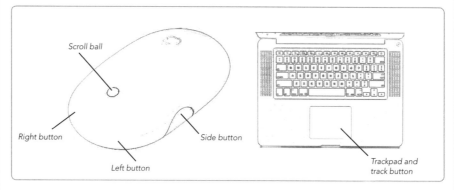

Scroll ball

Right button

Left button

Side button

Trackpad and track button

FIGURE 2-1: *The parts of the Mighty Mouse and trackpad*

* NOTE: Older mice do not have side buttons or a scroll ball. Instead, they may have a scroll wheel that rolls only up and down.

Project goal: Learn how to use your mouse to control your Macintosh.

What You'll Be Using

To learn how to use the mouse, you'll use the following:

▶   The mouse (or trackpad)

▶   The Finder

▶   The Dock

How to Point and Click the Mouse

Your Macintosh always displays a menu bar at the top of the screen. To choose a menu to open, move your mouse to move the pointer on the screen over a menu title, such as File or Edit. (Try it now!)

To move the pointer on a laptop Macintosh, press your finger on the trackpad and slide it along the surface.

Once you've moved the pointer to point to a menu on the screen, you can choose and open that menu by pressing and releasing the left mouse button. Pressing the left mouse button once and releasing it right away is known as *clicking*.

To press the left mouse button on a Mighty Mouse, press the left corner down and release. To press the left mouse button with a trackpad, press the trackpad button (or the entire trackpad if you have a new laptop) once and release.

Practice pointing and clicking the mouse:

1. Move the mouse pointer over the Apple menu in the upper-left corner of the screen.

2. Click the mouse (press and release the left mouse button). A pull-down menu appears, as shown in Figure 2-2.

3. Move the mouse up and down over the commands in the pull-down menu. Notice that each time you move the pointer over a command, the command appears highlighted. This is the Macintosh's way of asking you, "Is this the command you want to choose?"

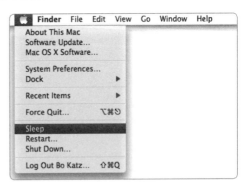

FIGURE 2-2: *Clicking a menu title displays a pull-down menu of commands.*

4. Move the mouse pointer anywhere away from the pull-down menu and click the left mouse button. The pull-down menu disappears. (You can also press the ESC key on the keyboard to make a pull-down menu disappear.)

Dragging the Mouse

Another common use for the mouse is called *dragging*. Dragging the mouse occurs when you move the pointer over something on the screen, hold the left mouse button down, move the mouse, and then release the left mouse button.

Dragging is often used to select multiple items, move or copy an item from one location to another, or, in many graphics programs, to draw lines on the screen or erase part of a picture, as shown in Figure 2-3.

Dragging can select multiple icons.

Dragging can move an object from one location to another.

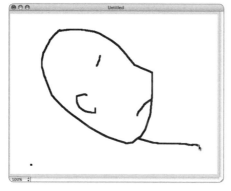

Dragging can draw or erase lines in a picture.

FIGURE 2-3: *Dragging the mouse performs different actions, depending on the program you're using.*

Practice dragging the mouse:

1. Move the mouse pointer over the Finder icon on the Dock and click the left mouse button. (From now on, this book will give this instruction in a shorter way: "Click the Finder icon on the Dock.") The Finder window appears.

2. Click the **Macintosh HD** icon that appears in the upper-left corner of the Finder window. The words *Macintosh HD* and the icon appear highlighted, so you know it has been selected. Several folder icons appear in the right pane of the Finder window, as shown in Figure 2-4.

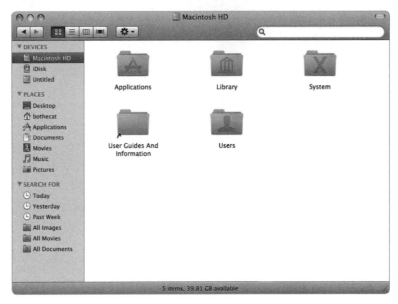

FIGURE 2-4: *Clicking the Macintosh HD icon displays the contents of your hard disk, which contains all your files and programs.*

* ***NOTE:*** **If the folder icons don't look like those shown in Figure 2-4, click the View menu and choose as Icons (select View ▸ as Icons), or press the ⌘ and 1 keys simultaneously (⌘-1).**

3. Move the mouse pointer over any folder (such as the Users folder), hold down the left mouse button, and move the mouse. (From now on, this book will use a shorter way to give this instruction: "Drag the folder.") Notice that as long as you hold down the left mouse button and move the mouse, a "ghost image" of the folder moves on the screen, following the mouse movement.

4. Move the mouse pointer to position the folder anywhere inside the right pane of the Finder window and then release the left mouse button. The folder now appears in its new location.

✳ *NOTE:* When dragging the mouse, always keep the left mouse button held down as you're moving. If you're using a trackpad on a laptop, hold down the trackpad button as you slide your fingertip along the trackpad surface.

Double-Clicking the Mouse

Although clicking is the most common way to use the mouse, the second most common way is called double-clicking. *Double-clicking* means pressing and releasing the left mouse button (or trackpad button) twice in rapid succession. Double-clicking is basically a shortcut for eliminating multiple single clicks to select an item and then choosing a menu command. For example, to open a file, you typically need to follow four steps:

1. Move the mouse pointer over the file you want to open.
2. Click the file to tell your Macintosh that this is the file you want to open.
3. Click the **File** menu title. A pull-down menu appears.
4. Click the **Open** command. (From now on, this book will explain how to choose a menu title and a command by using the shorter description: "Select **File ▸ Open**.")

Rather than click the mouse three different times, you could open a file just by double-clicking the mouse:

1. Move the mouse pointer over the file you want to open.
2. Double-click the file to tell your Macintosh that you want to open it.

Right-Clicking the Mouse

Most mice have a mouse button on the right side as well. To click the right mouse button on a Mighty Mouse, press down the right corner and release. To press the right mouse button on a trackpad, tap the trackpad once with two fingers. (If your laptop has a trackpad button, hold down the CTRL key, press the trackpad button, and then release both.)

When you point at something on the screen and right-click, a menu called a *shortcut menu* pops up on the screen. This shortcut menu provides a list of commands from which you can choose.

Here's how right-clicking works:

1. Move the mouse pointer over any icon that appears on the Dock.
2. Press and release the right mouse button (right-click). A shortcut menu appears, as shown in Figure 2-5.

FIGURE 2-5: *A shortcut menu appears when you right-click an item.*

3.   Move the mouse pointer away from the shortcut menu and click the left mouse button. The shortcut menu disappears. (You can also press the ESC key to make the shortcut menu disappear.)

Using the Scroll Ball

The scroll ball appears in the middle of the Mighty Mouse near the front of the mouse. By rolling the scroll ball, you can move the contents of a window in different directions, such as up and down or left and right.

* *NOTE:* **Laptop trackpads do not have a scroll ball. To simulate scrolling with a trackpad on a new Mac laptop, press two fingertips on the trackpad and slide both fingers up/down or left/right. You can also scroll by holding one fingertip still and sliding the second fingertip up/down or left/right.**

Here's how scrolling works:

1.   Click the Finder icon on the Dock. The Finder window appears.
2.   Click **Applications** in the left pane of the Finder window. The contents of the Applications folder appear in the right pane of the Finder window.
3.   Roll the scroll ball up and down. Notice as you roll the scroll ball up and down that the contents of the Finder window move up and down.

Using the Side Buttons

The Mighty Mouse provides two side buttons. If you squeeze these at the same time, all open windows on the screen slide out of sight to display the Desktop. If you squeeze these side buttons a second time, the windows reappear on your screen. The side buttons are useful if you have a lot of windows open and need to find something you've placed on your desktop.

Here's how the Mighty Mouse side buttons work:

1.   Click the Finder icon on the Dock. The Finder window appears.
2.   Click **Applications** in the left pane of the Finder window. The contents of the Applications folder appear in the right pane of the Finder window.
3.   Double-click any program icon in the Applications folder, such as Chess or iCal. Your chosen program window appears.
4.   Squeeze the side buttons of the Mighty Mouse. All windows on the screen disappear to reveal the Desktop.
5.   Squeeze the side buttons of the Mighty Mouse a second time. All windows pop back up on the screen again.

Customizing the Mouse

If you don't like the way your mouse behaves, you can modify its speed. To modify the mouse, do this:

1. Click the Apple menu and choose **System Preferences**. The System Preferences window appears.
2. Click the **Mouse** icon under the Hardware category. The Mouse dialog appears, as shown in Figure 2-6.

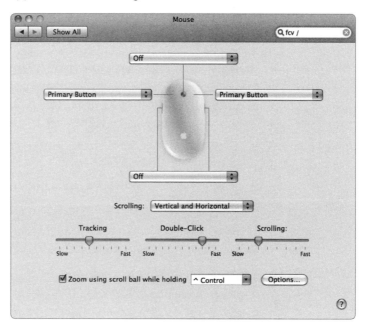

FIGURE 2-6: *The Mouse dialog lets you customize your mouse.*

> * *NOTE:* **The Mouse dialog in Figure 2-6 is for Apple's Mighty Mouse. If you have a different mouse connected to your computer, the Mouse dialog will show a similar Mouse dialog, but without options for customizing the side buttons.**

3. Choose one or more options for customizing how your mouse behaves, such as defining what happens if you click the right mouse button or squeeze the side mouse buttons (on a Mighty Mouse).
4. Click the close button in the upper-left corner of the Mouse dialog when you're done customizing your mouse.

Customizing the Trackpad

If you have one of the latest aluminum body Macintosh laptops, you'll have a unique trackpad that doubles as a giant button. (If you have an older plastic Macintosh laptop, you'll have a standard trackpad with a single button.)

The trackpad accepts four different finger gestures:

▶ **One Finger**   Pressing one finger on the trackpad acts like clicking the left button of an ordinary mouse.

▶ **Two Fingers**   Sliding two fingers horizontally or vertically scrolls in that direction, much like clicking the horizontal or vertical scrollbars of a window.

▶ **Three Fingers**   Sliding three fingers horizontally across the trackpad (left or right) displays the next item in certain programs, such as iPhoto.

▶ **Four Fingers**   Sliding four fingers up displays the desktop (similar to pressing F11), while sliding four fingers down displays all windows (similar to pressing F9). Sliding four fingers left or right displays the Application Switcher.

To customize the trackpad, do this:

1.   Click the Apple menu and choose **System Preferences**. The System Preferences window appears.

2.   Click the **Trackpad** icon under the Hardware category. The Trackpad dialog appears, as shown in Figure 2-7. A video plays in the right pane to show you how different finger gestures work.

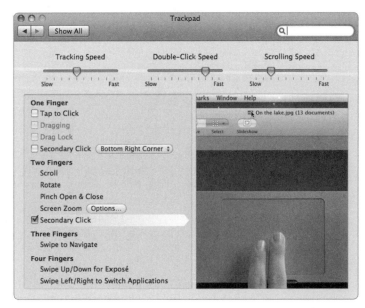

FIGURE 2-7: *The Trackpad dialog lets you customize finger gestures.*

3. Select (or clear) the checkboxes under the One Finger category. (If you select the Secondary Click checkbox under the One Finger category, you can select a corner of the trackpad that you can press to mimic pressing the right mouse button of a typical mouse.)
4. Select (or clear) the **Secondary Click** checkbox under the Two Fingers category. (If you click the Screen Zoom Options button, you can define how to zoom in and out using two fingers.)
5. Click the close button of the Trackpad dialog when you're done customizing the Trackpad.

Additional Ideas for Using the Mouse

Since the mouse is the primary way to control your Macintosh, you need to know the two most important uses for the mouse:

▶ **Point**   Move the pointer by moving the mouse.

▶ **Click**   Press the left mouse button once and let go.

You can control your entire Macintosh just by pointing and clicking the mouse. To make your Macintosh easier to use, learn the following additional ways to use the mouse:

▶ **Double-click**   Press the left mouse button twice in rapid succession.

▶ **Drag**   Point at something on the screen, hold down the left mouse button, move the mouse, and release the left mouse button.

▶ **Click and hold**   Point at something on the screen and hold down the left mouse button.

▶ **Right-click**   Press the right mouse button once and let go.

▶ **Scroll**   Roll the scroll ball up and down or left and right.

▶ **Squeeze**   Press the side buttons on the Mighty Mouse.

Start out by pointing and clicking, and when you get comfortable using your Macintosh and mouse, experiment with double-clicking, dragging, and right-clicking. If you have a Mighty Mouse, you can practice squeezing the side buttons as well. If you're worried about messing something up, practice double-clicking, dragging, and right-clicking on a Macintosh in a store or on someone else's Macintosh. That way, if you really mess things up, you can walk away and pretend you don't know what happened.

* *NOTE:* If you use a laptop, remember that you can still use a mouse simply by plugging one into your computer. You'll then have the choice of using the mouse or the trackpad to control your Macintosh. A spare mouse can be very handy when you're traveling—or even when you're using your Mac at home.

3 Choosing Commands on the Menu Bar

Using a computer is a bit like trying to communicate with someone. The computer starts off by asking you what you want to do. It's up to you to decipher the options the computer offers and tell it what to do next. The computer follows your command and asks what you want to do now, and so on.

To use a Macintosh, you must first understand the choices that are provided to you. Then you must tell your Macintosh what to do based on those choices.

You use the mouse and the keyboard to respond to information that is displayed on the screen to communicate with and control your Macintosh. That might mean clicking a menu and selecting a command, or clicking icons or buttons.

Since your Macintosh organizes most commands in menus, you first need to know how to find and use the commands stored in the menu bar, as shown in Figure 3-1.

Project goal: Learn to choose commands from the menu bar to control your Macintosh.

What You'll Be Using

To learn how to communicate with the Macintosh user interface, you'll use the following:

► The mouse

► The keyboard

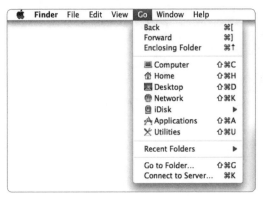

FIGURE 3-1: *The menu bar provides access to commands you use for controlling your Macintosh.*

Understanding the Menu Bar

When you visit a restaurant, the waiter hands you a menu. Likewise, when you turn on your Macintosh, it offers you menus of commands in its menu bar. But unlike that restaurant menu, you can select only one item at a time, and you must decide which menu to access to select the items you want.

The menu bar always appears at the top of the screen. Because the menu bar doesn't have enough room to display every command on the screen at once, it organizes related commands into categories, called *menu titles*. Two commonly used menu titles are File and Edit.

The File menu lists commands you use when working with files. Nearly every program creates files to store data on your Macintosh. A *file* can be a word processor document, a picture, or a spreadsheet of your budget. Typical commands found on the File menu let you open or print data stored in a file.

The Edit menu contains commands for modifying data, such as copying or deleting. Typically, the commands on the Edit menu let you modify data stored in a file.

To keep your screen from getting cluttered, the menu bar hides the list of available commands until you click a menu title. A menu typically displays three types of commands, as shown in Figure 3-2:

▶ Commands

▶ Submenu commands

▶ Ellipsis commands

Commands appear as a word or series of words, such as *Get Info* or *New Folder*. To select a command, just point to it and click the mouse. When you select a command from a menu, your Macintosh does something in response.

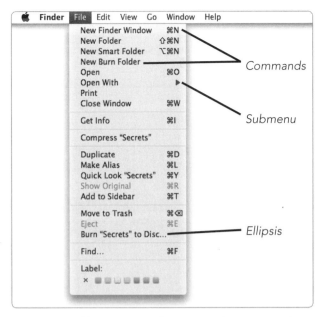

FIGURE 3-2: *Three types of commands are stored on menus.*

Normally you can choose a command by clicking it, but some commands display keyboard shortcuts on the right edge of a menu, using symbols to represent different keys on the keyboard. To choose a command like Open, you could press the Command key (⌘) and the O key at the same time.

Most keyboard shortcuts require pressing down two or more keys at the same time. By memorizing these keyboard shortcuts, you can choose common commands without the hassle of using the menus. However, not all commands offer keyboard shortcuts. If you don't see any keystrokes listed to the right of a command in a menu, that particular command doesn't have a keyboard shortcut.

Table 3-1: Common Keyboard Shortcut Symbols

Symbol	Key
⌘	Command
⇧	Shift
⌥	Option
∧	Control (CTRL)
⌫	Delete

Submenu commands always appear as a descriptive word or phrase with a triangle pointing to the right. To open a submenu, place your mouse over the command and wait for the submenu to pop up, as shown in Figure 3-3. This submenu lists additional commands from which you can choose.

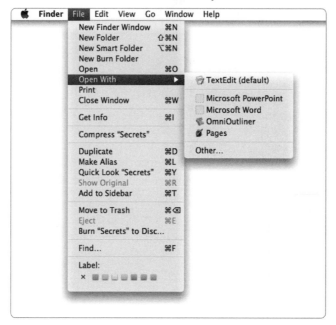

FIGURE 3-3: *Submenus always list additional commands from which you can choose.*

Ellipsis commands appear as a word or phrase followed by an ellipsis (...). To select an ellipsis command, place your mouse over the ellipsis command and click. After you click the mouse, you'll see a box with additional options, called a *dialog*. You use dialogs to give your Macintosh more information so it can complete some particular task. For example, as you're working on a file in an application, if you select the Save As command (a common ellipsis command) from the File menu, a Save As dialog pops up, asking you to type a name for the file, as shown in Figure 3-4.

FIGURE 3-4: *Choosing an ellipsis command always displays a dialog.*

One of the most important commands for any program is Quit, which exits or closes the program when you select it. Quit always appears in the *application menu* (the menu with the name of the application you're currently using, such as iPhoto or iCal), as shown in Figure 3-5.

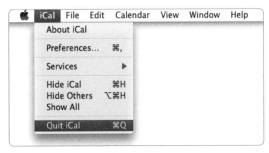

FIGURE 3-5: *The Quit command always appears in the application menu.*

Understanding Dialogs

A dialog typically contains one or more of the following items, as shown in Figure 3-6:

► Buttons

► Text boxes

► Pop-up menus

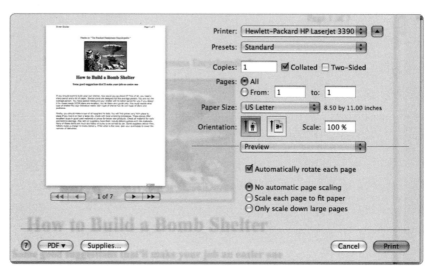

FIGURE 3-6: *Common parts of a dialog; note that the default button is the Print button, which is highlighted.*

Buttons can be clicked to open another dialog or to perform a single action. If a dialog displays multiple buttons, one button may be highlighted to identify it as the *default* button. To choose the command displayed by a default button, you can either click the button with your mouse or press the RETURN key on your keyboard. If you decide not to perform any action, you can click the Cancel button or press the ESC key.

Text boxes provide a space for you to type information, such as the number of copies or page numbers to print.

Pop-up menus provide a fixed list of possible options from which you can choose, as shown in Figure 3-7.

FIGURE 3-7: *A pop-up menu lets you choose from a fixed list of acceptable options.*

A dialog may appear condensed or expanded. A *condensed* dialog shows you the basic options available, and an *expanded* dialog lets you choose additional options. To condense or expand a dialog, click the Expand or Collapse button, as shown in Figure 3-8.

Expand button   *Collapse button*

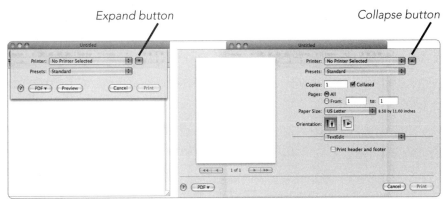

FIGURE 3-8: *A dialog can appear condensed (left) or expanded (right).*

Understanding the Parts of the Menu Bar

The menu bar consists of three separate parts, as shown in Figure 3-9:

▸ The Apple menu

▸ The Application menu

▸ Menulets

Apple menu   Application menu   Menulets

🍎 **Safari** File Edit View History Bookmarks Window Help   * ♡ ◀) ▭ Fri 8:18 AM Q

FIGURE 3-9: *The menu bar*

The *Apple menu* always appears on the left edge of the menu bar. It displays commands that provide information, let you customize Macintosh settings, or let you shut down your Macintosh, as shown in Figure 3-10.

The *application menu* consists of the name of the currently running program along with menus that contain commands used for that program.

No matter how many programs you may have running, only one menu bar appears at a time on the Macintosh. (If you're familiar with the Microsoft Windows user interface, every program window has its own menu bar, as shown in Figure 3-11.)

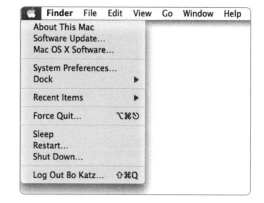

FIGURE 3-10: *The Apple menu always displays these commands.*

When two or more programs are running on your Macintosh, the application menu will show commands only for the *active* program (or application)—the program you're working with at that particular time. For example, when you're using iPhoto, the application menu displays *iPhoto* on the menu bar next to the Apple menu. If you're using iCal, the application menu displays *iCal* on the menu bar next to the Apple menu. If you're using Keynote, the application menu displays *Keynote* on the menu bar next to the Apple menu, as shown in Figure 3-12.

Menulets are little menus designed for controlling a single part of your Macintosh, such as the clock, the volume of your speakers, or battery and energy settings. They usually appear on the far right side of the menu bar and typically contain simple menus or sliders that control different parts of your Macintosh, as shown in Figure 3-13.

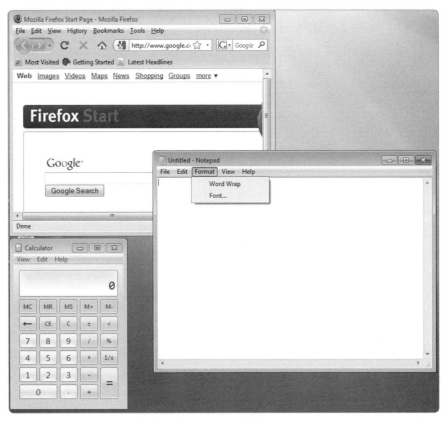

FIGURE 3-11: *When running multiple programs in Microsoft Windows, every program window has its own menu bar.*

FIGURE 3-12: *The name of the currently running application always appears to the right of the Apple menu.*

FIGURE 3-13: *Menulets appear on the menu bar to give you quick access to common features of your Macintosh.*

Additional Ideas for Using the Menu Bar

The menu bar gives you easy access to the commands you can use to control a program. The first time you use a program, browse through its menus to see how commands are grouped. Commands should be grouped logically to make them easy to find. For example, the Macintosh's Window menu contains commands for manipulating multiple windows on the screen, while the Edit menu contains commands for copying or pasting items.

The menu bar is also useful for identifying the active program. When you have multiple applications running and you're not sure which application the commands on the menu bar will affect, look for the name of the program next to the Apple menu. Figure 3-14 shows how the application name in the menu bar can help you identify the currently running application when multiple windows fill the screen. In this case, the currently running application is the Calculator program. The active application can also be identified by looking closely at the application windows, since the non-active program windows appear slightly dimmed.

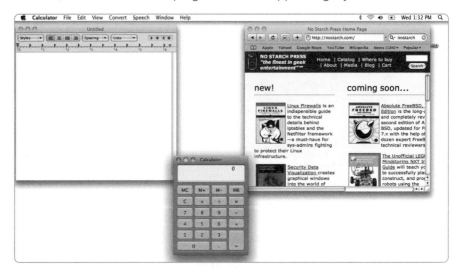

FIGURE 3-14: *When you have many windows open, you can identify the currently running program by looking for the application name in the menu bar.*

You'll also find menulets on the menu bar that you can use to adjust different parts of your Macintosh, such as the audio volume, time, and date. Since menulets are meant to give you one-click access to controlling different parts of your Macintosh, they always appear on the menu bar, no matter which program may be running.

Normally, the menu bar appears translucent, which means you can see part of the background image through the menu bar. If this annoys you, you can fix it by doing the following:

1. Click the Apple menu and choose **System Preferences**. A System Preferences window appears.
2. Click the **Desktop & Screen Saver** icon. A Desktop & Screen Saver window appears.
3. Click the **Desktop** tab.
4. Select or clear the **Translucent Menu Bar** checkbox, as shown in Figure 3-15.
5. Click the close button of the Desktop & Screen Saver window.

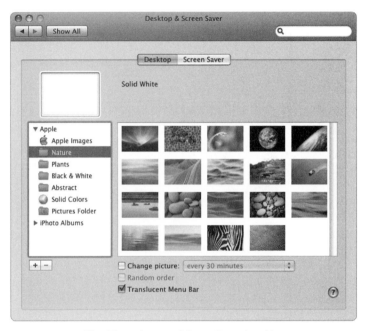

FIGURE 3-15: The Translucent Menu Bar checkbox appears on the Desktop tab in the Desktop & Screen Saver dialog.

By understanding the different parts and purposes of the menu bar, you'll always be able to control your Macintosh. Now you just have to figure out what you want to make it do.

4

Loading Programs and Files from the Dock

The point of owning a computer is to be able to run programs that make the computer perform something useful or fun. The types of programs you run determine what your computer can do. If you want to write letters or balance your budget, you can run a word processor or a spreadsheet program. If you want to do something a bit more fun, you can run astrology programs, horse-handicapping programs, or lottery-number-choosing programs. With the right program, you can make your Macintosh do practically anything that doesn't involve manual labor.

Your Macintosh can store literally thousands of different programs. You can make it easy to find and run programs by adding icons for each program to the Dock—the line of icons at the bottom of your screen. The Dock offers a convenient way to find, run, switch between, and shut down programs.

Project goal: Learn to use the Dock to run, switch, and quit programs on your Macintosh.

What You'll Be Using

To learn how to run programs on your Macintosh through the Dock, you'll use the following:

▶   The Dock

▶   The Finder

▶   The Chess program

▶   The Safari web browser

Understanding Program Icons

Every Macintosh program appears as an icon in the Applications folder on your hard disk. To run any program installed on your Macintosh, you must first find its icon. The most straightforward way to find a program icon is to look inside the Applications folder on your hard disk. The two ways to open the Applications folder are through the Finder or through the Dock.

A faster way to load a program is to place that program's icon on the Dock so it's within sight at all times. The main purpose of the Dock is to provide a place where you can find your most frequently used program icons without digging through the Applications folder. Table 4-1 shows the main differences between starting a program from the Applications folder and starting a program from the Dock.

Table 4-1: Program Icons in the Applications Folder vs. the Dock

	Applications Folder	Dock
Viewing program icons	Displays icons that represent all programs installed on your Macintosh.	Only displays icons of some programs installed on your Macintosh.
Starting a program	Double-click an icon to start a program (through the Finder) or single-click an icon (through the Applications folder on the Dock).	Single-click an icon to start a program.

Starting a Program Through the Finder

To start a program stored in the Applications folder, you have to use the Finder program and then double-click a program icon. To see how that works, try the following:

1. Click the Finder icon on the Dock. The Finder window appears.
2. Click the **Applications** folder icon that appears in the left pane of the Finder window. A list of all program icons stored in the Applications folder appears, as shown in Figure 4-1.
3. Double-click the **Chess** icon (or click the Chess program icon to select it and then select **File ▸ Open**, or press ⌘-O). The Chess program window appears. Notice that the Chess program icon now also appears in the Dock, as shown in Figure 4-2.
4. Select **Chess ▸ Quit** or press ⌘-Q. The Chess program window disappears and the Chess program icon disappears from the Dock.

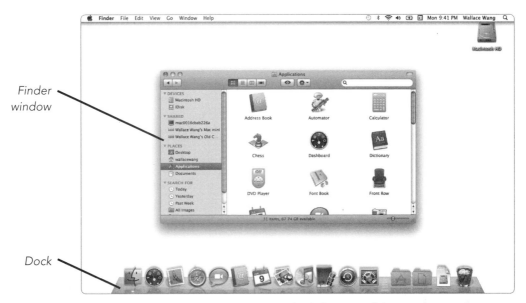

Finder window

Dock

FIGURE 4-1: *Clicking Applications in the left pane of the Finder window shows every program icon stored in the Applications folder.*

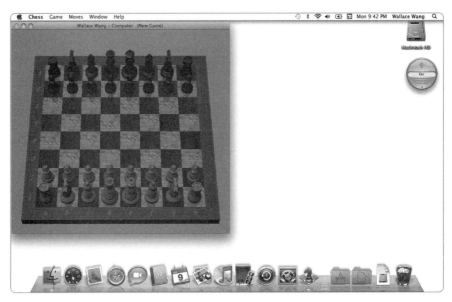

FIGURE 4-2: *Every running program displays its icon on the Dock with a blue dot underneath.*

Starting a Program Through the Applications Folder on the Dock

The Dock consists of two sides divided by a white dotted line. The left side of the Dock contains program icons. The right side of the Dock contains three folder icons next to the Trash icon, as shown in Figure 4-3. The right side of the Dock also holds the windows you've minimized (see Project 6 for more information on managing application windows).

The left side of the Dock shows your application shortcuts and what's currently running.

The right side shows any windows or applications you've minimized, commonly used folders, and the Trash.

FIGURE 4-3: *The left and right sides of the Dock*

The three folder icons on the right side of the Dock are the Applications folder, the Documents folder, and the Downloads folder. The purpose of these folder icons on the Dock is to give you quick access to your most commonly used folders.

✳ **NOTE: The Downloads folder displays the icon of the latest file stored in that folder.**

The Applications folder contains all the programs stored on your Macintosh. The Documents folder typically contains all the files you've created using different programs. The Downloads folder typically contains all files that you've downloaded from the Internet.

✳ **NOTE: The Applications folder on the Dock is simply another way to view the contents of the Applications folder. Likewise, the Documents folder on the Dock is just another way to access the Documents folder.**

For another way to view all the program icons in the Applications folder using the Dock, do this:

1. Click the Applications folder on the Dock. A window appears, listing program icons stored in the Applications folder, as shown in Figure 4-4.
2. (Optional) Click the scrollbar to view any program icons not currently visible in the window.
3. Click the **Chess** icon to load that program.
4. Select **Chess ▸ Quit** or press ⌘-Q. The Chess program window disappears and the Chess program icon disappears from the Dock.

FIGURE 4-4: *The Applications folder opens a window from the Dock.*

Starting a Program Through the Dock

The Dock displays icons of your most frequently used programs so you'll have one-click access to those programs. Initially, the Dock contains several different icons, but you can always add or delete these icons (see Project 5 to learn how to customize the Dock).

To see how to start a program from the Dock, do this:

1. Move the mouse pointer over the Safari icon on the Dock. Notice that when you move the mouse pointer over an icon in the Dock, the program name appears over that icon, as shown in Figure 4-5.

FIGURE 4-5: *The Safari icon loads the Safari web browser program.*

2. Click the Safari icon to load the Safari program. Notice that you only need to single-click an icon displayed in the Dock.
3. Select **Safari ▸ Quit** or press ⌘-Q. The Safari program window disappears, but the Safari program icon remains on the Dock.

Switching Programs and Windows from the Dock

Each time you run a program, its icon appears on the Dock with a blue dot underneath. For example, if you load both the iTunes and iPhoto programs, you'll see dots underneath both the iTunes and iPhoto icons on the Dock.

When you have two or more programs running at the same time, you can switch programs simply by clicking the icon on the Dock that represents the program you want to use. For example, to switch between iTunes and iPhoto, click the iTunes icon on the Dock and the iTunes window appears. Click the iPhoto icon on the Dock and the iPhoto window appears.

Many programs allow you to open multiple windows at once, such as Safari displaying two or more web pages in separate windows. To switch between multiple windows opened by the same program, you can use menus or thumbnails.

To see how to switch between different programs and program windows using menus and thumbnail images, do this:

1. Click the Finder icon on the Dock. A Finder window appears.
2. Click the Safari icon on the Dock. The Safari window appears. Notice that a blue dot now appears underneath the Safari icon. By default, Safari will display the Apple start page.
3. Click the Finder icon on the Dock. Notice that the Finder window appears over the Safari window and the Finder menu appears to the right of the Apple menu on the menu bar at the top of the screen.
4. Click the Safari icon on the Dock. Notice that the Safari window now appears over the Finder window and the Safari menu appears to the right of the Apple menu on the menu bar.
5. Select **File ▸ New Window**. A second Safari window appears.
6. Click in the Address text box, type **www.nostarch.com**, and press RETURN. The No Starch Press website appears.
7. Right-click the Safari icon on the Dock. A pop-up menu appears, listing the two Safari windows, as shown in Figure 4-6.

FIGURE 4-6: *Right-clicking an icon displays a list of all open windows created by that program.*

8. Click **Apple** in this pop-up menu. The Safari window displaying the Apple website appears.

9. Right-click the Safari icon and click **No Starch Press**. The window displaying the No Starch Press website appears.

10. Move the mouse pointer over the Safari icon on the Dock and hold down the left mouse button. After a few seconds, thumbnail images of all Safari windows appear, as shown in Figure 4-7.

FIGURE 4-7: *Clicking and holding on a program icon on the Dock displays a menu and thumbnail images of all currently opened windows created by that program.*

11. Click the thumbnail image of either the Apple or the No Starch Press website. Notice that your chosen window expands to fill the screen.

12. Select **Safari ▸ Quit** or press ⌘-Q. The Safari program windows disappear, but the Safari program icon remains on the Dock.

Quitting Programs from the Dock

Not only can the Dock help you start and switch between programs, but it can also help you quit programs. There are four common ways to quit a program, as shown in Figure 4-8:

▶ Click the program name (such as Safari or iTunes) on the menu bar and choose **Quit**.

▶ Press ⌘-Q.

▶ Point to a program icon on the Dock and hold down the left mouse button. When a menu appears, choose **Quit**.

▶ Right-click a program icon on the Dock and when a pop-up menu appears, choose **Quit**.

FIGURE 4-8: *The Quit command appears in the program menu on the Apple menu bar and in the pop-up menu on the Dock.*

✳ **NOTE:** If you try to quit a program with open files that you haven't saved, a dialog appears, asking if you want to save the files before quitting.

Accessing the Documents and Downloads Folders on the Dock

Initially the Dock contains three folders (Applications, Documents, and Downloads) that appear to the right of the white, dotted dividing line near the right side of the Dock. The Applications folder lets you access all stored programs on your Macintosh (see "Starting a Program Through the Applications Folder on the Dock" on page 40).

The Documents folder is meant to store all the files you've created using other programs, such as a word processor. The Downloads folder typically contains files you've downloaded off the Internet, although you can store anything in the Downloads folder if you wish.

To access the Documents or Downloads folder, you could click the Finder icon on the Dock and then search for the Documents or Downloads folder inside the Finder window. However, this can be confusing and tedious. A faster method is to access the Documents or Downloads folder directly from the Dock.

Browsing Through the Documents Folder

When you click the Documents folder on the Dock, a pop-up menu appears. The top part of the pop-up menu lists all the files and folders stored in your Documents folder, while the bottom part displays menu options such as Open in Finder, as shown in Figure 4-9.

If you click a file on the top part of the pop-up menu, you'll open that file. If you click a folder on the top part of the pop-up menu, you'll see a list of files and folders stored in that folder.

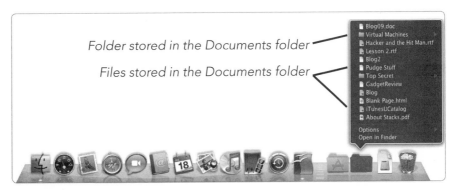

Folder stored in the Documents folder

Files stored in the Documents folder

FIGURE 4-9: *Clicking the Documents folder on the Dock displays a pop-up menu showing its contents.*

If you click the Open in Finder command near the bottom of the pop-up menu, you'll open the Documents folder inside a Finder window, which is identical to clicking the Finder icon on the Dock and then clicking the Documents icon in the left pane of the Finder window.

To open the Documents folder from the Dock, do this:

▸ Click the Documents folder on the Dock. A pop-up menu appears.

✳ **NOTE:** Your Documents folder pop-up menu will list different file and folder names than what you see in Figure 4-9.

▸ Click **Open in Finder**. The Documents window appears. This is identical to clicking the Finder icon on the Dock and then clicking the **Documents** icon in the left pane.

Browsing Through the Downloads Folder

The Downloads folder contains all the files you've downloaded off the Internet. To view the contents of the Downloads folder, do this:

▸ Click the Downloads folder icon on the Dock. A list of all files stored in the Downloads folder appears, as shown in Figure 4-10. (If the number of files stored in the Downloads folder is six or less, clicking the Downloads folder displays a curved fan list of file names. If the number of files stored is seven or greater, the list of files appears in a grid.)

▸ Click the **Open in Finder** icon (which looks like a curved arrow inside a circle). The Downloads window appears.

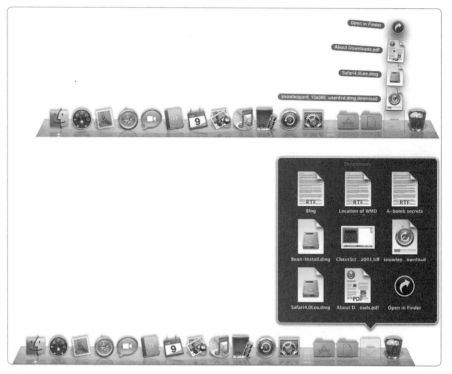

FIGURE 4-10: *Clicking the Downloads folder on the Dock displays a list of files.*

Additional Ideas for Using the Dock

The Dock acts like a shortcut, sparing you from using the Finder any time you want to run a program or open a file. In addition, the Dock also comes in handy for switching between programs and program windows, and quitting programs from one convenient location:

▶ Loading and switching programs: Click an icon on the Dock.

▶ Switching to a different open file: Right-click an icon on the Dock and click a filename.

▶ Shutting down a program: Right-click an icon on the Dock and choose Quit.

The more comfortable and familiar you get with the Dock, the easier it will be to use your Macintosh, no matter what you want to do, so take a few moments to practice using the Dock. You'll be spending most of your time using the Dock, so make sure you understand how it works so you can use it to do what you want.

5   Customizing the Dock

The Dock is a handy place for running programs. However, the Dock will likely also contain icons for programs that you never use, so you may want to remove those icons and replace them with icons of other programs.

In addition, you may want to rearrange the icons on the Dock so similar programs are grouped together, such as grouping all Internet programs in one part of the Dock.

Besides changing the icons that appear on the Dock, you can also rearrange the position of the Dock on the screen or the size of the icons on the Dock itself. Finally, you can store your own files and folders on the Dock to give you one-click access to the files or folders you need most often.

Project goal: Learn to customize the appearance of the Dock.

What You'll Be Using

To customize the Dock, you'll use the following:

▶   The Dock

▶   The System Preferences program

Hiding (and Showing) the Dock

Normally the Dock appears at the bottom of the screen, but if you find this annoying, you can make the Dock tuck itself out of view and then pop up again when you move the mouse pointer near its location.

There are two ways to hide the Dock: through the Apple menu or through the System Preferences window. To hide the Dock through the Apple menu, do the following:

1. Click the Apple menu and choose **Dock**. A menu appears, as shown in Figure 5-1.
2. Choose **Turn Hiding On**. (If you have already turned hiding on, you can turn it off by choosing **Turn Hiding Off**.)

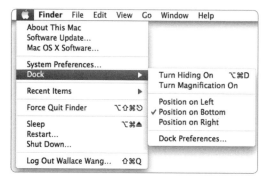

FIGURE 5-1: *The Dock command on the Apple menu gives you quick access to hiding the Dock.*

To hide the Dock through the System Preferences window, do this:

1. Click the Apple menu and choose **System Preferences**. The System Preferences window appears.
2. Click the **Dock** icon under the Personal category. The Dock window appears, as shown in Figure 5-2.
3. Select (or clear) the **Automatically hide and show the Dock** checkbox.
4. Click the close button of the Dock window to make it disappear.

Moving the Dock

The Dock normally appears on the bottom of the screen. However, you can make it appear on the left or right of the screen, as shown in Figure 5-3. To change the position of the Dock, you can use the Apple menu or the System Preferences window.

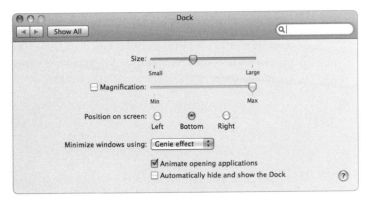

FIGURE 5-2: The Dock window lets you customize the Dock.

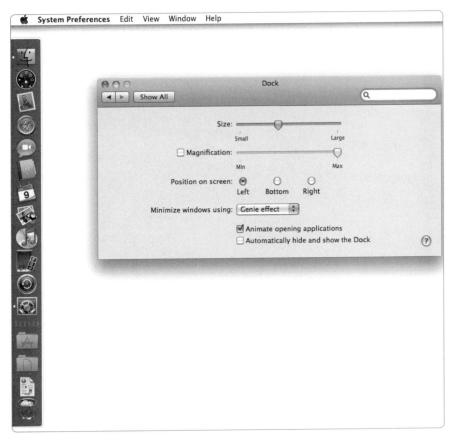

FIGURE 5-3: The Dock can appear on the left or right side of the screen instead of the bottom.

To change the location of the Dock using the Apple menu, do this:

1. Click the Apple menu and choose **Dock**. A menu appears (see Figure 5-1).
2. Choose **Position on Left**, **Position on Bottom**, or **Position on Right**. The Dock moves to its new location on the screen.

To change the location of the Dock using the System Preferences window, do this:

1. Click the Apple menu and choose **System Preferences**. The System Preferences window appears (see Figure 5-2).
2. Click the **Left**, **Bottom**, or **Right** radio button under the Position on screen group. The Dock moves to its new location on the screen.
3. Click the close button of the Dock window to make it disappear.

Making the Dock Easier to See

Depending on your preference, the size of the Dock may be too big or too small. To make the Dock easier to see, you can change its size and turn on magnification. Changing the size of the Dock simply makes the Dock icons bigger or smaller. However, depending on the number of icons stored on the Dock, you can only increase the size of the Dock to a certain limit.

That's why turning magnification on can be helpful, because when you move the mouse pointer over the Dock, the icon underneath the mouse pointer expands in size, as shown in Figure 5-4.

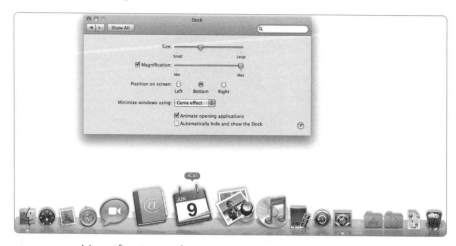

FIGURE 5-4: Magnification makes icons expand in size when you move the mouse pointer over them.

Changing the Size of the Dock

To change the size of the Dock, do this:

1. Click the Apple menu and choose **System Preferences**. The System Preferences window appears.
2. Click the **Dock** icon under the Personal category. The Dock window appears (see Figure 5-2).
3. Drag the **Size** slider left or right. As you drag the slider, the Dock will change in size.
4. Click the close button of the Dock window to make it disappear.

Turning Magnification On or Off

To turn magnification on (or off), do this:

1. Click the Apple menu and choose **System Preferences**. The System Preferences window appears.
2. Click the **Dock** icon under the Personal category. The Dock window appears (see Figure 5-2).
3. Select (or clear) the **Magnification** checkbox.
4. (Optional) Drag the **Magnification** slider left or right to control how much the Dock icons increase in size when you move the mouse pointer over them.
5. Click the close button of the Dock window to make it disappear.

* **NOTE:** You can also turn magnification on or off by clicking the Apple menu, choosing Dock, and choosing Turn Magnification On (or Off).

Rearranging Icons on the Dock

If you don't like the way the icons appear on the Dock, you can rearrange them. To rearrange an icon, do this:

1. Move the mouse pointer over the icon on the Dock that you want to move.
2. Drag the mouse left or right. Notice that as you move the mouse pointer, the icon you selected appears as a "ghost image" that you can see through. As you move this ghost image icon, the other icons on the Dock slide out of the way, as shown in Figure 5-5.

FIGURE 5-5: *Dragging an icon to move it to a different location on the Dock*

3.   Release the mouse button when you're happy with the location of your selected icon on the Dock.

Adding and Removing Icons on the Dock

The Dock contains icons for common programs you're most likely to use, such as Safari and iTunes. However, there's a good chance that the Dock currently contains icons that you'll rarely use, while it does not contain icons of programs that you do use often.

To fix this problem, you can add new program icons to the Dock and remove icons of programs that you don't need. There are two ways to add a program icon to the Dock:

▶   Drag a program icon from the Finder window to the Dock

▶   Open a program and choose the Keep in Dock command

Dragging an Icon to the Dock

The most straightforward way to place a new icon on the Dock is to drag it from the Finder window to the Dock by doing this:

1.   Click the Finder icon on the Dock. The Finder window appears.
2.   Click the **Applications** folder icon in the left pane of the Finder window. The right pane of the Finder window displays icons for all the programs installed on your Macintosh.
3.   Drag a program icon from the Finder window to the Dock, as shown in Figure 5-6. Your program icon now appears on the Dock.

FIGURE 5-6: *Dragging an icon from the Finder window to the Dock*

✳ **NOTE:** Dragging a program icon from the Finder window to the Dock still leaves the program icon in the Finder window.

Opening a Program and Keeping It on the Dock

Each time you start a program, its program icon automatically appears on the Dock with a blue dot underneath. When you quit that program, its program icon disappears from the Dock.

If you want to keep the program icon on the Dock after you quit the program, you can choose a Keep in Dock command, which will keep a program's icon on the Dock even after you quit that program.

To see how to use this method to keep a program icon on the Dock, do this:

1. Click the Finder icon on the Dock. The Finder window appears.
2. Click **Applications** in the left pane of the Finder window to display your program icons.
3. Double-click the **Calculator** icon. The Calculator window appears on the screen and the Calculator icon appears on the Dock.
4. Right-click the Calculator icon on the Dock. A pop-up menu appears, as shown in Figure 5-7. You can also move the mouse pointer over the Calculator icon on the Dock and hold down the left mouse button to display a menu, as shown in Figure 5-8.

FIGURE 5-7: *Right-clicking a running program's icon on the Dock displays a pop-up menu.*

FIGURE 5-8: *Clicking and holding on a running program's icon on the Dock displays a pop-up menu.*

5. Choose **Options ▸ Keep in Dock**.
6. Select **Calculator ▸ Quit** or press ⌘-Q. The Calculator program window disappears, but the Calculator program icon stays on the Dock.

Removing an Icon from the Dock by Dragging

Just as you can add an icon to the Dock by dragging it from the Finder window to the Dock, you can also remove an icon by dragging it off the Dock and dropping it anywhere away from the Dock, as shown in Figure 5-9.

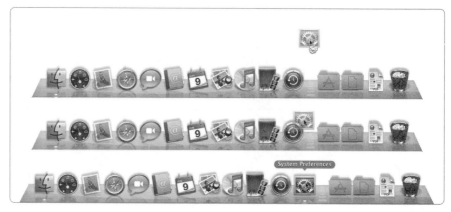

FIGURE 5-9: *To remove an icon from the Dock, just drag it off the Dock.*

To remove a program icon from the Dock by dragging it, do this:

1. Move the mouse pointer over an icon on the Dock that you no longer want, such as the Calculator program icon.
2. Drag the program icon away from the Dock.
3. Release the mouse button. Your program icon disappears in an animated puff of smoke.

✳ **NOTE:** Removing a program icon from the Dock does not delete the program; you can still find its program icon in the Applications window using the Finder.

Choosing the Remove from Dock Command

Another way to remove an icon from the Dock is to right-click the icon and then choose the Remove from Dock command. To see how this works, do this:

1. Right-click a program icon on the Dock that you want to remove, such as the Calculator or Address Book icon. A pop-up menu appears, as shown in Figure 5-10.
2. Choose **Options ▸ Remove from Dock**. Your chosen program icon disappears in an animated puff of smoke.

✳ **NOTE:** Removing a program icon from the Dock does not delete the program; you can still find its program icon in the Applications window using the Finder.

FIGURE 5-10: *Right-clicking a program icon on the Dock displays a pop-up menu.*

Adding and Removing Files and Folders on the Dock

If you have files or folders that you frequently use, you can store them on the right side of the Dock (right of the white dividing line) near the Applications, Documents, and Downloads folders and the Trash icon. (See Project 13 for further information on adding folders to the Dock.)

Adding a File or Folder to the Dock

You can add any file or folder to the Dock for one-click access to that file or folder. To add a file or folder to the Dock, do this:

1. Click the Finder icon on the Dock. The Finder window appears.
2. (Optional) Double-click the folder icons in the right pane of the Finder window to navigate to a different folder.
3. Drag a file or folder from the Finder window to the right side of the Dock. Your file or folder now appears on the Dock. If you click a file icon on the Dock, you'll open that file and load the program that created that file. If you click a folder icon on the Dock, you'll see a list of file icons stored in that folder.

✳ **NOTE:** Dragging a file or folder from the Finder window to the Dock does not delete that file or folder from its location.

Removing a File or Folder from the Dock

If you've added a file or folder to the Dock, you can always remove it by doing this:

1. Move the mouse pointer over the file or folder icon that you want to remove from the Dock.
2. Drag the icon away from the Dock.
3. Release the mouse button. Your file or folder icon disappears in an animated puff of smoke.

✳ **NOTE:** Removing a file or folder icon from the Dock does not erase that file or folder. It is still located in the folder you dragged it from.

Additional Ideas for Customizing the Dock

By changing the size of the Dock and turning on magnification, you can make the Dock easier to see, which can be handy if you have trouble seeing all the icons stored on the Dock. If you don't like other people using your computer when you're away, move the Dock to the left or right side of the screen and turn on hiding. Unless someone knows to move the mouse pointer to the left or right of the screen, they won't be able to find the Dock, which can keep them from running programs (unless they know how to start the Finder program without using the Dock).

Since the Dock contains lots of icons, take a moment to remove the ones you don't want and add new icons for programs that you need on a regular basis. Then consider dragging a file or folder to the Dock as well for quick access to that file or folder.

Just remember that the more icons you store on the Dock, the smaller each icon must appear to show the entire Dock. By customizing the Dock, you can make the Dock display your favorite programs so you can work more efficiently.

6

Manipulating Windows

Every program for the Macintosh displays windows that contain data. Although every program works with different data, every program's windows act and look alike. You can expand a window to fill your entire screen or open multiple windows to copy data between windows. By knowing how to manipulate program windows, you can make yourself as productive as possible with your favorite Macintosh programs.

For example, you might open a word processor window next to a window displaying a web page so you can copy text from the web browser window to your word processor window. During tax time, open a window containing last year's taxes next to a second window displaying your current year's taxes so you can compare the two sets of tax data. Windows let you organize your data so you can view and work with it as if you were laying different pieces of paper on a desk.

Project goal: Learn to manipulate windows on the screen to help you work with your data.

What You'll Be Using

To learn how to manipulate windows, you'll use the following:

▶ The Finder

▶ The Safari web browser

▶ Exposé

▶ Spaces

Arranging Windows

Every program window consists of several parts that allow you to manipulate the window, as shown in Figure 6-1:

▶ Close button (red)

▶ Minimize button (yellow)

▶ Zoom button (green)

▶ Title bar

▶ Toolbar toggle (appears only on windows that display icons underneath the title bar)

▶ Scrollbars and arrows

▶ Resize corner

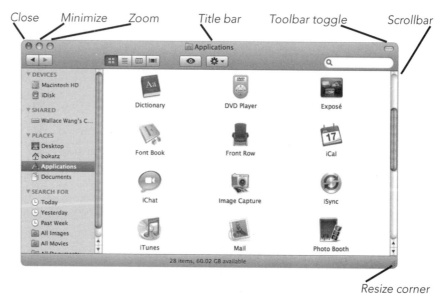

FIGURE 6-1: The parts used for manipulating a window

Closing a Window

Every time you open a window, you'll eventually need to close it again. You can close a window by clicking in the window you want to close and then selecting **File ▶ Close** or pressing ⌘-W.

Another way to close a window is to click the close button of that window. To see how the close button works, try the following:

1. Click the Finder icon on the Dock. The Finder window appears.
2. Click the close button of the Finder window. The Finder window disappears.

✳ *NOTE:* **Closing a window simply closes the file window, but the program keeps running. Quitting a program closes all of that program's windows and shuts down the program. If you want to stop using a file but still want to use that program, close a window. If you're done using a program, you can quit that program by choosing Quit from the Application menu, where the Application menu displays the name of the program, such as iPhoto or Safari. You can also quit an application by right-clicking its icon in the Dock, then clicking Quit.**

Moving a Window

Windows don't always appear where you want them, so you can move them to new positions on the screen. To move a window, use the mouse to drag the window's title bar. Try the following:

1. Click the Finder icon on the Dock. The Finder window appears.
2. Move the mouse over the title bar of the Finder window.
3. Drag the mouse. Notice that as long as you hold down the left mouse button, the Finder window moves wherever you move the mouse.
4. Release the left mouse button when you're happy with the position of the window.

Resizing a Window

A window may be too small or too large to display its contents. To fix this problem, you can resize a window by dragging the resize corner with the mouse. To see how the resize corner works, try the following:

1. Click the Finder icon on the Dock. The Finder window appears.
2. Move the mouse over the resize corner of the Finder window.
3. Drag the mouse. Notice that as long as you hold down the left mouse button, the window shrinks or expands as you move the mouse.
4. Release the mouse button when you're happy with the size of the window.

Scrolling a Window

Many times a window won't be large enough to display all of its contents at once, no matter how large you make the window. To view all the contents of a window, use the scrollbars located on the right side and bottom of a window. The *vertical scrollbar* (on the right side) lets you scroll up and down while the *horizontal scrollbar* (on the bottom) lets you scroll left and right. If a scrollbar isn't visible, that means the window already displays all of its contents on the screen.

To use a scrollbar, you have three choices, as shown in Figure 6-2:

▶   Click the scroll arrows.

▶   Drag the scroll box.

▶   Click in the scroll area.

Scroll box

Scroll area

Scroll arrows

FIGURE 6-2: A scrollbar lets you view the contents of a window.

To see how to scroll through a window, try the following:

1. Click the Finder icon on the Dock. The Finder window appears.
2. Move the mouse over the resize corner of the Finder window.
3. Drag the mouse to make the Finder window smaller and bigger. Notice that if you make the window too small, scrollbars appear. If you make the window large enough to display its contents, the scrollbars disappear.
4. Release the mouse button when the window displays at least one scrollbar.
5. Click the scroll arrows. Notice how the window scrolls a little bit each time you click a scroll arrow.
6. Click the scroll area of the scrollbar. Notice that clicking the scroll area makes the window scroll in large increments.
7. Drag the scroll box. Notice that dragging the scroll box lets you smoothly scroll in a window.

* **NOTE:** Rather than use the scrollbars on a window, you may find it easier to scroll by rolling the scroll ball on your mouse. If you have a trackpad on a new Mac laptop, press two fingertips on the trackpad and hold one finger still while sliding up and down on the trackpad (or right and left) with the second fingertip. You can also slide both fingers up and down (or right and left) in parallel.

Minimizing a Window

Moving a window or resizing a window to make it smaller may get a window out of the way, but sometimes you need to get a window off the screen altogether. Rather than closing the window (and opening it again later), you can temporarily hide a window by *minimizing* it.

A minimized window disappears from the screen and appears as a thumbnail image on the right side of the Dock near the Trash icon. When you want to view the window again, just click its thumbnail image on the Dock and the window springs back into view. To see how this works, try the following:

1. Click the Finder icon on the Dock. The Finder window appears.
2. Click the minimize button on the Finder window. The Finder window shrinks to a thumbnail image on the Dock, as shown in Figure 6-3. Notice that the Finder window no longer appears on the screen.

Minimized window

FIGURE 6-3: *A minimized window appears on the Dock as a thumbnail image.*

3. Click the thumbnail image of the Finder window on the Dock. The Finder window reappears on the screen.

Zooming a Window

Resizing a window can change a window's size, but a faster way to expand or shrink a window is to click the zoom button—the green button at the top-left corner of a window. When you click the zoom button with some programs (such as TextEdit), the window may expand in size to fill the entire screen. When you click the zoom button with other programs (such as Safari), the window expands in size just enough to display its contents so you don't have to scroll horizontally.

The next time you click the zoom button, the window shrinks back to its original size. Clicking the zoom button toggles a window's size from large to small. To experiment with the zoom button, try the following:

1. Click the Finder icon on the Dock. The Finder window appears.
2. Click the zoom button on the Finder window. The Finder window expands.
3. Click the zoom button on the Finder window again. The Finder window shrinks.

Hiding the Toolbar of a Window

Some (not all) windows display a row of icons, called a *toolbar*, at the top of the window. By clicking these icons, you can choose a command without using a menu.

Since the toolbar takes up space, you can hide toolbar icons by clicking the Toolbar toggle, which appears in the upper-right corner of a window. To view the toolbars again, click the Toolbar toggle once more. To see how to hide and display a window's toolbars selectively, try the following:

1. Click the Finder icon on the Dock. The Finder window appears.
2. Click the Toolbar toggle on the Finder window. The Finder window hides its toolbar icons, as shown in Figure 6-4.

Toolbar icons displayed   Toolbar icons hidden

FIGURE 6-4: *Clicking the Toolbar toggle switches between hiding and displaying the toolbar icons.*

3.   Click the Toolbar toggle on the Finder window again. The Finder window displays its toolbar icons once more.

Hiding and Displaying Windows with Exposé

When you have one or two windows on the screen, it's easy to manipulate those windows. However, manipulating three or more windows on the screen can get cumbersome. To make managing multiple windows easy, your Macintosh comes with a program called Exposé.

Exposé manages windows in three different ways:

▶   Hiding all windows out of sight

▶   Displaying only windows of a single program

▶   Displaying all windows as thumbnail images on the screen

Hiding All Windows out of Sight

If you open up too many windows, you may not be able to see your Desktop. To hide all windows, press the F11 key. Once you've hidden all windows, you can view them all by pressing the F11 key again.

To see how the F11 function key hides all windows, do the following:

1.   Click the Finder icon on the Dock. The Finder window appears.
2.   Click the Safari icon on the Dock. The Safari window appears.
3.   Press the F11 key. Notice that the Finder and Safari windows disappear.

4.	Press the F11 key again. Notice that the Finder and Safari windows appear again.

✳ *NOTE:* **If you have a Mighty Mouse, you can squeeze both side buttons to tuck all windows out of sight. Squeezing the side buttons again displays all windows once more.**

Displaying Only Windows from a Single Program

Rather than hide all windows, you can hide all windows except the windows that belong to a specific program. For example, if you're using a word processor and a spreadsheet, you can hide all spreadsheet windows while displaying only your word processor windows.

To see how the F10 function key displays only windows that belong to a single program, do the following:

1.	Click the Finder icon on the Dock. The Finder window appears.
2.	Click the Safari icon on the Dock. The Safari window appears.
3.	Select **File ▸ New Window** on the Safari menu bar. A second Safari window appears.
4.	Click in the Address text box of the Safari window, type `www.nostarch.com`, and press RETURN. The second Safari window displays the No Starch Press website.
5.	Click the Safari icon on the Dock.
6.	Press the F10 key. Notice that the Finder window disappears, but the two Safari windows still appear, as shown in Figure 6-5.

FIGURE 6-5: Pressing the F10 key displays only windows from a single program.

7. Click either of the Safari window images on the screen. Your chosen window appears on the screen.
8. Click the Finder icon on the Dock. The Finder window appears.
9. Press the F10 key. Notice that only the Finder window appears while the rest of the screen appears dimmed.
10. Press the F10 key again.

* **NOTE: As an alternative to pressing F10, you can also move the mouse pointer over a program icon on the Dock and hold down the left mouse button. After a few seconds, Exposé displays thumbnail images of all windows belonging to that program, as shown in Figure 6-6.**

FIGURE 6-6: *Pointing at a program icon on the Dock and holding down the left mouse button displays thumbnail images of open windows.*

Viewing All Windows as Thumbnail Images

If you have multiple windows open, you can click the one window you want to use. Since windows can overlap and hide other windows, Exposé can display all open windows as thumbnail images on the screen. That way you can click the thumbnail image of a window and switch to that window right away. If you have minimized windows, Exposé displays all currently open windows at the top of the screen and all minimized windows at the bottom of the screen.

To see how the F9 function key displays thumbnail images of all running programs, do the following:

1. Click the Finder icon on the Dock. The Finder window appears.
2. Click the Safari icon on the Dock. The Safari window appears.

3. Select **File ▸ New Window** on the Safari menu bar. A second Safari window appears.
4. Click in the Address text box of the Safari window, type `www.nostarch.com`, and press RETURN. The second Safari window displays the No Starch Press website.
5. Click the Safari icon on the Dock.
6. Press the F9 key. Notice that all windows appear as thumbnail images, as shown in Figure 6-7.
7. Click any thumbnail image of a window. Your chosen window appears on the screen in full size.

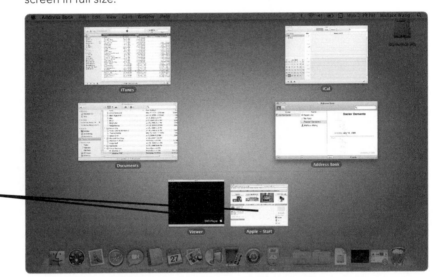

Minimized windows

FIGURE 6-7: *Pressing the F9 key displays all windows as thumbnail images. Minimized windows appear at the bottom and open windows appear at the top.*

Working with Multiple Desktops with Spaces

Pressing the F9, F10, or F11 key makes Exposé organize the windows on your Desktop in a hurry, but you can also organize windows using a program called Spaces. Instead of having one Desktop filled with windows, Spaces lets you fill up to sixteen Desktops with windows.

This would be like having up to sixteen different desks in your office—one desk for storing papers related to work, a second desk for storing papers related to your personal life, and a third desk for storing papers related to your upcoming family plans. Instead of cluttering a single desk with papers, multiple desks help you stay organized by isolating related papers to one desk. The Spaces program works the same way, except it provides your Macintosh with multiple Desktops that you can clutter with different windows.

Setting Up Spaces

To use the Spaces program, you must first turn it on and define how many virtual Desktops you want to create:

1. Click the Apple menu and select **System Preferences**. The System Preferences window appears.
2. Click the **Exposé & Spaces** icon under the Personal category. The Exposé & Spaces window appears.
3. Click the **Spaces** button. The Spaces window appears, as shown in Figure 6-8.

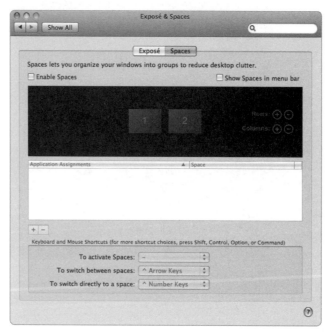

FIGURE 6-8: *The Spaces window lets you turn on Spaces and define how many Desktops you want to create.*

4. Select the **Enable Spaces** checkbox. This turns on Spaces so you can start using it.
5. Select the **Show Spaces in menu bar** checkbox. This lets you control Spaces through a menulet on the right side of the menu bar.

＊ **NOTE:** A menulet appears on the right side of the menu bar and displays a simple menu for controlling one part of your Macintosh, such as the volume or the number of virtual desktops you've created using Spaces.

6. Click the plus (+) button next to the Rows (or Columns) category to add additional rows or columns. To remove virtual Desktops, click the minus (–) button next to the Rows (or Columns) category. Add or remove columns until Spaces displays four virtual Desktops, as shown in Figure 6-9. (To create up to sixteen virtual Desktops, keep clicking the plus button next to the Rows or Columns category.)

7. Click the close button of the Exposé & Spaces window.

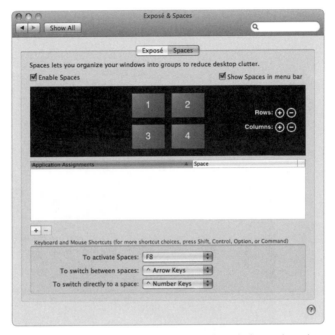

FIGURE 6-9: *You can add Desktops by clicking the plus buttons in the Rows and Columns categories.*

Switching Between Desktops

Once you've turned on Spaces and defined how many virtual Desktops to use, you can start placing windows on the Desktops and switch between them.

To switch Desktops, choose one of four options; the second option is shown in Figure 6-10:

▶ Click the Spaces icon on the Dock (or press F8) and then click a Desktop.

▶ Click the Spaces menulet on the right side of the menu bar and click the Desktop number you want.

▶ Press CTRL-left or right arrow key.

▶ Press CTRL-*number key* to switch to a specific numbered Desktop.

Spaces menulet

FIGURE 6-10: *You can switch between Desktops using the Spaces menulet.*

To see how to switch between Desktops in Spaces, try the following after you've configured Spaces to display two Desktops:

1. Click the Finder icon on the Dock. The Finder window appears.
2. Click the Spaces menulet and choose **2**. Notice that Desktop 2 appears, which currently doesn't have any open windows.
3. Click the Safari icon on the Dock. The Safari window appears.
4. Click the Spaces icon on the Dock or press the F8 key. Spaces displays two virtual Desktops on the screen, as shown in Figure 6-11.
5. Click any Desktop and it appears on the screen.

FIGURE 6-11: *Pressing F8 lets you see all your virtual Desktops at once.*

Moving Windows Between Desktops

If you open a window in one Desktop, you can always move it to another Desktop. To practice moving windows from one Desktop to another, try the following after you've configured Spaces to create two virtual Desktops:

1. Click the Finder icon on the Dock. A Finder window appears.
2. Click the Safari icon on the Dock. A Safari window appears.
3. Click the Spaces icon on the Dock or press F8. Spaces displays your two virtual Desktops on the screen.
4. Move the pointer over the Finder or Safari window. Notice that the pointer turns into a hand icon.

5. Drag the window over the other Desktop and release the left mouse button, as shown in Figure 6-12. Notice that your window now appears on the other Desktop.

FIGURE 6-12: *You can drag program windows from one Desktop to another.*

✳ **NOTE:** Another way to move windows from one Desktop to another is to view a Desktop in normal view, drag a window to the edge of the screen, and wait a few seconds until you see another Desktop appear. Then release the left mouse button.

Additional Ideas for Manipulating Windows

For more ways to manipulate windows, combine Spaces with Exposé. Turn on Spaces and load multiple program windows in two or more virtual Desktops. Then press F8 to display all your virtual Desktops. If you have too many program windows crammed into each Desktop, your virtual Desktops may look like Figure 6-13.

FIGURE 6-13: *Cramming too many program windows on a virtual Desktop can give it a cluttered look.*

If you press the F9 key, Exposé arranges your program windows within all virtual Desktops, as shown in Figure 6-14.

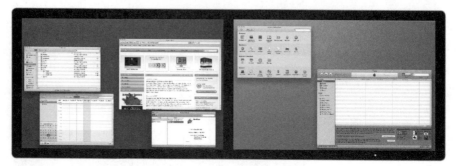

FIGURE 6-14: *Pressing F9 organizes program windows within virtual Desktops.*

Both Exposé and Spaces can keep you organized, while manipulating individual windows can let you control the exact appearance and position of a window on the screen. With so many ways to organize your windows, you have no excuse for not being organized on your Macintosh.

7 Navigating Through Folders with the Finder

Your Macintosh saves data, such as word processor documents, in files, and each file acts like a box for storing information. You can think of your hard disk as a big attic full of boxes of data.

After storing stuff in the attic, you may have trouble finding it again. The same is true after you store files on your hard disk. To help you look for files on your Macintosh, you can use a program called the *Finder*.

Project goal: Learn to use the Finder program to look for files stored on your Macintosh hard disk.

What You'll Be Using

To view the contents of your hard disk, you'll use the following:

▶ The Finder

Understanding Drives, Folders, and Files

Every Macintosh has a hard drive that stores data; you can also attach additional storage drives to your Macintosh, such as an external hard drive or a USB flash drive. Since any type of storage drive (hard drive, USB flash drive, and others) can store thousands (maybe even millions) of files, most drives use folders to divide stored contents into manageable pieces.

Folders provide separate compartments used for storing related files and folders in one place. To help you stay organized, the hard disk on every Macintosh already contains separate folders for storing related files, as shown in Figure 7-1.

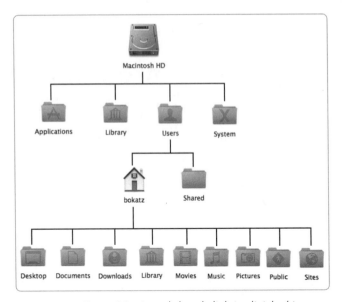

FIGURE 7-1: *Every Macintosh hard disk is divided into multiple folders.*

Your Macintosh hard disk is first divided into four folders:

▶ **Applications**   Contains all programs installed on your Macintosh

▶ **Library**   Contains files used by other programs

▶ **Users**   Contains a folder for each account created on the Macintosh; at least one Home folder is included inside the Users folder, and it is named after the person in charge of the account (in this case, bokatz)

▶ **System**   Contains all the files used by the Mac OS X operating system

Inside the Users folder, you'll find a separate folder for each account created on the Macintosh; this is called the *Home folder*. Inside the Home folder, you'll find additional folders:

▶ **Desktop**   Contains any files and folders placed on the Desktop

▶ **Documents**   Contains all files and folders created and saved in other programs, such as word processor programs, spreadsheet programs, presentation programs, and so on

▶ **Downloads**   Contains all files and folders downloaded from the Internet, such as programs you've purchased from a website or file attachments that other people have sent to you by email

▶ **Library**   Contains files that define how programs (stored in the Applications folder) work for this particular account
    The Library folder allows two different user accounts to access the same program, but the program can look and behave differently for each user. The Library folder also contains the *Fonts folder*, which stores all the fonts available on your Macintosh.

- ▶ **Movies** Contains digital video files, such as those created by iMovie
- ▶ **Music** Contains digital audio files, such as those stored by iTunes
- ▶ **Pictures** Contains digital photograph files, such as those stored by iPhoto
- ▶ **Public** Contains the *Drop Box folder*, where users working on other computers on a network can drop off files for you to retrieve
- ▶ **Sites** Contains all files and folders used to create web pages to display on a website; if you don't create any web pages, this folder will be empty

Understanding the Finder

The Finder lets you view the contents of one folder at a time. The left pane of the Finder window contains the *sidebar*, which lists four categories, as shown in Figure 7-2:

- ▶ **Devices** Lists all storage devices attached to your Macintosh, such as hard disks, flash drives, or CDs/DVDs
- ▶ **Shared** Lists all computers connected to the network; if your Macintosh isn't connected to a network, the Shared category will not appear
- ▶ **Places** Lists commonly used folders, such as Applications and Documents
- ▶ **Search For** Lists all files that you used on your Macintosh at a particular time, such as today, yesterday, or last week

FIGURE 7-2: The Finder window lets you switch to a different folder or drive and view the contents of that folder or drive.

To start the Finder, click the Finder icon (it looks like a square smiling face) on the Dock. If the Finder window doesn't appear on the Dock, select **File ▸ New Finder Window**. (Try it now!)

Viewing the Contents of a Drive

A *drive* is a separate storage item for holding files. Every Macintosh has at least one drive, called the *Macintosh HD (hard disk)*, but you can always add more storage devices (such as an external hard drive or a USB flash drive).

To view the contents of the Macintosh HD with the Finder, do the following:

1. Click the Finder icon on the Dock. The Finder window appears.
2. Click the **Macintosh HD** icon in the sidebar (the left pane of the Finder window) under the Devices category. The right pane of the Finder window displays the contents of the Macintosh hard drive, as shown in Figure 7-3, which contains the Applications, Library, System, and Users folders.

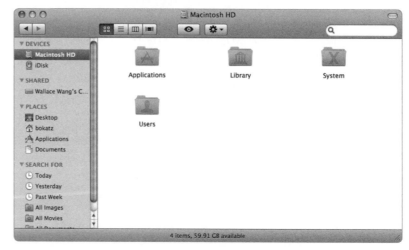

FIGURE 7-3: *Clicking the Macintosh HD icon displays its contents.*

To view the contents of another drive, click its icon under the Devices category in the sidebar.

Viewing a Folder Hierarchy

When you choose a drive in the Finder, you'll see files or folders (or both). Since folders can be buried inside other folders, opening several folders can get you lost in the hierarchy.

To keep yourself oriented as you navigate through multiple folders, you need to know how to open a folder, determine where you are, and return to your starting point.

Opening a Folder

To open a folder and view its contents, you have three choices:

▶ Double-click a folder.

▶ Click a folder and select **File ▶ Open** (or press ⌘-O).

▶ Right-click a folder and select **Open**.

To see how opening folders buries you deeper into the folder hierarchy, try the following:

1. Click the Finder icon on the Dock. The Finder window appears.
2. Click the **Macintosh HD** icon that appears in the sidebar of the Finder window. The right pane of the Finder window displays the Applications, Library, System, and Users folders.
3. Open the **Users** folder by using one of the three methods listed earlier (double-click, press ⌘-O, or right-click and select **Open**). The Shared and Home folders appear in the right pane of the Finder window.
4. Open the **Home** folder. The right pane of the Finder window displays the contents of the Home folder, which includes the Documents and Music folders.
5. Open the **Documents** folder. You have just navigated your way through the folder hierarchy shown in Figure 7-4.

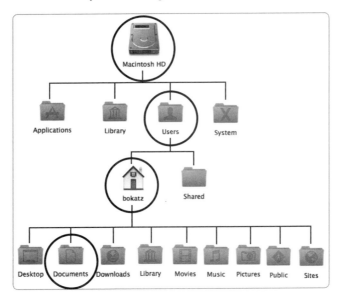

FIGURE 7-4: *You can go deep into the folder hierarchy.*

Identifying Your Location in the Folder Hierarchy

Each time you open a folder, you go deeper into the folder hierarchy. Unfortunately, you may open multiple folders and then lose track of exactly where you are. To help you identify your current location in the folder hierarchy, you can right-click a window's title bar to see a list of all the folders that lead to your current location, as shown in Figure 7-5.

FIGURE 7-5: *The list of folders shows your current location in the folder hierarchy.*

In this figure, the list of folders tells you the following:

▶ The Documents folder is the current folder displayed in the Finder window.

▶ The Documents folder is inside the Home folder named bokatz.

▶ The Home folder bokatz is inside the Users folder.

▶ The Users folder is stored on the Macintosh HD (hard disk).

▶ The Macintosh HD is connected to the computer identified as Bo Katz's Mac mini.

This list of the folder hierarchy serves two purposes. First, it helps you identify your current location in the folder hierarchy. Second, it provides a quick way to view the contents of any folder in this hierarchy list just by clicking its name.

To see how to display the folder hierarchy and switch to a different folder, do the following:

1. Click the Finder icon on the Dock. The Finder window appears.
2. Click **Documents** in the sidebar of the Finder window. The right pane displays the contents of the Documents folder.

3. Right-click the Finder window title bar (which displays *Documents* in the middle-top portion of the window). A list of the folder hierarchy appears.
4. Click **Macintosh HD**. The Finder window displays the contents of your Macintosh hard disk and now displays *Macintosh HD* in its title bar.

✳ **NOTE:** Right-clicking the title bar of a window works in other program windows as well, such as a Microsoft Word or Keynote window.

Navigating Back and Forth Through Folders

Each time you open a folder, you dig deeper into the folder hierarchy. To move back up a folder hierarchy, you have two choices:

▶ Select **Go ▸ Enclosing Folder**.

▶ Click the back arrow in the Finder window. (After you have clicked the back arrow once, you can click the forward arrow to move forward.)

To see how to navigate back and forth through a folder hierarchy, look at the folder hierarchy in Figure 7-1 and try the following:

1. Click the Finder icon on the Dock. The Finder window appears.
2. Click the **Macintosh HD** icon under the Devices category in the sidebar of the Finder window.
3. Double-click the **Users** folder. Your Home and Shared folders appear in the Finder window.
4. Double-click the Home folder (it looks like a little house icon). A variety of folders appear.
5. Double-click the **Downloads** folder. If you haven't downloaded anything from the Internet, the Downloads folder will be empty.
6. Click the back arrow. The Finder window displays the contents of the Home folder, which includes the Downloads folder you just opened.
7. Click the forward arrow. The Finder window displays the contents of the Downloads folder again.
8. Select **Go ▸ Enclosing Folder**. The Finder window displays the contents of the Home folder again.

Selecting the **Go ▸ Enclosing Folder** command always displays the folder that contains (encloses) the folder contents that appear in the Finder window. Clicking the back arrow always returns you to the previous Finder window viewed, which may not be the folder that contains (encloses) the currently displayed folder. To see the difference, try the following:

1. Click the Finder icon on the Dock. The Finder window appears.
2. Click the **Macintosh HD** icon. The Finder window displays the contents of your hard disk.
3. Select **Go ▸ Utilities**. The contents of the Utilities folder appear.
4. Click the back arrow. The Finder displays the contents of your hard disk.

5. Click the forward arrow. The Finder displays the contents of the Utilities folder again.
6. Select **Go ▸ Enclosing Folder**. Now the Finder window displays the contents of the Applications folder, which encloses the Utilities folder.

Shortcuts to Viewing Folders

Opening folders and backing out by using the **Go ▸ Enclosing Folder** command or the back and forward arrows lets you view folders. If you want to jump to a specific folder, you have two choices:

▸ The Go menu

▸ The sidebar

The *Go menu* displays commonly used folders, such as Applications and Home. Select **Go ▸ Recent Folders** to view a list of the last folders you opened. Or you can select the particular folder you want to view from the Go menu.

The sidebar displays icons of commonly used folders such as Applications and Documents. By clicking an icon in the sidebar, you can jump to that specific folder, as shown in Figure 7-6.

FIGURE 7-6: *The Go menu and the sidebar offer one-click access to commonly used folders.*

Additional Ideas for Navigating the Folder Hierarchy

If navigating through the folder hierarchy of your hard disk gets too cumbersome, you can place the folders that you access most often in the sidebar of the Finder window or as a stack on the right side of the Dock.

Placing a Folder in the Finder Sidebar

The Finder sidebar gives you one-click access to folders, and you can add your favorite folders to the sidebar by doing this:

1. Click the Finder icon on the Dock. The Finder window appears.
2. Open the folder that contains the folder you want to place in the sidebar. (So, for example, if you want to add the Downloads folder to the sidebar, open the Home folder, which contains the Downloads folder.)
3. Drag the chosen folder to the sidebar under the Places category. A horizontal line appears to show you where your folder will appear when you release the mouse button.
4. Release the mouse button when the horizontal line appears where you want your folder to appear in the sidebar.

* **NOTE:** To remove a folder from the sidebar, right-click the folder in the sidebar and select Remove From Sidebar. Removing a folder from the sidebar does not delete the folder or any files inside.

Placing a Folder as a Stack on the Dock

In addition to placing your favorite folders on the sidebar, you can also place a folder as a stack on the Dock for one-click access. Here's how:

1. Click the Finder icon on the Dock. The Finder window appears.
2. Open the folder that contains the folder you want to place on the Dock. (If, for example, you want to add the Movies folder to the Dock, open the Home folder, which contains the Movies folder.)
3. Drag your chosen folder to the right side of the divider (which looks like a thick dotted line) of the Dock. Any existing stacks slide out of the way.
4. Release the mouse button to place your chosen folder as a stack on the Dock. Now you can click this stack any time to access the files inside.

* **NOTE:** To remove a stack from the Dock, drag the stack off the Dock and release the mouse button. The stack disappears in a puff of animated smoke. Removing a stack from the Dock does not delete the folder or any files inside.

By storing your favorite folders in the sidebar or on the Dock, you'll never lose track of your files again.

<table>
<tr><td>**8**</td><td># Managing and Viewing Your Files and Folders</td></tr>
</table>

Your Macintosh stores data in files. To create a file, you need to use a program such as a word processor program, a paint program, a spreadsheet program, or a presentation program. Every time you create a file that you want to keep, you must save it, name it, and specify where it will be stored.

Filenames are for your benefit, so you should choose descriptive names, such as *Letter to the Ex-Wife* or *Tax Returns 2010*. You can store files on any storage device or drive, but you'll probably store similar files together in a folder to make it easy to find them when you need them later.

After you've created a file or folder, you can copy or move that file or folder to a new location at any time. You might also want to rename a file or folder. Just as you can store and rearrange stuff in your home, you can store and rearrange stuff saved on your Macintosh.

Project goal: Learn to create, view, copy, move, and rename files and folders stored on your Macintosh.

What You'll Be Using

To create, view, copy, move, and rename files and folders, you'll use the following:

▶   The Finder

▶   The TextEdit program

Creating Files and Folders

To create a file, you first need to create new data (by typing text or drawing a picture, for example) using a program (such as a word processor or paint program). You then select **File ▸ Save** to save the file. To create a folder, you have two options:

▸ Create a new folder in the Save dialog.

▸ Create a new folder in the Finder window.

Creating a Folder in the Save Dialog

When you save a file for the first time, you will name the file and define where to store it. At this time, you can store a file in an existing folder or create a new folder in which to store the file.

To see how to create a new folder using the Save dialog, do this:

1. Click the Finder icon on the Dock. The Finder window appears.
2. Double-click the **TextEdit** icon to load the TextEdit program.
3. Type a sentence.
4. Select **File ▸ Save**. A Save As dialog appears, as shown in Figure 8-1.

FIGURE 8-1: *The Save As dialog typically appears in a condensed version.*

5. Click the downward-pointing arrow button that appears to the right of the Save As text box. The Save As dialog expands, as shown in Figure 8-2.
6. Click a drive in the left pane of the Save As dialog, such as the Macintosh HD. The middle pane displays any folders already stored on the chosen drive.

FIGURE 8-2: *Expanding the Save As dialog displays the New Folder button and other options.*

7.   (Optional) Click a folder in the middle pane, such as the Users folder, if you clicked the Macintosh HD in the preceding step. The right pane displays the contents of this folder. Repeat this step for each additional folder you want to open.
8.   Click the **New Folder** button. A New Folder dialog appears.
9.   Type a descriptive name for your folder and click **Create**. At this point, you can type a name for your file to store it in your newly created folder by clicking the **Save** button.

Creating a Folder in the Finder Window

You can also create a new folder using the Finder window. Here's how:

1.   Click the Finder icon on the Dock. The Finder window appears.
2.   Open the folder in which you want to create a new folder.
3.   Select **File ▸ New Folder**. An untitled folder appears.
4.   Type a descriptive name for your folder and press RETURN.

Changing the View of Folders

The Finder window can display the contents of a folder in four different ways, as shown in Figure 8-3:

▸   **Icons**   Displays files and folders as large icons or pictures

▸   **List**   Displays files and folders as tiny icons, with names and the dates and times that they were last modified

▶ **Columns**   Displays files and folders in columns so you can easily see the folder hierarchy

▶ **Cover Flow**   Displays files and folders as a combination of the Icons and List views

Icons   *List*

Columns   *Cover Flow*

FIGURE 8-3: *Views let you see your files and folders in different ways.*

To change the view of a folder, do the following:

1. Click the Finder icon on the Dock. The Finder window appears.
2. Click the **Applications** folder in the sidebar (the left pane) of the Finder window. The contents of the Applications folder appears in the Finder window.
3. Click the List button or select **View ▸ as List**. Notice how the Finder window changes the way your files and folders appear.
4. Click the Columns button or select **View ▸ as Columns**.
5. Click the Cover Flow button or select **View ▸ as Cover Flow**.
6. Click the Icons button or select **View ▸ as Icons**.

* **NOTE:** When you display Finder window contents in the as Icons view, you can magnify the size of the icons by dragging the slider that appears in the bottom-right corner of the Finder window, as shown in Figure 8-4.

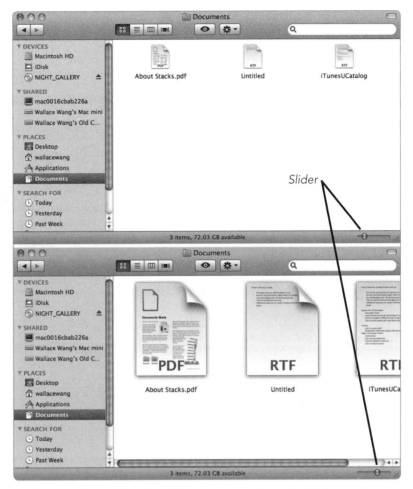

Slider

FIGURE 8-4: *Dragging the slider can magnify or shrink icons displayed in the as Icons view.*

Peeking Inside a File

The Finder window can show you where your files are located. If you want to see the contents inside your files, you could double-click a file to open it, but a faster method is to use the Quick Look feature.

The *Quick Look* feature lets you peek at a file's contents without having to start a program. To use the Quick Look feature, click a filename and then do one of the following:

▸ Click the Quick Look button (it looks like an eye in the top of the Finder window).

▸ Press ⌘-Y.

▶ Select **File ▶ Quick Look**.

▶ Right-click a filename and select **Quick Look**.

To exit the Quick Look feature, click the close button on the Quick Look window, as shown in Figure 8-5.

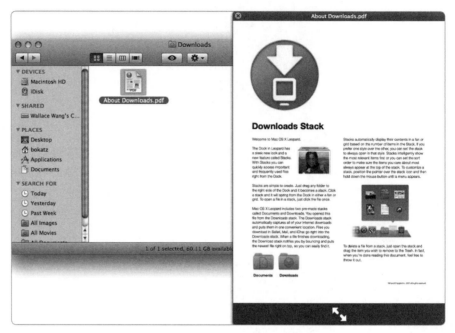

FIGURE 8-5: *Quick Look displays the contents of a file without opening that file in a program.*

Renaming a File or Folder

After you've created a file or folder, you might want to rename it, especially if you misspelled the filename or folder name. To rename a file or folder, do this:

1. Click the Finder icon on the Dock. The Finder window appears.
2. Open the folder that contains the file or folder you want to rename.
3. Click the file or folder you want to rename. The filename or folder name appears highlighted.
4. Press RETURN. A text box appears around the filename or folder name so you can edit it.
5. Type a new name or use the arrow and DELETE keys to edit the existing name.
6. Press RETURN. Your file or folder displays its new name.

Deleting a File or Folder

When you no longer need a file or folder, you can get rid of it to save space on your hard disk and keep things organized. Just remember that when you delete a folder, you also delete all files and folders within it. Before deleting a folder, be sure you want to delete everything inside that folder. You can play it safe and delete files individually.

Here's how to delete a file or folder:

1. Click the Finder icon on the Dock. The Finder window appears.
2. Open the folder that contains the file or folder you want to delete.
3. Click the file or folder you want to delete. (Hold down the ⌘ key while clicking to select multiple files and folders.)
4. Drag the selected file(s) or folder(s) over the Trash icon on the Dock, or select **File ▸ Move to Trash**, or right-click the file or folder and choose **Move to Trash**.

* *NOTE:* **To retrieve a file or folder from the Trash, click the Trash icon to open the Finder window, then right-click a file or folder. When a pop-up menu appears, choose Put Back, which returns the file or folder back to its last location before you deleted it. You can also select and drag the deleted files or folders to a new location on your hard disk. If you right-click the Trash icon on the Dock and click Empty Trash, your Macintosh erases any deleted files or folders permanently. Until you click the Empty Trash option, your deleted files and folders still take up physical space on your hard disk.**

Copying a File or Folder

The most straightforward way to copy a file or folder is to use the Edit menu's Copy and Paste commands. Here's how:

1. Click the Finder icon on the Dock. The Finder window appears.
2. Open the folder that contains the file or folder you want to copy.
3. Click to select the file(s) or folder(s) you want to copy. (Hold down the ⌘ key as you click to select multiple files and folders.)
4. Select **Edit ▸ Copy**, or press ⌘-C.
5. Open the folder in which you want to store the copy or copies of your selected file(s) or folder(s).
6. Select **Edit ▸ Paste**, or press ⌘-V, to paste your copied files or folders in your chosen folder.

* *NOTE:* **If you change your mind about copying and pasting a file or folder to a new location, press ⌘-Z or select Edit ▸ Undo Copy immediately after you've pasted the file.**

You can also copy files and folders from one drive to another by dragging them with the mouse. To copy a file or folder by dragging, do the following:

1. Click the Finder icon on the Dock. The Finder window appears.
2. Open the folder that contains the file or folder you want to copy.
3. Click the file or folder you want to copy. (Hold down the ⌘ key to click and select multiple files and folders.)
4. Drag the selected file(s) or folder(s) over a drive listed in the sidebar of the Finder window. A plus sign appears in a green circle by the pointer to let you know that the dragging mouse is moving a copy of the file or folder rather than the actual file or folder itself.

✳ *NOTE:* **If you hold the pointer over a drive for a few seconds, the Finder window displays the contents of that drive, so you can then move the pointer over a folder on that drive.**

5. Release the mouse button to copy your chosen file or folder to the location displayed inside the Finder window.

✳ *NOTE:* **If you try these steps to copy a folder or file from one folder to another on the same drive, hold down the OPTION key as you drag. A plus sign appears in a green circle by the pointer to let you know that the mouse is dragging copies of the item(s).**

Moving a File or Folder

You can move a file or folder in two ways, depending on whether you're moving a file or folder on the same drive or between two different drives. To move a file or folder between folders on the same drive, do the following:

1. Click the Finder icon on the Dock. The Finder window appears.
2. Open the folder that contains the file or folder you want to move.
3. Click the file or folder you want to move. (Hold down the ⌘ key to click and select multiple files and folders.)
4. Drag the selected file(s) or folder(s) over another folder on the same drive (either inside the right pane of the Finder window or over a folder in the sidebar) and wait until the Finder window opens the contents of that folder. Keep holding down the left mouse button.
5. Move the mouse pointer over the folder in which you want to move the file(s) or folder(s), and then release the left mouse button when the Finder highlights the appropriate folder.

To move a file or folder between two different drives, rather than copy it, you must hold down the ⌘ key while dragging the item between the drives. (If you don't hold down the ⌘ key, you'll copy the file or folder instead of moving it.)

To move a file or folder from one drive to another drive, do the following:

1. Click the Finder icon on the Dock. The Finder window appears.
2. Open the folder that contains the file or folder you want to move.
3. Click the file or folder you want to move. (Hold down the ⌘ key and click to select multiple files and folders.)
4. Hold down the ⌘ key and drag your selected file(s) or folder(s) over the receiving drive in the sidebar of the Finder window. Wait a few seconds until the Finder window opens the contents of that drive. Keep holding down the left mouse button.
5. Move the mouse pointer over a folder and wait a few seconds until the Finder opens that folder. Repeat this for each additional folder you want to open.
6. Release the left mouse button and the ⌘ key when the Finder highlights the folder where you want to move your selected file(s) or folder(s).

* **NOTE:** **If you change your mind about copying and pasting a file or folder to a new location, press ⌘-Z or select Edit ▸ Undo Move immediately after pasting.**

Additional Ideas for Managing and Viewing Files and Folders

Folders can help you stay organized, so you should create additional folders in your Documents folder to arrange and organize your files. Whenever your files or folders start looking cluttered or disorganized, you should think about creating a new folder, moving files to another folder, or deleting files to keep things tidy. By peeking inside files using the Quick Look feature, you can quickly see which files you need to keep and which files you can safely delete.

Keeping your files and folders organized is an ongoing task, like brushing your teeth or filling your car with gas, and it lets you spend more time working and less time searching for information on your Macintosh. Spend a little time periodically to keep your files and folders organized. You'll be glad you did.

9

Conserving Energy While Using Your Macintosh

If you're concerned about global warming, you can do something about it with your Macintosh. Every computer needs electricity to work, but too often people leave computers running when they're not using them, which gobbles up power unnecessarily. While you could turn your computer off and then on again when you need it, doing so several times a day can actually harm your computer since every time you turn it back on again, it receives a jolt of electricity to start it up.

As a safer alternative to turning your Macintosh on and off repeatedly, you can let it go to sleep when it's not in use. This reduces the amount of power consumed by your Macintosh, yet keeps it turned on so it's ready for use at the touch of the keyboard.

When your Macintosh is turned on, it needs power to spin its hard disk, display images on the screen, and do actual work with its processor. Such normal use typically consumes 60 to 120 watts, which is about the same amount of power used by an ordinary light bulb. However, if you let your Macintosh go to sleep, you can reduce the amount of power it uses to 5 watts or less.

Project goal: Learn how to conserve power by letting your Macintosh go to sleep.

What You'll Be Using

To make a Macintosh sleep and wake up, you need only the following:

▶ The System Preferences program

The Parts of Your Macintosh That Will Go to Sleep

The three biggest power-consuming parts of your Macintosh are the following:

▶ **Processor**   This is the part that does all the work, such as calculating mathematical equations in a spreadsheet or determining the trajectory of a missile fired in a video game based on the movement of the mouse.

▶ **Display**   This part is the screen that shows windows, menus, and icons so you can control your Macintosh and read information.

▶ **Hard disk**   This is where your Macintosh stores programs and data.

You can choose to put only one or two of these items to sleep, but for maximum energy conservation, you should put all of them to sleep after a fixed amount of time. This fixed amount of time is known as the *inactivity time*. You define the inactivity time, which is the amount of time your Macintosh waits after it detects no activity (such as your moving the mouse or typing) before going to sleep. Everyone has his or her own idea of the most appropriate inactivity period. Some people use a short inactivity period, such as 5 minutes, but you may find that's too short and your Macintosh will actually go to sleep in the middle of your work! On the other hand, if you define a long inactivity time, such as 1 hour, your computer could waste electricity while you're away from it. Around 15 to 20 minutes can be a reasonable amount of inactivity time, but see what works for you.

＊*NOTE:* **You can define specific inactivity times for your processor and monitor but not for your hard disk, since your hard disk could be saving files or running additional programs while you're not using your computer.**

To define an inactivity time for your processor and monitor, and to make your Macintosh's hard disk go to sleep whenever possible, do the following:

1. Click the Apple menu and select **System Preferences**. A System Preferences window appears.
2. Click the **Energy Saver** icon under the Hardware category. The Energy Saver window appears, as shown in Figure 9-1.
3. (Optional) If you have a laptop, you'll see two tabs labeled Battery and Power Adapter. This lets you define different sleep settings for when your laptop is running off its Battery or Power Adapter. Click the Battery or Power Adapter tab.

＊*NOTE:* **If you have a laptop, you'll see both Settings for and Optimization pop-up menus, which let you define different power-saving settings when running a laptop using batteries or a power adapter. If you have a desktop, you won't see these pop-up menus.**

4. Drag the **Computer Sleep** slider to specify a time, such as 15 minutes. This slider defines when to put the processor to sleep.

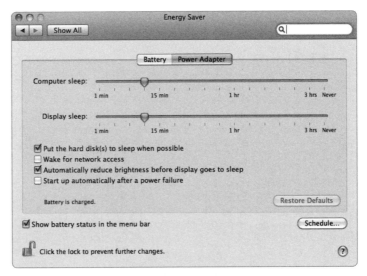

FIGURE 9-1: *The Energy Saver window lets you define an inactivity time for the processor and monitor.*

5. Drag the **Display Sleep** slider to specify a time, such as 15 minutes. This slider defines when to put the monitor to sleep (it tends to consume the most electricity).

6. Select or clear the **Put the hard disk(s) to sleep when possible** checkbox. If selected, this option waits until the hard disk isn't busy to put it to sleep.

7. Click the close button on the Energy Saver window.

* **NOTE: To wake up a Macintosh that's sleeping, just tap any key on the keyboard.**

Forcing Your Macintosh to Sleep

If you know you're going to be away from your Macintosh, you can wait for your Macintosh to go to sleep automatically or you can make it go to sleep right away.

If you have a laptop, the fastest way to make it go to sleep is to close the screen.

Of course, you can't close up a desktop like a laptop, but you can define a *hot corner* on your desktop or laptop to tell your Macintosh to sleep when you move your mouse to that corner. Here's how to define a hot corner to put your Macintosh to sleep:

1. Click the Apple menu and choose **System Preferences**. A System Preferences window appears.

2. Click the **Desktop & Screen Saver** icon that appears under the Personal category. A Desktop & Screen Saver window appears.

3. Click the **Screen Saver** tab. The Screen Saver options appear, as shown in Figure 9-2.

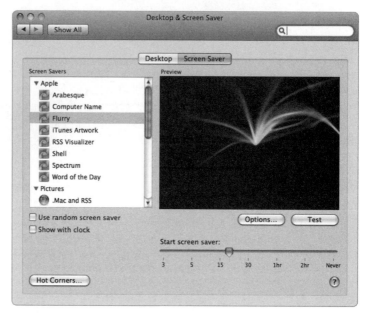

FIGURE 9-2: *The Desktop & Screen Saver window displays a list of different screensavers you can choose.*

4. Click the **Hot Corners** button in the bottom-left corner of the Desktop & Screen Saver window. A sheet drops down and displays pop-up menus at each of the four corners of a thumbnail image of a screen.
5. Click a pop-up menu near the corner you want to define as a hot corner and a menu of options appears, as shown in Figure 9-3. Choose **Put Display to Sleep**.
6. Click **OK**.
7. Click the close button of the Desktop & Screen Saver window, or select **System Preferences ▸ Quit System Preferences**. Now you can force your Macintosh to go to sleep by moving the mouse into the hot corner you defined as Sleep Display.

✳ **NOTE:** You can define more than one hot corner at a time, such as the two bottom corners or the two right corners.

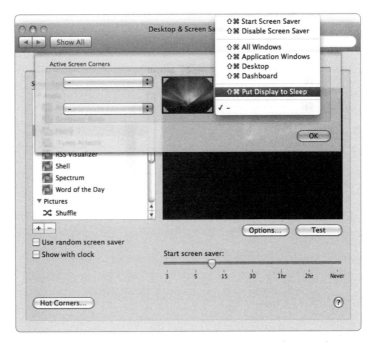

FIGURE 9-3: *Choose Put Display to Sleep to indicate where the hot corner will be located on the screen.*

Making Your Macintosh Sleep on a Schedule

You can make your Macintosh fall asleep according to a particular schedule. (This is similar to scheduling your Macintosh to turn itself on and off, as described in Project 1.)

Here's how to schedule a time to make your Macintosh sleep and wake up:

1. Click the Apple menu and select **System Preferences**. The System Preferences window appears.
2. Click the **Energy Saver** icon under the Hardware category. An Energy Saver window appears (see Figure 9-1).
3. Click the **Schedule** button in the bottom-right corner of the Energy Saver window. A scheduling sheet drops down and displays different time options, as shown in Figure 9-4.
4. Select the **Start up or wake** checkbox.
5. Click the pop-up menu next to the Start up or wake checkbox and choose an option such as Every Day or Monday.
6. Click in the time text box and type a time or click the up/down arrows to set a time, such as 7:00 AM.

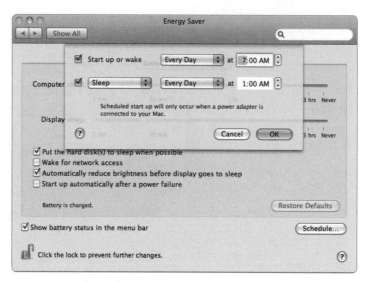

FIGURE 9-4: *The scheduling sheet lets you define a wake-up and sleep time.*

7. Select the second checkbox underneath the Start up or wake checkbox, click the pop-up menu, and choose **Sleep**.
8. Click the next pop-up menu and choose a day such as Every Day or Friday.
9. Click in the time text box and type a time or click the up/down arrows to set a time, such as 5:15 PM.
10. Click **OK**. The Energy Saver window appears again.
11. Click the close button of the System Preferences window, or select **System Preferences ▸ Quit System Preferences**.

Additional Ideas for Conserving Energy

To conserve even more energy when using your computer, consider using a laptop instead of a desktop. Laptop models use less electricity. You can even attach a mouse, keyboard, and monitor to a laptop so you can use a bigger screen and keyboard at your desk while still having the option of carrying your laptop around wherever you need it.

If you have a desktop Macintosh, shut it down when you know you won't be using it for an extended period of time, such as over the weekend or when you're on vacation. Although a Macintosh doesn't consume a large amount of electricity, every little bit that you save can help, and that also means a lower electricity bill for you.

PART 2

Making Life Easier with Shortcuts

10 Working Faster with Shortcut Commands

Using pull-down menus from the menu bar is the most straightforward way to control your Macintosh, but it's not the only way. Since the two-step process of clicking a pull-down menu and then clicking a command can be cumbersome, your Macintosh offers three different types of shortcuts to help you choose commands faster:

► Keyboard shortcuts

► Buttons

► Shortcut menus

Project goal: Learn how to choose your favorite commands quickly using a shortcut rather than the menu bar.

What You'll Be Using

You'll be using the following:

► The Finder

► The TextEdit program

Using Keyboard Shortcuts

Every Macintosh program provides shortcut keys you can use for choosing common commands. You'll find that using these keyboard shortcuts is often faster than clicking through various menus to select commands. Table 10-1 displays the most common keyboard shortcuts that work in any program.

Table 10-1: Common Keyboard Shortcuts

Shortcut	Action	Equivalent Menu Selection
⌘-N	Create a new file	File ▶ New
⌘-O	Open a file	File ▶ Open
⌘-W	Close the active window	File ▶ Close
⌘-S	Save a file	File ▶ Save
⌘-F	Find	Edit ▶ Find
⌘-Q	Quit a program	*Program name* ▶ Quit *Program name*
⌘-Z	Undo	Edit ▶ Undo
⌘-C	Copy	Edit ▶ Copy
⌘-X	Cut	Edit ▶ Cut
⌘-V	Paste	Edit ▶ Paste
⌘-A	Select all	Edit ▶ Select All

Along with the general shortcuts listed in Table 10-1, every program includes shortcuts that are specific to that program. To view a program's particular command shortcuts, load the program and open the pull-down menus. If a command offers a keyboard shortcut, it appears to the right of the command, as shown in Figure 10-1.

To save space, pull-down menus use symbols to represent different keys. For example, to choose the Print command, you hold down the Command key (⌘), press P, and then release both keys. Table 10-2 lists some of the common symbols you'll see on pull-down menus.

Table 10-2: Common Keyboard Shortcut Symbols

Symbol	Key
⌘	Command
⇧	Shift
⌥	Option
⌃	Control (Ctrl)
⌫	Delete

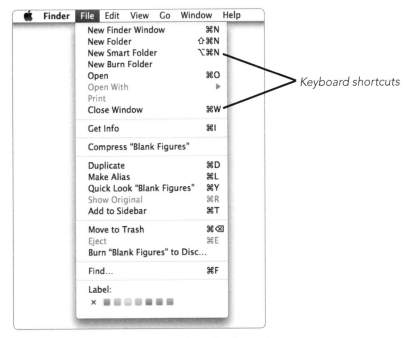

FIGURE 10-1: *Program menus show keyboard shortcuts directly to the right of specific commands.*

Using Buttons

Many programs also display graphical icons or buttons at the top of the window to represent a specific command, such as an icon of a printer to represent the Print command. By clicking one of these buttons, you can choose a command quickly and easily.

Since the purpose of each button may not be obvious from its icon, you can move the mouse over a button and wait a moment until a short description of that button's purpose appears, as shown in Figure 10-2.

To see some examples of these one-click buttons, try the following:

1. Click the Finder icon on the Dock. The Finder window appears.
2. Click **Applications** in the left pane of the Finder window.
3. Click the Icons, List, Columns, and Cover Flow buttons to switch the appearance of the Finder window. Notice how fast and easy clicking buttons can be compared to using pull-down menus.

* **NOTE:** **Not every command has an equivalent icon button or keyboard shortcut.**

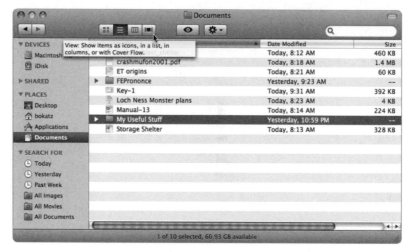

FIGURE 10-2: *Moving the mouse pointer over an icon button displays a short description of that button's purpose.*

Using Shortcut Menus

Pull-down menus can overwhelm you with too many choices. To display a limited list of useful commands, use *shortcut menus*, which appear when you right-click an item. For example, if you want to delete a file, right-click the filename, and when the shortcut menu appears, select **Move to Trash**.

To see how shortcut menus work, try this:

1. Click the Finder icon on the Dock. The Finder window appears.
2. Click **Applications** in the left pane of the Finder window.
3. Move the mouse over an icon, such as the System Preferences icon, and right-click the mouse. (If you're using a laptop, hold down two fingers on the trackpad or hold down the CTRL key and press the trackpad button to simulate a right-click.) A shortcut menu appears, listing commands, as shown in Figure 10-3.
4. Press ESC or click the mouse away from the shortcut menu to make the shortcut menu disappear.

To see how shortcut menus can work with text, do the following:

1. Click the Finder icon on the Dock. The Finder window appears.
2. Click **Applications** in the left pane of the Finder window.
3. Double-click the **TextEdit** icon. The TextEdit window appears.
4. Type a sentence.
5. Select all or part of your sentence by dragging the mouse over the text.
6. Move the mouse over the selected text and right-click. A shortcut menu appears, as shown in Figure 10-4. Notice that the shortcut menu displays several commands depending on the items you've selected and right-clicked.

FIGURE 10-3: *Right-clicking displays a shortcut menu.*

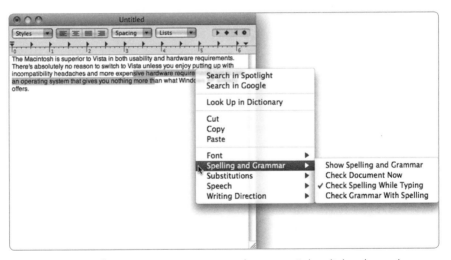

FIGURE 10-4: *A shortcut menu appears when you right-click selected text.*

To see how you can delete files or folders using a shortcut menu, try the following:

1. Click the Finder icon on the Dock. The Finder window appears.
2. Click **Documents** in the left pane of the Finder window.

3. Select **File ▸ New Folder**. An untitled folder appears in the right pane of the Finder window.
4. Right-click the untitled folder to display a shortcut menu.
5. Select **Move to Trash**.

Additional Ideas for Using Shortcuts

You'll be able to work more efficiently with programs if you memorize basic shortcuts to save a file, print a file, quit a program, and perform other common tasks. Browse through the pull-down menus of your favorite programs and see which commands offer keyboard shortcuts or command buttons. Get in the habit of right-clicking items to view a shortcut menu of commands. By using shortcuts, you'll be able to control your Macintosh quickly and conveniently.

11

Learning to Drag and Drop

To copy or move items, you can select the Cut or Copy command from the Edit menu or use the equivalent keyboard shortcuts, such as ⌘-X and ⌘-C. For an even faster way to copy or move items, you can use your mouse to drag and drop the items.

Dragging means pointing the mouse at an item and moving the mouse while holding down the left mouse button. *Dropping* means releasing the left mouse button when the pointer appears where you want to place a dragged item. Since dragging and dropping can be used as a shortcut to copy and move items, learning how to drag and drop can make any program easier to use.

Project goal: Learn different ways to drag and drop text and graphics in different programs.

What You'll Be Using

To practice dragging and dropping, you'll need the following:

▶ The TextEdit program

▶ The Safari web browser

▶ An Internet connection

▶ The Finder

Dragging and Dropping Text

When you're editing text, you may need to copy or move words, sentences, or entire paragraphs from one place to another. As a shortcut, you can use the mouse to drag and drop text within nearly every program, such as word processors (like Microsoft Word or Pages) and email programs (like Mail).

Use these steps to drag and drop text:

1. Start TextEdit. (Double-click the **TextEdit** icon in the Applications folder.) The TextEdit window appears.
2. Type a few sentences of text, and then use the mouse to select some text to drag it to a new location.
3. Holding down the left mouse button, drag the mouse and the selected text to a new location. The cursor moves to show you where your text will appear when you release the left mouse button.
4. Release the left mouse button to drop the selected text.

If you repeat these steps but hold down the OPTION key while dragging the mouse, you'll copy and paste the selected text, instead of moving it. You can tell when dragging and dropping is copying, rather than moving, an item because during a copy, a plus sign appears inside a green circle near the pointer as you move the mouse.

To see how dragging and dropping text works to copy text, try the following:

1. Start TextEdit. (Double-click the **TextEdit** icon in the Applications folder.) The TextEdit window appears.
2. Type three paragraphs of text.
3. Select the third (last) paragraph.
4. Move the mouse pointer over the selected text, hold down the Option key, and drag your selected text below the first paragraph. Your selected text appears as a "ghost image," as shown in Figure 11-1.
5. Release the left mouse button to move your copied text to the new location.

Dragging and Dropping Website Addresses in Safari

Safari lets you browse the Internet and visit websites. If you find an interesting website, you can save that website's address by dragging it out of the Address text box and dropping it over the Bookmarks Bar, as shown in Figure 11-2.

To drag a website address and store it on your Bookmarks Bar, do this:

1. Start Safari.
2. Visit a website, such as *http://www.nostarch.com/*. Notice that an icon or a blue dot appears to the left of the website's address in the Address text box.

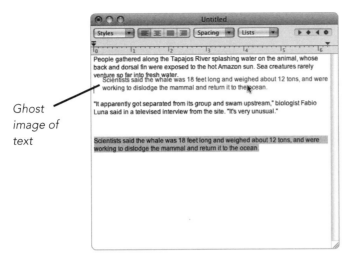

Ghost image of text

FIGURE 11-1: *When dragging text, your selected text's "ghost image" moves with the mouse pointer.*

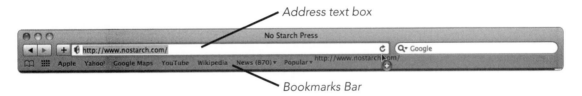

Address text box

Bookmarks Bar

FIGURE 11-2: *You can drag a website's address out of the Address text box and onto the Bookmarks Bar in Safari.*

3. Move the pointer over the icon that appears on the left side of the Address text box.
4. Drag the website icon over the Bookmarks Bar and release the left mouse button to drop it. A dialog appears, asking you to give your bookmark a name.
5. Type a descriptive name for your bookmark, or edit the existing bookmark name.
6. Click **OK**. Your chosen website address appears on the Bookmarks Bar.

✳ **NOTE: To remove a bookmark from the Bookmarks Bar, just drag the bookmark off the Bookmarks Bar and release the left mouse button.**

Dragging and Dropping Graphics

You can also copy a picture from one program to another, such as copying an image from a website or from iPhoto and pasting it into a word processor document or an email message.

To copy a picture and paste it into a word processor document or email message, do this:

1. Start your word processor or email program.
2. Start Safari (if you want to copy pictures off a web page) or iPhoto (if you want to copy a picture out of your iPhoto collection).
3. Move the windows of the two programs side by side so both are visible, such as placing the Safari window next to a word processor window, or the iPhoto window next to an email window.
4. Drag a picture (displayed in Safari or iPhoto) over your word processor or email window.
5. Release the left mouse button to drop the picture into the word processor document or email message, as shown in Figure 11-3.

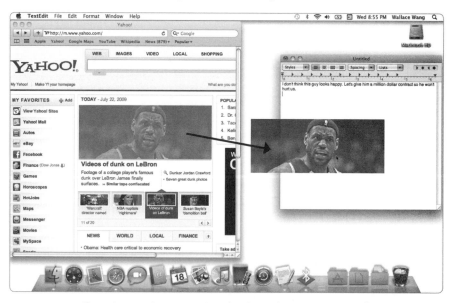

FIGURE 11-3: *Copying a picture is simple: Just drag it to a new location.*

Dragging and Dropping Files into Programs

When you double-click a file icon displayed in the Finder, your Macintosh usually starts the program that originally created that file. However, many files can be opened by different programs.

For example, a Microsoft Word file can be opened by Microsoft Word, TextEdit, Pages (the word processor found in the iWork suite, sold separately by Apple), or even an old copy of AppleWorks. A Microsoft Excel spreadsheet can be opened by Microsoft Excel or Numbers (the spreadsheet found in the iWork suite).

If you want to open a file in a program other than the one used to create it, you have two choices. First, you can right-click (or CTRL-click) the file, choose **Open With**, and then choose the name of the program to open the file, as shown in Figure 11-4.

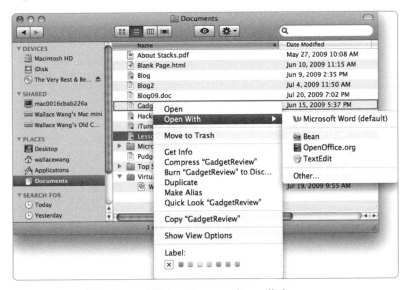

FIGURE 11-4: *The Open With submenu lists all the programs on your Macintosh that can open a particular file.*

Alternatively, you can drag a file icon from the Finder window and drop it over a program icon displayed in the Dock. So, for example, if you want to open a Microsoft Word file in the Pages word processor, you can drag and drop the Microsoft Word file over the Pages icon on the Dock.

Use the following steps to drag and drop a file over a program icon on the Dock:

1. Make sure that the program you want to use to open the file appears on the Dock.
2. Click the Finder icon on the Dock. The Finder window appears.
3. Find the file you want to open.
4. Drag the file out of the Finder window and drop it over a program icon on the Dock.

＊ *NOTE:* **If you drag and drop a file over a program icon on the Dock and nothing happens, that means the program can't open that particular file.**

Additional Ideas for Dragging and Dropping

Dragging and dropping can make any program easier to use—just as long as you know what to drag and drop in the first place. Since many programs don't make it obvious what you can drag and drop, feel free to experiment with different programs.

Just point the mouse to any text or graphic image and drag it. If the text or graphic image moves along with the mouse pointer, you've discovered something you can drag. Once you discover text or graphics that you can drag, practice dropping them in likely places, such as inside another window or in a different location in the current window.

Dragging and dropping may take practice, especially if you're new to computers. But once you get the hang of dragging and dropping, you'll find it offers some unique shortcuts to making your Macintosh even easier to use.

12 Controlling Your Macintosh with Hot Corners

Like most computers, your Macintosh provides shortcuts for accessing certain features, and one of the most useful shortcuts is called a hot corner. A *hot corner* is simply one corner of the screen that makes your Macintosh do something when you move your mouse pointer into that corner.

By using hot corners, you can control your screensaver, put your Macintosh to sleep, hide and display Dashboard programs, and manipulate windows with your mouse. Hot corners provide another way to make your Macintosh easier to use.

Project goal: Define hot corners to control different parts of your Macintosh.

What You'll Be Using

To control your Macintosh using hot corners, you'll be using one program:

► The System Preferences program

Defining a Hot Corner

You can define each corner of the screen as a hot corner to make your Macintosh do one of the following:

▶ **Start Screen Saver** or **Disable Screen Saver** Turns on the screensaver right away without waiting for the screensaver's inactivity period (or prevents the screensaver from running)

▶ **All Windows** Displays all windows as thumbnail images on the screen (equivalent to pressing F9)

▶ **Application Windows** Displays thumbnail images of windows belonging to the currently active program (equivalent to pressing F10)

▶ **Desktop** Hides all windows (equivalent to pressing F11)

▶ **Dashboard** Loads or hides the Dashboard program (equivalent to pressing F12)

▶ **Sleep Display** Puts Display to sleep

Here's how to define a hot corner:

1. Click the Apple menu and select **System Preferences**. A System Preferences window appears.
2. Click the **Desktop & Screen Saver** icon under the Personal category. The Desktop & Screen Saver window appears.
3. Click the **Screen Saver** tab. Different screensaver options appear, as shown in Figure 12-1.

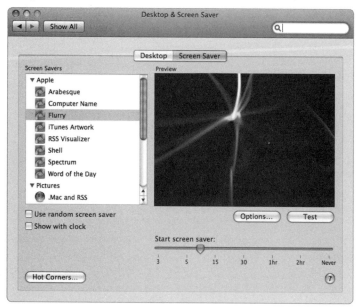

FIGURE 12-1: *The Screen Saver part of the Desktop & Screen Saver window displays screensaver options.*

4.   Click the **Hot Corners** button. A sheet drops down, as shown in Figure 12-2.

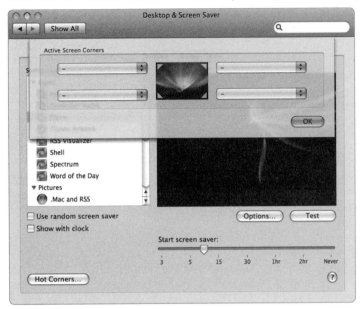

FIGURE 12-2: *A sheet drops down, where you can define each corner of the screen as a hot corner.*

5.   Click the pop-up menu for the corner of the screen that you want to designate as a hot corner. A pop-up menu appears, listing all your choices, as shown in Figure 12-3.
6.   Click a choice, such as **Desktop** or **All Windows**. Your choice appears in the pop-up menu next to your chosen hot corner.
7.   Click **OK**.
8.   Click the close button of the Desktop & Screen Saver window.

✳ NOTE: **To turn off a hot corner, select the dash (–) option in the pop-up menu next to your chosen hot corner.**

Using a Hot Corner

Once you've defined a hot corner, you can trigger the hot corner action by moving the mouse pointer into the hot corner. To turn off the action designated by the hot corner, just move the pointer out of the corner.

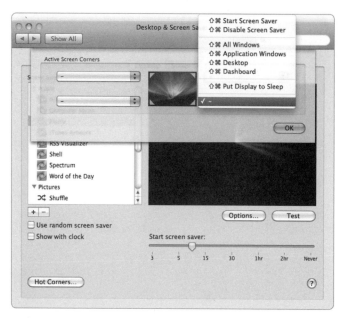

FIGURE 12-3: *Clicking a pop-up menu displays choices for defining a hot corner.*

Additional Ideas for Using Hot Corners

No matter which features you prefer, hot corners will help you to access those features quickly and easily. Experiment with hot corners to determine which features are most convenient. Once you start using hot corners, you may find lots of uses for them. Following are some ideas.

The Start Screen Saver option can be handy when you want to run the screensaver right away, such as when you're shopping online for a birthday present and the birthday boy or girl wanders into the room. By moving the mouse into a Start Screen Saver hot corner, the screensaver kicks in immediately, hiding your activity.

The Disable Screen Saver option can be handy when you're working on something on the screen and your Macintosh keeps turning on your screensaver. Rather than turn off the screensaver through the System Preferences window (and have to turn it back on again later), move the pointer into a hot corner designated as Disable Screen Saver to keep the screensaver from starting up.

The All Windows (F9), Application Windows (F10), and Desktop (F11) options mimic the features of Exposé and can be a fast way to organize and view multiple windows on the screen. Just choose a hot corner to organize your windows the way you like best, such as viewing all program windows as thumbnail images, and your Macintosh will obediently arrange your windows every time you move the pointer into that particular hot corner.

If you use the Dashboard often, designate a hot corner for loading and hiding the Dashboard so you don't have to press F12 every time.

13 Finding Files Fast

The longer you use your Macintosh, the more files you'll create and save. And the more files you create, the more effort you'll need to put into keeping everything organized. To stay organized, you could store all files in the Documents folder. Of course, the more files you save, the more crowded the Documents folder will get.

One solution is to create additional folders inside the Documents folder. But then again, as you create more folders and use them to hold various files, you'll find it even harder to find what you want when you need it.

Fortunately, your Macintosh offers two ways to help you find files. You can use a feature called *Spotlight* to search for a specific file just by typing a single word or phrase. For example, if you search for the word *Taxes*, Spotlight will find all files that contain the word *Taxes* either in the filename or anywhere inside the file itself.

You can also keep things organized by storing files in folders that can be quickly accessible. Instead of wading through multiple folders stored inside the Documents folder to find what you want, you can store a folder in the Finder window or on the Dock so that you can view it quickly with a single click.

By using Spotlight to search for files and the Finder and Dock to access folders, you'll make it easier to find files when you need them.

Project goal: Learn to find files using Spotlight and store folders in the Finder window and Dock.

What You'll Be Using

To find files and store them in easily accessible folders, you'll use the following:

- ► Spotlight
- ► The Finder
- ► The Dock
- ► The TextEdit program (to create files for test purposes)

Finding Specific Files with Spotlight

Spotlight finds files by name or content. For example, to find a file named *Customers*, you could type *Customers* or just *Cust*.

✳ **NOTE: If you don't know the name of the file that you want, just type a word that appears in that file. For example, to find a file that contains a report about Microsoft, tell Spotlight to search for the word *Microsoft*.**

You can access Spotlight through the Finder window or the menu bar.

Using Spotlight Through the Finder

To see how Spotlight works through the Finder, follow these steps:

1. Click the Finder icon on the Dock. The Finder window appears.
2. Click in the Spotlight search box, as shown in Figure 13-1.

Spotlight search box

FIGURE 13-1: *The Spotlight search box appears in the upper-right corner of the Finder window.*

3.   Type **book** (or whatever word you want to find in a file) in the Spotlight search box and press RETURN. Spotlight displays all files that contain the word you typed in their filenames, as shown in Figure 13-2.

FIGURE 13-2: *All files that Spotlight finds appears in the Finder window.*

4.   Click the close button in the Spotlight search box to clear the search box.
5.   Click the **Applications** folder in the left pane (called the sidebar) of the Finder window.
6.   Double-click the **TextEdit** icon. The TextEdit window appears.
7.   Type this sentence: `This book is about stone soup.`
8.   Select **File ▶ Save**. A dialog appears.
9.   Click in the **Save As** text box and type `My File`.
10.   Select **TextEdit ▶ Quit TextEdit**.
11.   Click the Finder icon on the Dock. The Finder window appears.
12.   Click in the Spotlight search box.
13.   Type **book** in the Spotlight search box and press RETURN. Notice that Spotlight now displays your TextEdit file that contains the word *book* in its contents, as shown in Figure 13-3.
14.   Double-click this file. TextEdit should load and display the contents of the file.
15.   Select **TextEdit ▶ Quit TextEdit**.
16.   Click the close button in the Spotlight search box.
17.   Click the close button of the Finder window.

FIGURE 13-3: *Spotlight can find text stored inside a file.*

Using Spotlight from the Menu Bar

In addition to accessing Spotlight through the Finder, you can also access Spotlight directly from the menu bar:

1. Click the Spotlight icon on the right side of the menu bar. A Spotlight search box appears, as shown in Figure 13-4.

FIGURE 13-4: *Clicking the Spotlight icon on the menu bar displays a Spotlight search box.*

2. Click in the Spotlight search box and type a word or phrase, such as **book**. Spotlight displays a menu of items that contain the word or phrase that matches what you typed, as shown in Figure 13-5.
3. Click a file to view it, or click the close button in the Spotlight search box.
4. Click anywhere away from the Spotlight menu to make it go away.

Using Smart Folders

Spotlight can find specific types of files by name or contents. The problem with Spotlight, however, is that you must type a word or phrase each time you want to find certain files. For example, if you're organizing tax information, you could type the word *Taxes* in Spotlight every time you need to find a file related to your taxes.

If you added a new tax file or deleted an old tax file, you'd have to retype *Taxes* into the Spotlight search box to see all the current tax-related files.

To automate this process, you can use a Smart Folder instead. A Smart Folder saves a Spotlight search (such as the word *Taxes*), so every time you add or delete files that contain the word *Taxes*, the Smart Folder updates its contents automatically to include those files. No matter how many times you add new tax files or delete old ones, the Smart Folder always displays the updated list of tax files without forcing you to retype *Taxes* into Spotlight ever again.

✱ NOTE: Smart Folders don't physically contain files. Instead, they contain links to the actual files stored elsewhere on your hard disk.

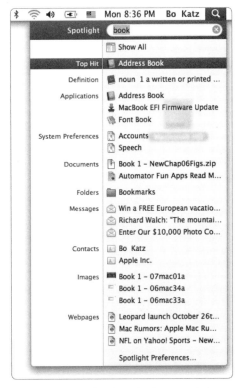

FIGURE 13-5: *The Spotlight search box displays a menu of items that contain a match of your search word or phrase.*

Here's how to create a Smart Folder:

1. Click the Finder icon on the Dock. The Finder window appears.
2. Click the **Documents** folder in the sidebar of the Finder window.
3. Select **File ▸ New Smart Folder**. A New Smart Folder window appears.
4. Click in the **Spotlight** search box, type a word or phrase (such as *Stone*), and press RETURN. Spotlight displays all files that contain the word you typed in their filenames.

✱ NOTE: If you search for *stone*, you should find the TextEdit file you created earlier that contains the sentence *This book is about stone soup*.

5. Click the **Save** button underneath the Spotlight search box. A dialog appears.
6. Click in the **Save As** text box and type a descriptive name for your Smart Folder (or just leave its name as New Smart Folder).
7. Click the **Where** pop-up menu and choose **Desktop**.

8.   Click **Save**. Your Macintosh saves your Smart Folder on the Desktop and in the sidebar of the Finder, as shown in Figure 13-6.

FIGURE 13-6: *Smart Folders appear in the sidebar of the Finder window and in your chosen location, such as the Desktop.*

9.   Click **Applications** in the sidebar of the Finder window.
10.   Double-click the **TextEdit** icon. The TextEdit window appears.
11.   Type `Another file with the word stone in it`.
12.   Select **File ▸ Save**. A dialog appears.
13.   Click in the **Save As** text box and type `My Secret File`.
14.   Click **Save**.
15.   Select **TextEdit ▸ Quit TextEdit**.
16.   Double-click the **Smart Folder** icon on the Desktop. The Smart Folder window appears, listing your *My Secret File* (which contains the sentence *Another file with the word stone in it*). From now on, this Smart Folder displays every file you create or modify that contains the word *stone* in it.

✻ **NOTE: You may want to delete this Smart Folder from your Desktop and the sidebar of the Finder window when you're done with this exercise. To delete the Smart Folder from the Desktop, drag the Smart Folder icon over the Trash icon on the Dock. To delete the Smart Folder from the sidebar of the Finder window, drag the Smart Folder icon off the sidebar and release the mouse button to see your Smart Folder disappear in an animated puff of smoke. Deleting a Smart Folder deletes only the Smart Folder itself; it never deletes any files whose names are displayed inside that Smart Folder.**

Placing Folders on the Sidebar

Besides putting Smart Folders on the sidebar, you can add any folders on the sidebar to give you one-click access to your favorite folders. To create and place a folder on the sidebar, do the following:

1. Click the Finder icon on the Dock. The Finder window appears.
2. Click the **Documents** folder in the sidebar of the Finder window.
3. Select **File ▸ New Folder**. A new folder icon appears in the right pane of the Finder window.
4. Type a descriptive name for your folder, such as *My Useful Stuff*, and press RETURN.
5. Drag your newly created folder over the sidebar, directly underneath Documents in the Places category, until you see a horizontal line appear in the sidebar.
6. Release the left mouse button. Now whenever you need to access the contents of this particular folder, you can click the folder name in the sidebar.

* **NOTE: To delete the folder from the sidebar of the Finder window after this exercise, drag its icon off the sidebar and release the mouse button to see your folder disappear in an animated puff of smoke. Deleting a folder from the sidebar removes the folder only from the sidebar but never deletes any files displayed inside that folder.**

Placing Folders on the Dock

Another way to get one-click access to a folder is to store the folder on the right side of the Dock. When folders appear on the Dock, the folders are called a *stack*. Here's how to place a folder on the Dock to create a stack:

1. Click the Finder icon on the Dock. A Finder window appears.
2. Open the folder that contains the folder that you want to place on the Dock.
3. Drag the folder over the right side of the Dock near the Trash icon. Wait until any existing stacks on the Dock slide apart to make room.
4. Release the left mouse button to add the stack to the Dock.

Clicking the stack icon displays the contents of that folder. You can choose how to display the contents of a stack in one of three ways, as shown in Figure 13-7:

▸ Fan

▸ Grid

▸ List

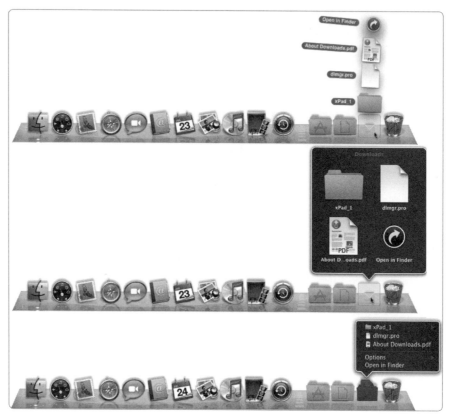

FIGURE 13-7: *Displaying folder contents in a fan, grid, and list.*

To define how to display the contents of a stack, do this:

1. Right-click the stack that you want to define. A pop-up menu appears, as shown in Figure 13-8.

FIGURE 13-8: *Right-clicking a stack displays a pop-up menu.*

2.   Click Fan, Grid, List, or Automatic. (If you choose Automatic, clicking a stack will display its contents as a fan if it contains eight or fewer items, or as a grid if it contains nine or more items.)

* **NOTE:** To delete a stack from the Dock of the Finder window, drag the stack icon off the Dock and release the mouse button to see your folder disappear in an animated puff of smoke. Deleting a stack from the Dock removes the stack only from the Dock but never deletes any files displayed inside that folder.

Peeking at Files Without Opening Them

Sometimes the fastest way to find a particular file is to browse through files individually. To browse individual files quickly and easily, the Macintosh offers two features called *Quick Look* and *Cover Flow*. Both Quick Look and Cover Flow let you view the contents of a file without having to open it. Here's how to use Quick Look:

1.   Click the Finder icon on the Dock. A Finder window appears.
2.   Click **Documents** on the sidebar of the Finder window.
3.   Click a file icon and click the Quick Look button (it looks like an eye at the top of the Finder window). (You can also select **File ▸ Quick Look** or press ⌘-Y.) A window appears, displaying the contents of that file. If the file is large, you may be able to scroll and read the entire file contents, as shown in Figure 13-9.
4.   Click the close button of the Quick Look window.

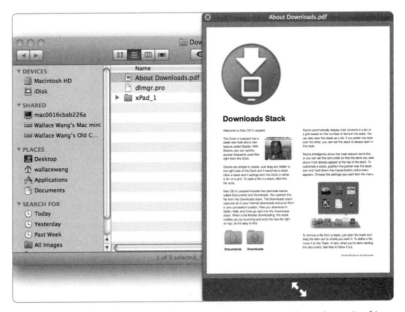

FIGURE 13-9: *The Quick Look feature lets you peek and read a file without opening it.*

Cover Flow lets you peek inside a file and can be useful when you need to browse quickly through several files to find the one you want. Here's how to use Cover Flow:

1.	Click the Finder icon on the Dock. A Finder window appears.
2.	Click **Documents** on the sidebar of the Finder window.
3.	Select **View ▸ as Cover Flow** (or press ⌘-4, or click the Cover Flow button). The Finder window displays all files as icons that you can flip through just by clicking them, as shown in Figure 13-10.

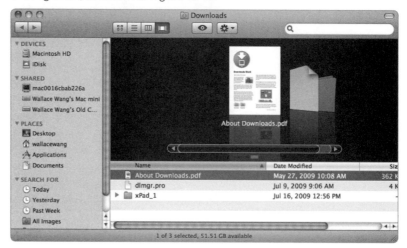

FIGURE 13-10: *Cover Flow displays all files as icons and lists.*

4.	Click the file icon displayed in the Cover Flow or in the list. If the file is large, two arrows may appear, allowing you to click to see another page of your selected file.

Additional Ideas for Finding Files

For speedier file searching, you can combine the various file-searching techniques. For example, use Spotlight to find files and then use Quick Look to peek inside each file before opening it. Or open a Smart Folder and view its contents in Cover Flow to browse through each file without opening it.

Even if you can't stay organized, you'll find that with the help of your Macintosh, finding your important files can be a lot easier than you might think.

14

Organizing Files and Folders by Color and Weird Words

Organizing files is like organizing clothes. It's much easier just to toss them in a pile when you're done with them, but then finding them later can prove difficult. Just as you need to take time to organize your clothes so you can quickly find them again, so should you create separate folders to store your files and give each file a descriptive name that will always help you remember what that file contains.

Of course, sometimes the best way to search for a file is through your own unique system of mental association that may make sense to nobody else. You may not remember that you named a file *January Monthly Budget* or that you stored it in a folder called *Budgets*. However, you may never forget that January was the month you won a jackpot playing a slot machine in a casino while wearing your lucky green shirt, so you can identify your *January Monthly Budget* file using the color green and adding the keyword *casino* or *slot machine*.

Now the next time you want to find this file, you have two additional choices besides searching for the filename or the contents of that file:

▶ Look for the green file.

▶ Search for the phrase *casino* or *slot machine*.

By labeling files using colors or keywords that don't appear as part of the filename or inside the file itself, you can identify files your own way to help you find them when you need them.

Project goal: Learn to label files by color or keywords and find them by looking for specific colors or keywords using Spotlight.

What You'll Be Using

To label and color code your files, you'll be using the following:

▶ The Finder

▶ Spotlight

Labeling Files and Folders by Color

Normally when you look for files in the Finder window, all files appear as icons and a name. Trying to find the one file you want out of a dozen or more files can be like trying to find a single airline flight on a screen full of a dozen other airline flight listings.

To make visually browsing for a file much easier, you can identify it by one of seven color labels: red, orange, yellow, green, blue, purple, or gray.

Here's how to label a file or folder with a color:

1. Click the Finder icon on the Dock. A Finder window appears.
2. Open the drive and folder that contain the file or folder you want to label with a color.
3. Click the file or folder you want to label with a color.
4. Select **File ▸ Get Info**, or press ⌘-I. A Get Info window appears, as shown in Figure 14-1.

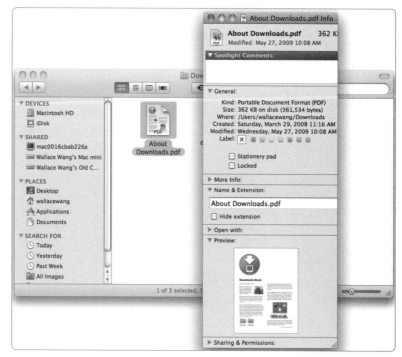

FIGURE 14-1: *The Get Info window lets you choose a color label for your chosen file or folder.*

5. Click a color in the Label category.
6. Click the close button of the Get Info window. The name of your chosen file or folder now appears highlighted in your chosen color.

✳ *NOTE:* **For a faster way to add a color label to a file or folder, right-click that file or folder to display a pop-up menu. Then click a color label, as shown in Figure 14-2.**

FIGURE 14-2: Right-clicking a file or folder offers a faster way to choose a color label.

Searching Files and Folders by Color

After you've labeled one or more files or folders with a color, you can browse through the Finder window and quickly see all files or folders of specific colors. To make finding color labeled files and folders even faster, you can sort all files and folders by color.

Here's how to sort files or folders by color:

1. Click the Finder icon on the Dock. The Finder window appears.
2. Open the drive and folder that you want to sort by color.
3. Select **View ▸ as Icons** (or **as Columns**). The Finder window displays all your files and folders.
4. Select **View ▸ Arrange By ▸ Label**. The Finder window displays all your color labeled files and folders at the bottom of the window. (You may need to scroll down to see them.)

Adding Spotlight Comments

Your Macintosh comes with a search feature called Spotlight, which lets you type a word or phrase to find a file. By using Spotlight, you can search for all or part of a filename, a word stored inside a file, or a word specifically designated as a Spotlight comment.

Of course, if you want to find a particular file, but you can't remember any part of its name or its contents, Spotlight won't help you find it. To avoid this problem, you can add Spotlight comments to the file. Spotlight comments give files additional labels that can help you find a particular file. These labels can be any word or phrase that you associate with that particular file, such as the name of the person who relies on the information stored in that file (such as your boss) or a general description of the file's purpose (such as *tax information* or *business expenses*).

Here's how to add Spotlight comments to a file:

1. Click the Finder icon on the Dock. A Finder window appears.
2. Open the drive and folder that contain the file in which you want to add a Spotlight comment.
3. Select **File ▸ Get Info**, or press ⌘-I. A Get Info window appears (see Figure 14-1).
4. Click in the **Spotlight Comments** text box, as shown in Figure 14-3, and type a descriptive word or phrase. (If the Spotlight Comments text box is not visible, click the triangle that appears to the left of Spotlight Comments.)
5. Click the close button of the Get Info window.

To see how Spotlight comments work, try labeling files with certain words and then searching for those words using Spotlight:

1. Click the Finder icon on the Dock. A Finder window appears.
2. Click the **Applications** folder that appears in the left pane (sidebar) of the Finder window. The contents of the Applications folder appear in the right pane of the Finder window.
3. Click the **Chess** file.
4. Select **File ▸ Get Info**, or press ⌘-I. A Get Info window appears (see Figure 14-1).
5. Click in the **Spotlight Comments** text box and type a word, such as *frustrating*.

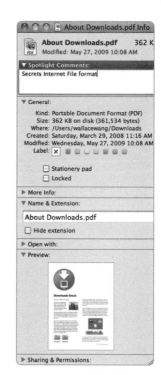

FIGURE 14-3: *The Spotlight Comments text box lets you type additional words to help you find a file using Spotlight.*

6. Click the close button of the Get Info window.
7. Click in the Spotlight search box in the upper-right corner of the Finder window, and type the word you typed in the Spotlight Comments text box earlier, such as *frustrating*.
8. Press RETURN. Spotlight searches for the word *frustrating* stored in the Spotlight Comments text box of any file. In this case, it finds the Chess program file, as shown in Figure 14-4.
9. Click the clear button in the Spotlight search box.

FIGURE 14-4: *Typing text in the Spotlight search box searches for filenames, file contents, and Spotlight comments.*

Additional Ideas for Labeling Files and Folders with Colors and Comments

Use colors liberally to associate files and folders with certain ideas or categories. For example, if you're going through a divorce or doing your taxes, label all divorce- or tax-related files with the color red. By associating red with anger and indirectly with divorce or filing taxes, you'll remember what all your red files represent.

For help with finding files again, label files and folders with certain colors that represent emotions or ideas, and then type those same emotions or ideas as Spotlight comments. Now if you forget that the color red represents anger, just type *anger* in the Spotlight search box and Spotlight will find all your divorce- or tax-related files that you associated with anger.

Think of colors and Spotlight comments as just one more way to identify and find files and folders again. Since it's so easy to store files and folders, but not as easy to find them again, using colors and Spotlight comments can help you keep a little bit more organized.

15

Putting Information at Your Fingertips with Dashboard

While using your Macintosh, you may suddenly need to look at a calendar, a clock, a weather forecast, or a calculator. Rather than reach for a paper calendar, a clock, a newspaper weather forecast, or a pocket calculator, you can use your Macintosh to display these items using a program called Dashboard that comes with every new Macintosh.

Dashboard provides a variety of simple programs, called *widgets*, that you can pop on the screen at any time and make disappear at a moment's notice. You can be typing in a word processor, run Dashboard to view a calendar or sport score, and then shove Dashboard out of the way again to keep working in your word processor. If you need information at your fingertips, you'll find Dashboard a valuable asset when doing anything with your Macintosh.

Project goal: Learn to use and modify Dashboard to view different types of widgets on the screen.

What You'll Be Using

To learn how to display simple programs on the screen, you'll be using the following:

▶   The Dock

▶   Dashboard

▶   The Safari web browser

Starting Dashboard

The Dashboard program starts and manages miniature programs called widgets. A *widget* performs a single function, such as displaying a calendar or calculator on the screen. Every time you want to use a widget, you have to start Dashboard.

You can start Dashboard in three ways:

▶ Press F12.

▶ Click the Dashboard icon on the Dock.

▶ Double-click the Dashboard icon stored in the Applications folder.

As soon as you start Dashboard, every widget currently loaded into Dashboard will appear on your screen, as shown in Figure 15-1.

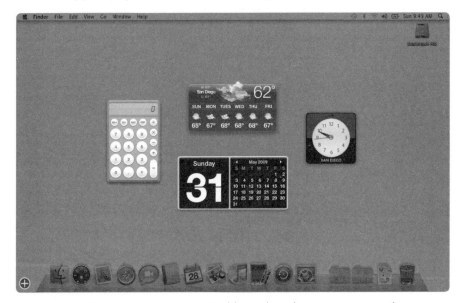

FIGURE 15-1: Every time you start Dashboard, widgets appear on the screen.

✱ *NOTE:* **Some widgets won't work without an Internet connection, such as the weather forecasting widget.**

To tuck all widgets out of the way and exit Dashboard, choose one of the following:

▶ Press F12.

▶ Click the mouse anywhere on the screen except on a widget.

Adding and Removing Dashboard Widgets

Each time you start Dashboard, it displays a handful of widgets on the screen, such as the Calculator, Calendar, and Clock widgets. In case you don't need a certain widget, such as the Clock widget, you can remove it and replace it with another widget that you find more useful, such as a widget that tracks stock prices.

You can add or remove as many widgets as you want, although the more widgets you display, the more crowded your screen appears. At the very least, you'll need at least one widget to appear when you start Dashboard. You can choose from the following default library of Dashboard widgets:

▶ **Address Book**   Lets you search for a person stored in your Address Book

▶ **Business**   Lets you search the Yellow Pages for a business (requires an Internet connection)

▶ **Calculator**   Displays a four-function calculator

▶ **Dictionary**   Lets you look up words in the Macintosh dictionary or thesaurus

▶ **ESPN**   Displays the latest sports news and scores (requires an Internet connection)

▶ **Flight Tracker**   Lets you track flights by airline or cities (requires an Internet connection)

▶ **Google**   Lets you type a word or phrase to search for with Google (requires an Internet connection)

▶ **iCal**   Displays a calendar and any events you've scheduled in iCal

▶ **iTunes**   Lets you control iTunes to play, pause, rewind, or fast-forward

▶ **Movies**   Displays currently playing movies, show times, and theaters (requires an Internet connection)

▶ **People**   Lets you search the White Pages for a person (requires an Internet connection)

▶ **Ski Report**   Displays ski conditions at your favorite ski resort (requires an Internet connection)

▶ **Stickies**   Displays sticky notes for typing and saving notes

▶ **Stocks**   Displays delayed stock prices (requires an Internet connection)

▶ **Tile Game**   Displays a simple game for sliding tiles to create a picture

▶ **Translation**   Translates words from one language to another

▶ **Unit Converter**   Converts units of measurement, such as from inches to centimeters

▶ **Weather**   Displays a six-day weather forecast (requires an Internet connection)

▶ **World Clock**   Displays a clock for the time zone of your choice

Adding Widgets to Dashboard

To browse the Dashboard library of widgets and choose one to appear on your screen, do the following:

1. Press F12 to start Dashboard. Dashboard displays its widgets.
2. Click the plus button that appears in the lower-left corner of the screen. Dashboard displays its current library of widgets at the bottom of the screen, as shown in Figure 15-2.

Widget library

FIGURE 15-2: *The Dashboard library contains additional widgets to display.*

3. Choose a widget that you want to display when Dashboard starts, and drag and drop the widget anywhere on the screen. (You can also click a widget to place it in the middle of the screen.) The widget appears to create ripples when you release the left mouse button.
4. Repeat the preceding step for each additional widget you want to appear when Dashboard starts.
5. Click the close button in the lower-left corner of the screen when you're done adding widgets to the screen.

Removing Widgets from Dashboard

You can customize Dashboard by adding new widgets or by removing current widgets that you may no longer need. When you remove a widget, you're just stopping the widget from appearing—you don't physically erase the widget from your hard disk.

Here's how to remove a widget:

1. Press F12 to start Dashboard. Dashboard displays its widgets.
2. Click the plus button that appears in the lower-left corner of the screen. Dashboard displays close buttons in the upper-left corner of every currently displayed widget, as shown in Figure 15-3.

Close buttons

FIGURE 15-3: *Clicking the plus button displays close buttons on all widgets on the screen.*

3. Click the close button of a widget that you no longer want to appear when you start Dashboard. The chosen widget disappears. (You can always add this widget back to Dashboard later if you want.)
4. Press F12, click the Dashboard icon on the Dock, or click anywhere on the screen except on a widget to make the widgets disappear.

Rearranging Widgets on Dashboard

After you've added new widgets or removed some from the screen, you may want to move widgets around to display them the way you like best. Here's how to rearrange widgets:

1. Press F12 to start Dashboard. Dashboard displays its widgets.
2. Move the mouse pointer over a widget that you want to move.
3. Drag the mouse to move the widget to a new location on the screen.
4. Release the left mouse button when you're happy with the new location of the widget on the screen.
5. Press F12, click the Dashboard icon on the Dock, or click anywhere on the screen except on a widget to make the widgets disappear.

Customizing Widgets

Some widgets allow you to customize the type of information they display. For example, the World Clock widget lets you choose a specific city, so you can view the current time in New York or Paris; the Stocks widget lets you decide which stock quotes you want to display; and the Weather widget lets you choose to display the forecast for a specific city, such as San Diego or Chicago.

Although you can't customize every widget, such as the Calculator widget, you can customize many of them. Here's how to customize a widget:

1. Press F12 to start Dashboard. Dashboard displays its widgets.
2. Move the mouse pointer over the lower-right corner of the widget you want to customize. An i button appears, as shown in Figure 15-4.
3. Click the **i** button. The widget appears to flip around to display various options for customizing its appearance or functionality, as shown in Figure 15-5.

FIGURE 15-4: *You can customize any widget that displays an i button in its lower-right corner.*

FIGURE 15-5: *The backside of a widget displays options for customizing how the widget behaves.*

4. Click or choose any options for changing the appearance of the widget, and then click **Done**.
5. Press F12, click the Dashboard icon on the Dock, or click anywhere on the screen except on a widget to make the widgets disappear.

Finding More Widgets

Although Dashboard includes a library of widgets from which you can choose, you can always find more widgets on the Internet that you can download and install. To find more widgets, visit one of the following websites:

▸ Apple (*http://www.apple.com/downloads/dashboard/*)

▸ Dashboard Widgets (*http://www.dashboardwidgets.com/*)

Here's how to download and install a widget:

1. Start the Safari program and visit a website that offers Dashboard widgets.
2. Click the widget you want to download and click **Download**. A Downloads window appears, showing you the progress in saving your chosen widget to your Macintosh. When the widget is finished downloading onto your hard disk, a dialog appears, asking if you want to install the widget in Dashboard, as shown in Figure 15-6.

FIGURE 15-6: As soon as you've downloaded a widget, a dialog appears, asking if you want to install the widget in Dashboard.

3. Click **Install**. Your widget appears on the screen and asks if you want to keep the widget or not.
4. Click **Keep** (or Delete).
5. Move the widget on the screen where you want it to appear.
6. Press F12, click the Dashboard icon on the Dock, or click anywhere on the screen except on a widget to make the widgets disappear.

Erasing Widgets

The only widgets you can erase from your hard disk are those you've downloaded and installed from the Internet. Here's how to erase a downloaded widget from your hard disk:

1. Press F12 to start Dashboard. Dashboard displays its widgets.
2. Click the plus button that appears in the lower-left corner of the screen. Dashboard displays its library of available widgets.
3. Click the **Widgets** icon. The Manage Widgets widget appears, as shown in Figure 15-7.

FIGURE 15-7: The Manage Widgets widget lets you erase additional widgets you may have installed.

4. Click the red minus button that appears to the right of the widget you want to erase. (You cannot erase any of Dashboard's built-in library of widgets.) A dialog appears, asking if you want to send your selected widget to the Trash.
5. Click **OK**.
6. Click the close button of the Manage Widgets widget to make it disappear.
7. Press F12, click the Dashboard icon on the Dock, or click anywhere on the screen except on a widget to make the widgets disappear.

Additional Ideas for Using Dashboard

Some widgets can be useful (Calculator or World Clock), while others can be for fun (Ski Report or Movies). If you regularly need to consult a calendar or an address book, you may find the iCal and Address Book widgets particularly useful.

The Address Book widget lets you type all or part of a name to search for contact information about a person or company stored in your Address Book, as shown in Figure 15-8. By using the Address Book widget, you can view your stored contact information without the nuisance of starting Address Book, searching for a name, and then quitting Address Book when you're done.

FIGURE 15-8: *The Address Book widget lets you search for names and contact information without starting and quitting the Address Book program.*

The iCal widget can be handy when you want to review any scheduled events (appointments) for the day. Rather than start iCal and browse through your scheduled events, just display the iCal widget on Dashboard. Each time you click the iCal widget, it toggles between three states, as shown in Figure 15-9:

▶ Displays today's date

▶ Displays today's date and a monthly calendar

▶ Displays today's date, a monthly calendar, and today's scheduled events

FIGURE 15-9: *Clicking the iCal widget toggles the calendar appearance.*

By using widgets, you'll find Dashboard handy for displaying information that you need quickly while using your Macintosh. By taking the time to customize Dashboard, you can make your Macintosh more useful and convenient than any other computer you've used in the past.

16 Giving Your Macintosh Multiple Personalities with User Accounts

The best way to accommodate multiple people who want to use a Macintosh is to buy everyone a separate Macintosh so they'll leave your computer alone. Unfortunately, it's not always practical to buy a separate computer for everyone, so you can do the next best thing and split your Macintosh into "multiple personalities" by creating user accounts instead.

When you divide a Macintosh into separate user accounts, each user can customize his or her account to make the Macintosh take on a different personality. One account might have a purple background with pictures of cats scattered on the screen, while another account might have a plain white background, for example.

More importantly, each account lets a user isolate his or her own personal files from those of other users. So if you create important business records and tax returns in one account, your 10-year-old daughter can't accidentally erase all your financial records from a second account. Even better, if a rare Macintosh computer virus infects one account, the account prevents the virus from spreading to files created and stored in other accounts. User accounts simply isolate multiple users from each other while giving the illusion that each person has complete control over every part of the Macintosh.

Project goal: Learn to create, switch, and delete user accounts on a Macintosh.

What You'll Be Using

To create, use, and remove accounts on your Macintosh, you'll be using the following:

▶ The System Preferences program

Understanding User Accounts

The first time you plugged in and set up your Macintosh, it guided you through the process of typing your name and a password, which essentially created the first user account on your computer. Every Macintosh needs at least one user account, but if you want to share your Macintosh with other people, you'll need to set up additional accounts. You can create four types of user accounts:

▶ **Administrator** This account allows full access to modifying all parts of the Macintosh, including creating and deleting additional accounts. In addition, only an Administrator account is able to install software. When you unpacked your Macintosh, the first account you created was the Administrator account.

▶ **Standard** This account allows full access to all parts of the Macintosh with no ability to create, modify, or delete other user accounts. A Standard account cannot install software.

▶ **Managed with Parental Controls** This account allows restricted access to the Macintosh including time limitations, restricted Internet access, and limited program access.

▶ **Guest** This account allows access to the Macintosh without requiring a password, but does not allow saving files or customizing any part of the Macintosh.

As a general rule, you probably want to create only one Administrator account on your Macintosh that you control. If you create a second Administrator account, that second account can delete your Administrator account and all your files, too. The only reason to create two Administrator accounts is if you trust another person not to abuse his or her privileges, such as parents using separate Administrator accounts so both can create and monitor their children's accounts.

A Standard account is handy if you want to give someone full access to the Macintosh except for the ability to create, modify, or delete other accounts and install applications system-wide. For example, if you're the most computer-savvy person in your family, you might want to set up an Administrator account for yourself but set up Standard accounts for your spouse and kids.

A Managed with Parental Controls account is useful for tracking and restricting someone's access to your Macintosh. Managed with Parental Controls accounts are commonly used by parents to give their children limited Internet and computer access. (To learn more about creating a Managed with Parental Controls account, see Project 17.)

A Guest account is typically used for a Macintosh that is located in an area where anyone can use it. By eliminating the need for a password, a Guest account gives everyone access to the Macintosh. By refusing to save files or allow customizing of the Macintosh, a Guest account prevents anyone from messing up your computer. You can create only one Guest account on a Macintosh (but you can create an unlimited number of other types of accounts). By default, your Macintosh has already defined a guest account, so you won't have to bother going through the motions to create one unless you delete the default guest account.

Creating User Accounts

When creating a user account on your Macintosh, you need to determine these three items:

▶ The type of account you want to create (Administrator, Standard, Managed with Parental Controls, Guest)

▶ A username that uniquely identifies that account

▶ A password (mandatory for Administrator accounts, but optional for all other types of accounts)

✳ **NOTE:** **The only type of account that can create other user accounts is an Administrator account.**

Here's how to create an account:

1. Click the Apple menu and choose **System Preferences**. A System Preferences window appears.
2. Click the **Accounts** icon under the System category. An Accounts window appears, as shown in Figure 16-1.

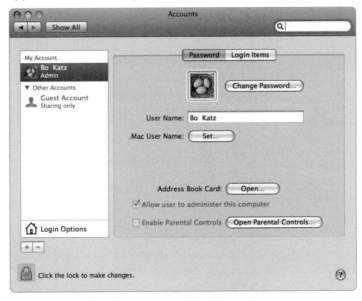

FIGURE 16-1: *The Accounts window lists all accounts on your Macintosh and lets you create (or delete) them.*

3. Click the lock icon that appears in the bottom-left corner of the Accounts window. A dialog appears, asking for your password.
4. Type your password and click **OK**.

5. Click the plus button to add a user account. A dialog appears, as shown in Figure 16-2.

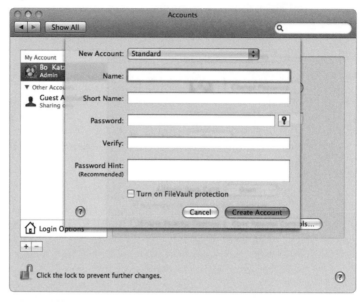

FIGURE 16-2: *When adding an account, you must define the account type, username, and password.*

6. Click the **New Account** pop-up menu and choose an account type (such as Standard or Managed with Parental Controls).
7. Click in the **Name** text box and type a name for the account, such as the name of the person who will be using this account.
8. Click in the **Short Name** text box. A condensed version of the name appears. At this point, you can edit the short name created by your Macintosh if you want.
9. Click in the **Password** text box and type a password for your newly created account.
10. Click in the **Verify** text box and retype the password a second time.
11. Click in the **Password Hint** text box and type a short phrase that can help you remember your password.
12. Click **Create Account**. A dialog appears, asking if you want to turn automatic login on or off. *Automatic login* means that each time you turn on your Macintosh, it uses one account without requiring anyone to type a password. If you're the only person using your Macintosh, automatic login can be convenient. However, if you create multiple accounts, you probably don't want automatic login turned on since it will allow anyone to access your Macintosh without a password.
13. Click **Keep Automatic Login** or **Turn Off Automatic Login**.
14. Click the close button of the Accounts window.

Logging Out of and In to an Account

After you've created two or more accounts on your Macintosh, you can switch between them. One way to switch between accounts is to log out of one account and then log in to a second account.

Here's how to log out of an account:

1. Click the Apple menu. A drop-down menu appears, as shown in Figure 16-3.

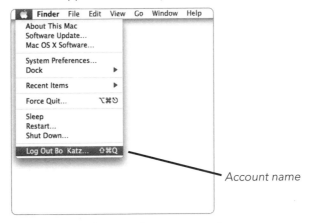

FIGURE 16-3: The Log Out command appears on the Apple menu and displays the name of the currently active account.

2. Select **Log Out**. A dialog appears, asking if you really want to log out of your account.
3. Click **Log Out**. Your Macintosh displays a screen that lists all account names.
4. Click the name of the account you want to use. A Password text box appears.
5. Click in the **Password** text box and type the password for your chosen account. The Desktop of the chosen account appears on the screen.

Fast Switching Between Accounts

One problem with logging out of one account and logging in to a second account is that each time you log out of an account, you have to shut down any running programs. When you log back in to that account, you have to start up your programs again.

For a faster and more convenient way to switch between accounts, you can use *Fast User Switching*, which lets you switch accounts without shutting down any programs. That way, when you return to an account, all your programs are still running, ready for you to start using them again.

The advantage of using Fast User Switching is that it lets you switch accounts without having to shut down all programs running under another account. However, the drawback is that each time you switch out of an account, your Macintosh keeps all programs running, which can gobble up memory. If you leave too many programs running in multiple accounts, your Macintosh may run low on memory and begin responding slowly or be unable to run additional programs.

Turning On Fast User Switching

Before you can use Faster User Switching, you must turn it on through an Administrator account:

1. Click the Apple menu and choose **System Preferences**. A System Preferences window appears.
2. Click the **Accounts** icon under the System category. An Accounts window appears.
3. Click the lock icon that appears in the bottom-left corner of the Accounts window. A dialog appears, asking for your password.
4. Type your password and click **OK**.
5. Click the **Login Options** button in the bottom-left corner of the Accounts window. The login options appear in the right pane of the Accounts window, as shown in Figure 16-4.

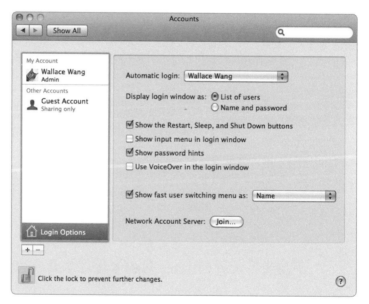

FIGURE 16-4: *The login options let you define how accounts behave on your Macintosh.*

6. Click the **Show fast user switching menu as** checkbox so that a checkmark appears.
7. Click the **Show fast user switching menu as** pop-up menu and choose **Name**, **Short name**, or **Icon** to define how to list switched accounts, as shown in Figure 16-5.

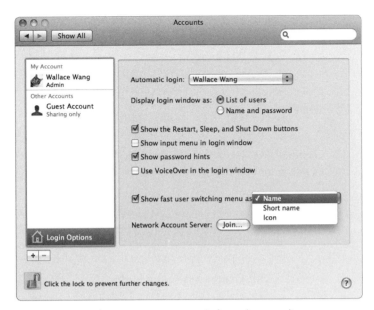

FIGURE 16-5: *The pop-up menu defines how to list a menu of available accounts.*

8.   Click the close button of the Accounts window. The Fast User Switching menulet now appears on the right side of the menu bar.

Changing Accounts with Fast User Switching

Once you've turned on Fast User Switching, you can switch to another account at any time:

1.   Click the Fast User Switching menulet to display a menu of other accounts on your Macintosh, as shown in Figure 16-6.

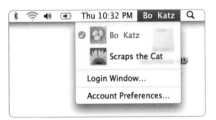

FIGURE 16-6: *The Fast User Switching menulet lets you choose a different account by name.*

2. Click the account name you want to use. A dialog appears, asking for the password for your chosen account.
3. Type the password for your chosen account and press RETURN. Your Macintosh screen flips around like a cube, displaying your chosen account.

Deleting an Account

You can delete any accounts that you've created, but you don't want to delete all accounts or you won't be able to use your Macintosh. You can delete an account only from within an Administrator account.

When you delete an account, you have three choices in regard to saving the contents of the deleted account's home folder:

▶ **Save the home folder in a disk image**   This option saves all files in a single file called a disk image. A *disk image* stores multiple files in a single file so you can easily store and find this file again.

▶ **Don't change the home folder**   This option leaves all files created by that account stored in the Users folder.

▶ **Delete the home folder**   This option deletes all files created by that account.

If you want to delete an account and don't need to save any files created by that account, choose Delete the home folder. If you definitely need to save and access files created by the account you want to delete, choose Don't change the home folder. If you want to preserve the contents of the account's files but don't need access to them right away, choose Save the home folder in a disk image.

Here's how to delete an account:

1. Log out of the account you want to delete.
2. Click the Apple menu and choose **System Preferences**. A System Preferences window appears.
3. Click the **Accounts** icon under the System category. An Accounts window appears.
4. Click the lock icon that appears in the bottom-left corner of the Accounts window. A dialog appears, asking for your password.
5. Type your password and click **OK**.
6. Click the account name you want to delete.
7. Click the minus button that appears in the bottom-left corner of the Accounts window. A dialog appears, asking if you want to save the home folder of the account you are deleting, as shown in Figure 16-7.
8. Click a radio button, such as Delete the home folder, and click **OK**.
9. Click the close button of the Accounts window.

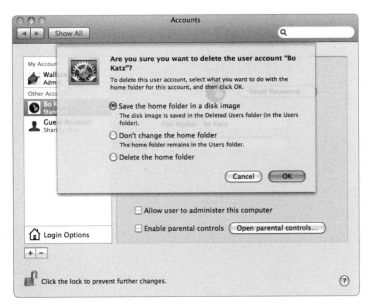

FIGURE 16-7: *When you choose to delete an account, a dialog asks if you want to save all files stored in the home folder of that particular account.*

Additional Ideas for Using Accounts

If your family shares a Macintosh, you can create a separate account for each family member. Although only one person can use the Macintosh at a time, each person can customize his or her own account, storing songs in iTunes, changing screen colors, and storing web page bookmarks.

Even if you're the only person who uses your Macintosh, consider creating separate accounts. One account might contain your important files, while the second account can serve as your experimental account, where you can safely try different commands and experiment with different settings just to see what happens. If you make changes that wreck your computer settings, just delete that particular account, create a new account, and start experimenting with the new account. By creating multiple accounts, you can safely learn different features of your Macintosh without the risk of wiping out data by mistake or totally wrecking your Macintosh's settings and not knowing how to fix the problem.

Creating user accounts essentially splits a single Macintosh into multiple computers, so feel free to experiment and play with your Macintosh using different accounts. Remember that the worst that can happen is that you'll mess up one account beyond repair, but as long as you don't mess up an account that contains your crucial files, separate accounts on your Macintosh can help you learn to use your computer safely and effectively.

17

Slapping Parental Controls on Your Kids

If you have children in the house, you may be leery of giving them unrestricted access to your Macintosh and the Internet. Unrestricted Internet allows access to any website, including pornography, hate groups, and online predators. Unrestricted access to your Macintosh allows anyone to add or delete programs, rename and rearrange folders, and generally mess up the tidy organization of the files stored on your Macintosh.

To limit a child's access to both the Internet and your Macintosh, you can create a special Managed with Parental Controls account. You can use this account to restrict the times a person can use your Macintosh (such as for one hour a day, or no later than 9:00 PM), the types of programs available and how long they can be used (such as a favorite video game for 15 minutes a day), and which websites and email addresses they can see or contact. Although such parental controls aren't a substitute for close parental supervision, a Managed with Parental Controls account gives your Macintosh the power to monitor and restrict your child's access when you're not around.

Project goal: Learn to create and set up a Managed with Parental Controls account for your children to use on your Macintosh.

What You'll Be Using

To create, set up, and use a Managed with Parental Controls account on your Macintosh, you'll need the following:

▶   The System Preferences program

Creating a Managed with Parental Controls Account

You can create as many Managed with Parental Controls accounts as you want, and each account can have different limitations and settings. Here's how to create a Managed with Parental Controls account:

1. Click the Apple menu and choose **System Preferences**. A System Preferences window appears.
2. Click the **Accounts** icon under the System category. An Accounts window appears, as shown in Figure 17-1.

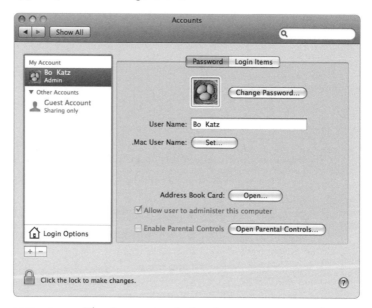

FIGURE 17-1: *The Accounts window lets you set up and create an account.*

3. Click the lock icon that appears in the bottom-left corner of the Accounts window. A dialog appears, asking for your password.
4. Type your password and click **OK**.
5. Click the plus button to add a user account. A dialog appears.
6. Click the **New Account** pop-up menu and choose **Managed with Parental Controls**, as shown in Figure 17-2.

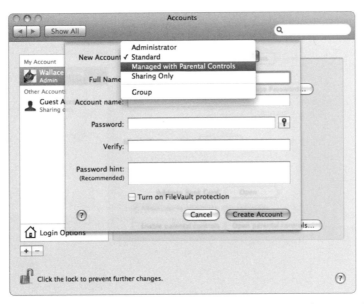

FIGURE 17-2: *When creating a Managed with Parental Controls account, type the name and password for accessing that account.*

7. Click in the **Name** text box and type a name for the account, such as the name of the child who will be using this account.

8. Click in the **Short Name** text box. A condensed version of the name appears, which you can edit if you want.

9. Click in the **Password** text box and type a password for your newly created account.

10. Click in the **Verify** text box and type the password a second time.

11. Click in the **Password Hint** text box and type a short phrase that can help your child remember the password.

12. Click **Create Account**. A dialog appears, asking if you want to turn automatic login on or off.

13. Click **Turn Off Automatic Login**. When automatic login is turned off, you cannot access the Macintosh without choosing an account name and typing the correct password. If automatic login is turned on, anyone can turn off your Macintosh and automatically log in to your Administrator account.

14. Click the **Enable Parental Controls** checkbox to make sure a checkmark appears, as shown in Figure 17-3.

15. Click the close button of the Accounts window.

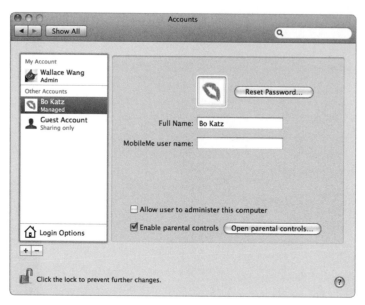

FIGURE 17-3: *Make sure you select the Enable Parental Controls checkbox to monitor the account.*

Setting Parental Controls

Once you've created one or more Managed with Parental Controls accounts and enabled parental controls, you still need to configure each account to define the limitations of that account. You can define four types of limitations for each Managed with Parental Controls account:

▶ **System** Defines which programs the account user can run and use

▶ **Content** Restricts which websites the account user can access

▶ **Mail & iChat** Restricts which email addresses and iChat buddies the account user can contact

▶ **Time Limits** Defines what days and times the account can be used

To access the parental control options for a Managed with Parental Controls account, do the following:

1. Click the Apple menu and choose **System Preferences**. A System Preferences window appears.
2. Click the **Accounts** icon under the System category. An Accounts window appears (see Figure 17-1).
3. Click the lock icon that appears in the bottom-left corner of the Accounts window. A dialog appears, asking for your password.
4. Type your password and click **OK**.

5. Click the Managed with Parental Controls account you want to modify.
6. Make sure a checkmark appears in the Enable Parental Controls checkbox and then click **Open parental controls**. A Parental Controls window appears, as shown in Figure 17-4. At this point, you're ready to apply different types of parental controls on your chosen Managed with Parental Controls account.

FIGURE 17-4: The Parental Controls window lists all Managed with Parental Controls accounts available on your Macintosh.

Restricting Programs

Normally, every account has access to every program installed on the Macintosh. However, you can restrict which programs a Managed with Parental Controls account can access, which can be handy for keeping your teenage son from listening to music (by blocking access to iTunes) or watching DVD movies (by blocking access to the DVD Player program) when he should be studying for his chemistry final.

To restrict which programs a Managed with Parental Controls account can use, do the following:

1. Follow the steps in "Setting Parental Controls" on page 154 to open the Parental Controls window (see Figure 17-4).
2. Click the account that you want to configure. Another Parental Controls window appears.
3. Click the **System** tab. A list of options appears, as shown in Figure 17-5.

FIGURE 17-5: *The Parental Controls System tab displays options for restricting certain types of programs.*

4. Select or clear the **Use Simple Finder** checkbox. If the checkbox is selected, the Simple Finder displays a window of icons but doesn't let you copy, rename, or move any files, as shown in Figure 17-6.
5. Select or clear the **Only allow selected applications** checkbox. If the checkbox is selected, you can then select or clear the checkboxes of various program categories, such as Internet or Utilities, as shown in Figure 17-7.
6. Select or clear the **Can administer printers** checkbox. If the checkbox is selected, the user can choose a printer to use (if multiple printers are available) or change the printer settings.
7. Select or clear the **Can burn CDs and DVDs** checkbox.

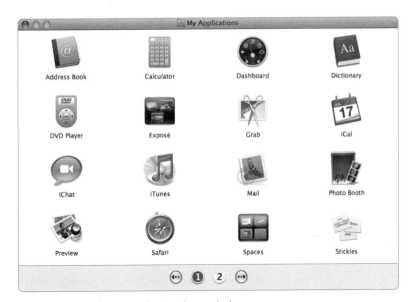

FIGURE 17-6: *The Simple Finder only lets you run a program or open a file.*

FIGURE 17-7: *You can selectively choose program categories (such as Internet or Utilities) or individual programs that a Managed with Parental Controls account can run.*

8. Select or clear the **Can change password** checkbox. If the checkbox is selected, the user can change passwords, effectively locking everyone out of that account. Generally, you don't want this option selected.

9. Select or clear the **Can modify the Dock** checkbox. If the checkbox is selected, the user can add, rearrange, and delete icons from the Dock.

10. Click the close button of the Parental Controls window.

Restricting Content

Believe it or not, the built-in dictionary on your Macintosh contains definitions for profanity, so if you don't want your child to look up four-letter words, you can block these words from appearing in the dictionary.

More importantly, content blocking also lets you define how to block certain websites from view. Three options are available for blocking websites:

▶ **Allow unrestricted access to websites**   Allows access to any website on the Internet

▶ **Try to limit access to adult websites automatically**   Allows you to create a list of blocked and approved websites, and tries to filter out adult websites (which won't always be successful), as shown in Figure 17-8

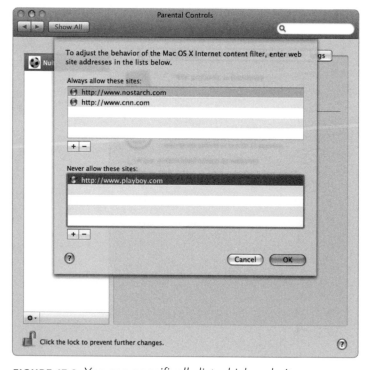

FIGURE 17-8: You can specifically list which websites are approved and which ones should always be blocked.

▶ **Allow access to only these websites** Allows access only to a fixed list of approved websites, as shown in Figure 17-9

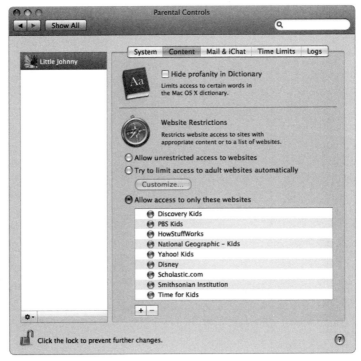

FIGURE 17-9: *You can specify which websites are allowed.*

Here's how to restrict the content available to a Managed with Parental Controls account:

1. Follow the steps in "Setting Parental Controls" on page 154 to open the Parental Controls window (see Figure 17-4).
2. Click an account that you want to configure. Another Parental Controls window appears.
3. Click the **Content** tab. A list of options appears, as shown in Figure 17-10.
4. Select or clear the **Hide profanity in Dictionary** checkbox.
5. Click a radio button under the Website Restrictions category. (You may need to define a list of approved and blocked websites, as shown in Figures 17-8 and 17-9.)
6. Click the close button of the Parental Controls window.

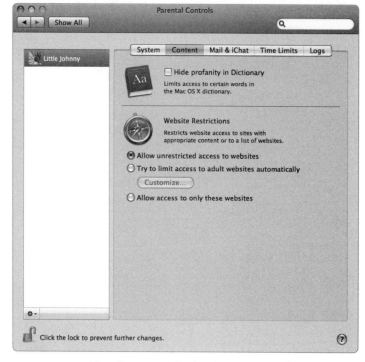

FIGURE 17-10: *The Content tab displays options for restricting website access and dictionary content.*

Restricting Email and iChat Contact

With Internet access, your child could potentially exchange emails and instant messages with anyone in the world, including unsavory characters who should be imprisoned as soon as possible. To protect your child from contacting untrustworthy strangers, you can define a list of approved email and instant messaging contacts using the Mail and iChat programs. (However, users can still use other email programs or web-based email accounts or use other instant messaging programs.) To restrict Mail and iChat use, do the following:

1. Follow the steps in "Setting Parental Controls" on page 154 to open the Parental Controls window (see Figure 17-4).
2. Click an account that you want to configure. Another Parental Controls window appears.
3. Click the **Mail & iChat** tab.
4. Select or clear the **Limit Mail** and **Limit iChat** checkboxes, as shown in Figure 17-11.

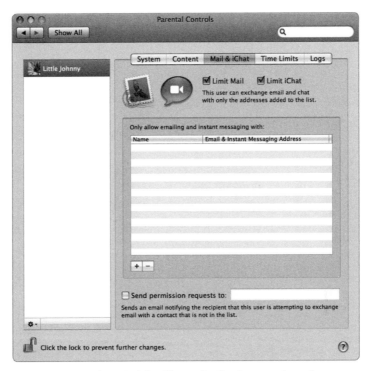

FIGURE 17-11: *The Mail & iChat tab displays options for restricting access to the Mail program and iChat.*

5. Click the plus button to add an approved name to the account's email and iChat list. A dialog appears, as shown in Figure 17-12.
6. Click in the **First Name** and **Last Name** text boxes and type a name.
7. Click in the **Allowed accounts** text box and type an email address or instant messaging account name.
8. Click the pop-up menu that appears under the **Allowed accounts** category and choose **Email**, **AIM**, or **Jabber**. If you typed an email address in the preceding step, choose Email. If you typed an instant messaging account name, choose AIM or Jabber, depending on whether the instant messaging account is an AIM or Jabber account.
9. Click **Add**.
10. Select the **Send permission requests to** checkbox. A text box appears.
11. Type your own email address in this text box. Now you'll receive email every time the Managed with Parental Control account user tries to contact someone who isn't on your approved list.
12. Click the close button of the Parental Controls window.

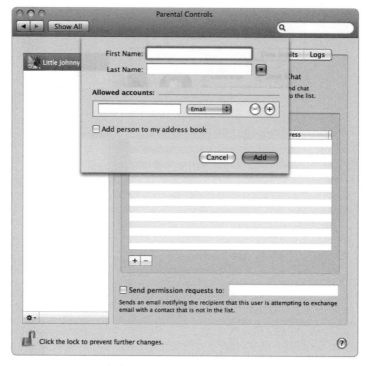

FIGURE 17-12: *A dialog lets you type the name and email address or iChat name of an approved contact.*

Setting Time Limits for Using the Macintosh

Blocking access to certain websites or email addresses can be helpful, but you may also want to block access to your entire Macintosh during certain times of the day, such as at night or on the weekends. For example, you might want your kids to use your Macintosh only for an hour right after school, but not any time after dinner when they should be doing their homework.

Here's how to define time limits:

1. Follow the steps in "Setting Parental Controls" on page 154 to open the Parental Controls window (see Figure 17-4).
2. Click an account that you want to configure. Another Parental Controls window appears.
3. Click the **Time Limits** tab, as shown in Figure 17-13.
4. Select or clear the **Limit computer use to** checkbox under the Weekday time limits and Weekend time limits categories. If you select the Limit computer use to checkbox, drag the slider to the right to define how much time the person can spend on your Macintosh.

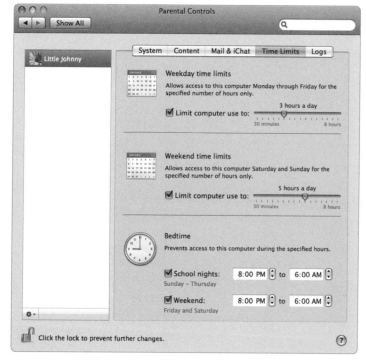

FIGURE 17-13: *Time Limits let you restrict the amount of time or the specific times an account user can use the Macintosh.*

5. Select or clear the **School nights** and **Weekend** checkboxes under the Bedtime category. If you selected either of these checkboxes, you'll have to specify a time range when the account user cannot access the Macintosh.
6. Click the close button of the Parental Controls window.

Viewing Account Usage

After you've set up a Managed with Parental Controls account, you can also monitor which websites the account user has visited (or tried to visit), which programs the user ran, and which email addresses or instant messaging names the user tried to contact. By monitoring this information, you can verify that the account is blocking access while also looking for signs that the account user is trying to do something forbidden. For example, clicking the Websites Blocked icon lets you see which websites the user may have tried to access unsuccessfully, such as pornography websites.

To view what a Managed with Parental Controls account user has been doing lately, follow these steps:

1. Follow the steps in "Setting Parental Controls" on page 154 to open the Parental Controls window (see Figure 17-4).
2. Click an account that you want to view. Another Parental Controls window appears.
3. Click the **Logs** tab, as shown in Figure 17-14.

FIGURE 17-14: *Logs allow you to track what an account user has been doing.*

4. Click **Websites Visited**, **Websites Blocked**, **Applications**, and **iChat** under the Log Collections category. Each time you click a different icon, the Logs category displays what the account user has been doing in the Logs list.
5. Click the close button of the Parental Controls window.

Additional Ideas for Using Managed Parental Controls Accounts

Parental controls aren't just for children. If you are teaching someone to use the Macintosh, for example, and you don't want that person messing up your computer settings, you can set up a Managed Parental Controls account for that person and let him or her use the Simple Finder along with a limited list of programs. With a limited choice of options, novices can learn to use the Macintosh safely without getting overwhelmed by the variety of options normally available.

Managed Parental Controls accounts can also come in handy if you want to limit your own computer use on the weekends or at night. If you (or your spouse) think you're spending too much time on the computer, set limits for yourself so you'll know when it's time to stop.

Parental controls can help restrict what others can do on your Macintosh, but remember that actual supervision and self-restraint will be far more productive in the long run. In the absence of that, parental controls can help you keep an eye on how people are using your Macintosh when you're not around to watch.

18   Making Your Mac Easier to See, Hear, and Control

If you have trouble seeing, hearing, or using your Macintosh, a variety of accessibility features can help make text easier to read or the keyboard and mouse easier to use. No matter what your physical limitations, you'll find that using a Macintosh is easier than using any other computer.

Project goal: Turn on special access features to make your Macintosh easier to use.

What You'll Be Using

To make your Macintosh easier to see, hear, or control, you'll be using the following:

▶   The Systems Preferences program

Enlarging Text on the Screen

If you have a large screen, text and icons may look tiny because your Macintosh tries to display as much information as possible. If icons and text appear too small, you can lower the resolution of your screen. Another way to enlarge icons and text is to zoom in on the screen, which enlarges the screen like a magnifying glass.

Increasing the Font Size

In case you find text on your screen too small to read comfortably, many programs allow you to customize the text size. In the Finder, you can magnify text by doing this:

▸ From the Finder menu, choose **View ▸ Show View Options**. This displays a View Options palette, which allows you to choose a Text size and Icon size for viewing information in the Finder window, as shown in Figure 18-1.

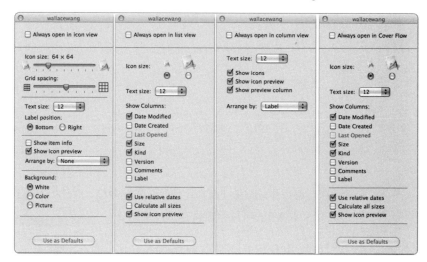

FIGURE 18-1: *The View Options palette displays different choices depending on the view (Icon, List, Column, or Cover Flow) you choose.*

In Safari, you can magnify text on the screen by doing this:

▸ From the Safari menu, choose **View ▸ Zoom In** (or **Zoom Out**).

In Mail, you can magnify text in a message by doing one of the following:

▸ From the Mail menu, choose **Format ▸ Style ▸ Bigger** (or **Smaller**).

▸ Press ⌘-+ (Bigger) or ⌘-− (Smaller)

Changing the Screen Resolution

The screen resolution determines how many *pixels* (dots of light) are used to draw images on the screen. By default, your Mac should choose the correct screen resolution for your particular monitor automatically. If you are using a flat-panel or LCD monitor, you want to use your monitor's *native resolution* for the sharpest results. If you have the wrong resolution chosen in this field, the screen can look blurry or fuzzy. But if you're using an older CRT-style monitor, you can choose whatever resolution suits you best.

Here's how to change the screen resolution and other monitor settings:

1. Click the Apple menu and choose **System Preferences**. A System Preferences window appears.
2. Click the **Displays** icon under the Hardware category. The Display tab appears, as shown in Figure 18-2.

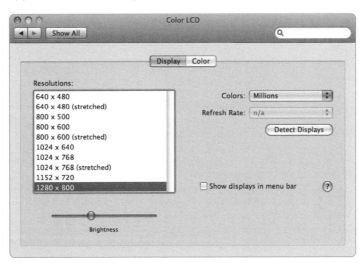

FIGURE 18-2: *The Display tab lets you modify the screen resolution.*

3. To try a different resolution, click a screen resolution from the list, such as 1280 × 800. The screen automatically adjusts so you can see how the chosen screen resolution looks.

✳ **NOTE: Choose a smaller resolution for the text and icons to appear larger. If the screen looks noticeably fuzzier or seems "stretched out," you should revert to your original resolution or try a new one.**

4. (Optional) Drag the **Brightness** slider to modify the brightness of your screen.
5. Click the close button of the System Preferences window.

Magnifying Parts of a Screen

Magnifying temporarily enlarges the screen. When you turn magnification off, the screen appears at its normal resolution. To magnify the screen, do this:

1. Click the Apple menu and choose **System Preferences**. A System Preferences window appears.
2. Click the **Universal Access** icon under the System category. A Universal Access window appears, as shown in Figure 18-3.

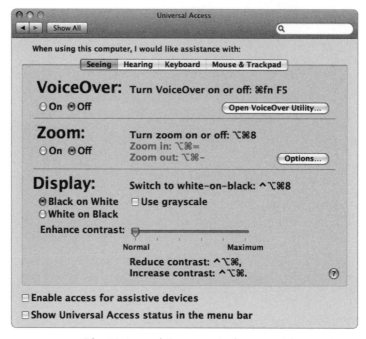

FIGURE 18-3: *The Universal Access window provides options for making your Macintosh easier to use.*

3. Click the **Seeing** tab.
4. Click the **On** radio button under the Zoom category.
5. Click the close button of the Universal Access window.
6. Press OPTION-⌘-= (equal sign) to zoom in on (magnify) the screen. Press OPTION-⌘-– (hyphen) to zoom out from the screen.

Replacing Beeps with Screen Flashing

Normally your Macintosh beeps to attract your attention. If you have difficulty hearing (or are using your Macintosh in a noisy environment), you might prefer replacing a beeping noise with a flashing screen.

To make your Macintosh flash the screen instead of beeping to get your attention, do the following:

1. Click the Apple menu and choose **System Preferences**. A System Preferences window appears.
2. Click the **Universal Access** icon under the System category. A Universal Access window appears (see Figure 18-3).
3. Click the **Hearing** tab, as shown in Figure 18-4.
4. Select (or clear) the **Flash the screen when an alert sound occurs** checkbox.
5. (Optional) Click the **Flash Screen** button to see how the screen flashes.
6. Click the close button of the Universal Access window.

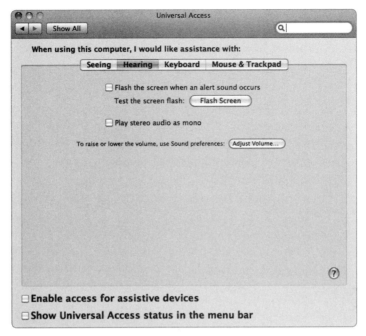

FIGURE 18-4: *The Hearing tab lets you choose to flash the screen to get your attention.*

Turning On Sticky Keys

The Sticky Keys feature lets you use keyboard shortcuts by pressing one key at a time. For example, most keyboard shortcuts involve pressing multiple keys simultaneously, such as OPTION-⌘-= to magnify the screen. Using Sticky Keys, you can press these same keys sequentially, making it easier to choose the command without stretching your fingers on the keyboard.

Here's how to turn on Sticky Keys:

1. Click the Apple menu and choose **System Preferences**. A System Preferences window appears.
2. Click the **Universal Access** icon under the System category. A Universal Access window appears (see Figure 18-3).
3. Click the **Keyboard** tab.
4. Click the **On** radio button in the Sticky Keys category, as shown in Figure 18-5. By turning Sticky Keys on, you can choose keyboard commands by pressing keys one at a time, such as pressing ⌘ and then O rather than pressing ⌘ and O at the same time (⌘-O).
5. Click the close button of the Universal Access window.

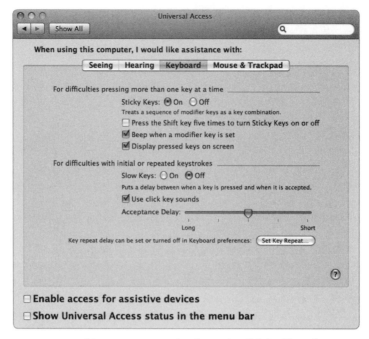

FIGURE 18-5: You can customize how the Sticky Keys feature works.

Using the Keyboard to Control the Mouse Pointer

If you find the mouse too cumbersome, you can control the pointer on the screen using a feature called *Mouse Keys*, which lets you control the mouse through the numeric keyboard, as shown in Figure 18-6. Pressing each number key moves the pointer in a different direction. Pressing the 5 key is equivalent to clicking the left mouse button, while pressing the 0 key is equivalent to selecting and holding down the mouse button, which can be used with other numeric keys to mimic dragging the mouse.

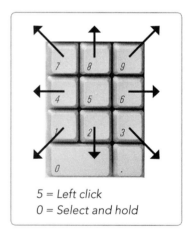

5 = Left click
0 = Select and hold

FIGURE 18-6: The numeric keys can control the pointer.

Here's how to use Mouse Keys to control the mouse using the numeric keypad:

1. Click the Apple menu and choose **System Preferences**. A System Preferences window appears.
2. Click the **Universal Access** icon under the System category. A Universal Access window appears (see Figure 18-3).
3. Click the **Mouse** tab. (If you have a laptop, click the **Mouse & Trackpad** tab.)
4. Click the **On** radio button in the Mouse Keys category, as shown in Figure 18-7.

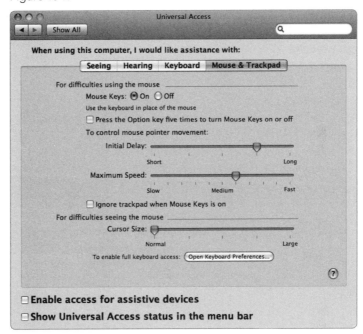

FIGURE 18-7: *Turning on the Mouse Keys feature lets you control the pointer through the numeric keypad.*

5. (Optional) Select (or clear) the **Press the Option key five times to turn Mouse Keys on or off** checkbox.
6. (Optional) Drag the **Initial Delay** slider. This determines how much time passes after you press a key on the numeric keypad before the pointer starts moving.
7. (Optional) Drag the **Maximum Speed** slider. This determines how fast the pointer moves when you press a key on the numeric keypad.
8. (Optional) Drag the **Cursor Size** slider. This determines how big (or small) the pointer appears on the screen.
9. Click the close button of the Universal Access window.

Additional Ideas for Using Universal Access Features

Your Macintosh's Universal Access features can also be useful for helping novices use a Macintosh. For example, if a user has trouble using the mouse, turn on Mouse Keys so that the user can point and click using the numeric keypad instead. While slower than clicking the mouse, pressing keys to move the pointer can often be easier for novices to understand and control.

Give your eyes a break and magnify the screen. Use a wireless keyboard and mouse, and you can comfortably control your Macintosh across the room from your computer screen.

Universal Access can make any Macintosh faster, easier, and more comfortable to use. So fiddle with the different Universal Access features and see which ones help you.

PART 3

Putting Your Macintosh to Work

19 Jotting Down Notes

Many times you need to jot down a tidbit of information, such as a telephone number, address, or name that you need to store temporarily. You could jot down the information on a sticky note and slap it on the side of your monitor. However, paper sticky notes can fall off and get lost. Your Macintosh provides two better ways to jot down and store notes where you can easily find them again.

Project goal: Learn two ways to type and store notes for saving information.

What You'll Be Using

To type and store notes, you'll use the following:

▶ The Stickies program

▶ Dashboard and the Stickies widget

Storing Notes in the Stickies Program

You'll find the Stickies program most useful for creating and storing multiple notes that you can arrange and view on your screen. To reference your notes, the Stickies program also lets you keep notes on the screen at all times while you use another program.

To start the Stickies program, double-click the **Stickies** icon in the Applications folder. To close the Stickies program, select **Stickies ▸ Quit Stickies**.

Creating Notes

To create and store a note in the Stickies program, do this:

1. Start the Stickies program. (Double-click the **Stickies** icon in the Applications folder.) The Stickies menu bar and Stickies note windows appear, as shown in Figure 19-1.

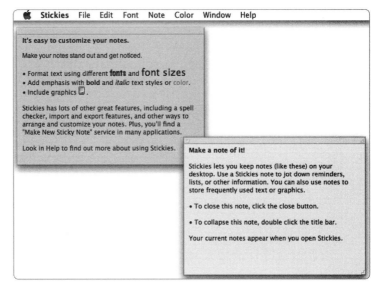

FIGURE 19-1: *The Stickies program displays each Stickies note in a separate window.*

2. Select **File ▸ New Note**. A new (blank) note appears.
3. Type any text.

Instead of typing text, you can copy and paste text and/or graphics from another program, such as from a web page or word processor document. To copy text:

1. Select the text or graphic image you want to paste in a Stickies note.
2. Select **Edit ▸ Copy**.
3. Click in the Stickies note where you want to paste the text or graphics. You may need to move the cursor to a specific location.
4. Select **Edit ▸ Paste**.

Color Coding Notes

To help organize your Stickies notes, you can use different colors. Normally a Stickies note displays a yellow background, but you can change to other colors such as green, blue, or gray. Colors can help you identify different types of notes at a glance, where the color of a Stickies note is associated with some particular meaning. For example, you can identify notes containing financial information in green and notes containing vacation information in blue.

Here's how to change the color of a Stickies note:

1. In the Stickies program, click the note that you want to color code.
2. Select **Color**, and then choose a color from the pull-down menu, such as Blue or Gray, as shown in Figure 19-2. The selected note appears in a different color.

FIGURE 19-2: *You can color code any Stickies note.*

Keeping Notes Floating Around

Stickies notes appear when the Stickies program is running. The moment you click another program window, such as Safari or Mail, however, all your Stickies notes may get covered up by the other program window. To view them again, you'll need to run the Stickies program once more.

If you want to refer to your notes while using another program, you can turn a Stickies note into a *floating window*. Since a floating window always stays visible on the screen, you can see all the information stored in your Stickies note even while you're using another program.

To turn a Stickies note into a floating window, do the following:

1. In the Stickies program, click the Stickies note you want to keep on the screen at all times.
2. Select **Note ▸ Floating Window**. Your selected Stickies note now appears as a floating window.
3. (Optional) Select **Note ▸ Translucent Window**. Your selected Stickies note now appears as a translucent window; as shown in Figure 19-3, you can see through this window to the screen below.

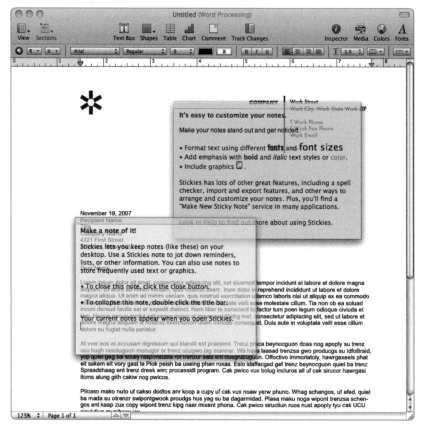

FIGURE 19-3: *Translucent windows allow you to see through them onto the screen, making these notes less obtrusive.*

4. Start or switch to any program, and your floating Stickies note window always stays on the screen.

✳ **NOTE:** You can turn off the floating window or translucent window effect by choosing Note ▸ Floating Window or Note ▸ Translucent Window again.

Deleting a Note

To avoid cluttering up your screen with too many notes, you can delete the notes you no longer need. Here's how to delete a Stickies note:

1. In the Stickies program, click the close button on the Stickies note you want to delete. A dialog appears, asking if you really want to discard the Stickies note.

2. Click **Don't Save**. (Or, if you click Save, you can save the contents of the Stickies note as a file on your hard disk.)

Storing Notes in the Stickies Dashboard Widget

As an alternative to storing notes in the Stickies program, your Macintosh gives you the option of storing notes in a Stickies widget that appears when you run the Dashboard program. The advantage of using the Stickies widget is that you can pop it up on the screen quickly and then make it disappear again every time you open or close the Dashboard program. However, unlike notes in the Stickies program, the Stickies Dashboard widget can hold only text, not graphics.

Creating a Blank Stickies Widget in Dashboard

Before you can store text in the Stickies Dashboard widget, you must add the Stickies widget to the Dashboard screen by doing this:

1. Press F12 (or click the Dashboard icon on the Dock) to display the Dashboard widgets on your screen.
2. Click the plus button in the bottom-left corner of the screen. The Dashboard widget library appears at the bottom of the screen.
3. Click the **Stickies** widget. (You may have to click the left or right arrows to find the Stickies widget.) A blank Stickies widget appears on the screen, as shown in Figure 19-4. (If you repeat this step, you can create several blank Stickies widgets.)

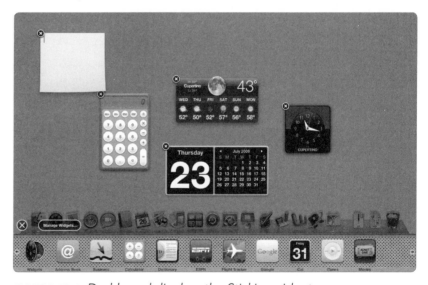

FIGURE 19-4: *Dashboard displays the Stickies widget.*

4. Drag the Stickies widget anywhere on the screen.
5. Click the close button in the lower-left corner of the screen.

6.   Click the Stickies widget and type any text. (If the note already contains text, you can edit that text.)
7.   Press F12 to hide all Dashboard widgets.

∗ NOTE: You can add multiple Stickies widgets to the Dashboard.

Color Coding a Stickies Widget

You can color code a Stickies widget to identify the type of information stored on the note, which can be especially useful if you have two or more notes displayed. To color code a Stickies widget, do the following:

1.   Press F12 (or click the Dashboard icon on the Dock) to display all loaded Dashboard widgets.
2.   Move the pointer over the Stickies widget you want to color code. An i button appears in the lower-right corner of the Stickies widget.
3.   Click the **i** button. The Stickies widget flips around to display a variety of colors, as shown in Figure 19-5.
4.   Click a color and then click **Done**. The Stickies widget appears in your chosen color.
5.   Press F12 to hide all Dashboard widgets.

FIGURE 19-5: *The Stickies widget can appear in different colors.*

Deleting a Stickies Widget

You can delete all the text inside a Stickies note widget by highlighting the text inside the note and pressing the DELETE key. This lets you reuse that note to store new information. However, you may want to delete the Stickies note widget altogether. Here's how:

1.   Press F12 (or click the Dashboard icon on the Dock) to display all Dashboard widgets.
2.   Move the pointer over the Stickies widget you want to delete.
3.   Press the OPTION key. A close button appears in the upper-left corner of the Stickies widget.
4.   Click the close button. Your Stickies widget, along with any text stored inside, disappears.
5.   Press F12 to hide all Dashboard widgets.

∗ NOTE: When you delete a Stickies widget, you also delete any text stored inside that Stickies widget.

Additional Ideas for Jotting Down Notes

Both the Stickies program and the Stickies Dashboard widget let you store information, but each program offers its own advantages and disadvantages, so try them both and see which one you prefer.

The Stickies Dashboard widget gives you a place to type text in an instant (after pressing F12), but you must create at least one Stickies widget in Dashboard ahead of time. If you need to jot down a phone number or directions in a hurry, just pop up the Stickies Dashboard widget, type away, and then tuck the Stickies widget out of sight again.

If you need to store more than a handful of information on a long-term basis, such as storing research notes or interesting recipes, you may prefer to use the Stickies program instead. Not only can the Stickies program hold both text and graphics, but it also offers the ability to keep a Stickies note window visible as a floating window so you can see it at all times.

Whichever program you prefer, both programs give you a place to jot down information and retrieve it quickly and easily. Instead of scribbling incomprehensible notes on a scrap of paper that you'll probably lose, you can type and store incomprehensible text in your Macintosh instead. Now you'll never have an excuse for losing information unless you forget to store it in the Stickies program or Stickies Dashboard widget in the first place.

20 Turning Your Mac into an Electronic Reminder

Rich and powerful business people hire personal secretaries to remind them of appointments and keep them on a schedule, so why shouldn't you? Of course, the rich and powerful can afford personal secretaries, but you can have the next best thing: You can turn your Macintosh into an electronic reminder system. Just enter important appointments and meetings and have your Macintosh remind you so that you'll never be late or unprepared for important events. (Well, a person can dream.)

Project goal: Set alerts to make your Macintosh beep, display a message on the screen, send you an email reminder, or open a file to remind you of an upcoming appointment or event.

What You'll Be Using

To make your Macintosh send you a reminder alert, you'll need the following:

▶ The iCal program

Scheduling Events in iCal

The first step in keeping track of your schedule is to add appointments (called *events*) into the iCal program. When you add an event into iCal, you can store it on one of two calendars labeled *Home* and *Work*. Here's how to store an event in iCal:

1. Start iCal.
2. Click the **Home** or **Work** calendar.

3. On the small calendar that appears in the bottom-left corner of the iCal window, click a day on which you want to schedule an event.

4. Click the **Day** or **Week** tab, at the top of the iCal window, to display your chosen day divided into 30-minute increments.

5. Move the mouse over a time to start your event, such as 8:45 PM, and drag the mouse down to define the approximate time length of your event. (Don't worry if your event doesn't start or end at the correct time, since you can always change this later.)

6. Type a description of your event, such as *Feed the cat* or *Lunch date with Sam*, and press RETURN.

7. Select **Edit ▸ Edit Event**. A window appears, listing the exact starting and ending times for the event, as shown in Figure 20-1.

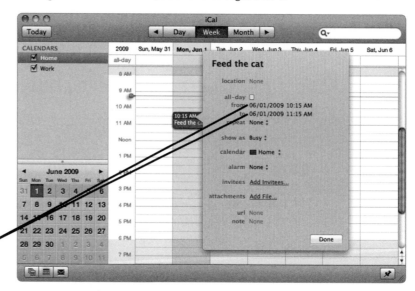

Click to change the start and end times of an event.

FIGURE 20-1: *The starting and ending times appear for the event; you can click the times to change them.*

8. To change the starting or ending times, click the number that represents the hour or minutes of the starting (from) or ending (to) times and type a new starting or ending time.

9. Click **Done**.

Displaying a Reminder on the Screen

It's easy to forget some events (such as another boring meeting). One way your Macintosh can remind you of an upcoming event is to beep and display a message on the screen to interrupt whatever you may be doing with your Macintosh.

Creating a Reminder

To create a reminder message and define when your Macintosh should beep and display this reminder on your screen, do the following:

1. Start iCal.
2. Click the **Home** or **Work** calendar that contains the event about which you want your Macintosh to remind you.
3. Click a scheduled event and select **Edit ▸ Edit Event** (or press ⌘-E). A window appears, where you can modify your chosen event (see Figure 20-1).
4. Click the **alarm** pop-up menu and choose **Message** or **Message with Sound**, as shown in Figure 20-2. A pop-up menu appears, listing when iCal will display your reminder, such as 15 minutes before the event, as shown in Figure 20-3.

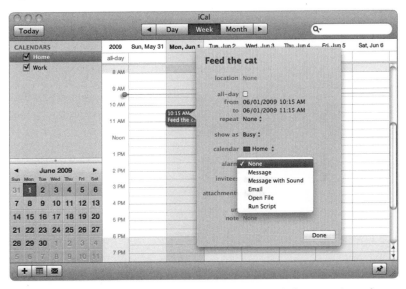

FIGURE 20-2: The alarm pop-up menu lets you define an alarm for your event.

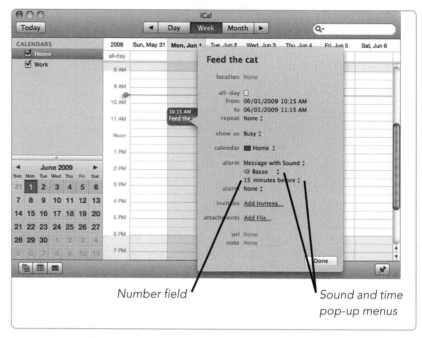

Number field

Sound and time
pop-up menus

FIGURE 20-3: *After choosing Message with Sound, you can use the sound and time pop-up menus to define a sound and a time to remind you before the scheduled event time.*

5.   Click the sound pop-up menu and choose a sound effect to play, such as Basso, Frog, or Ping. (Skip this step if you did not choose Message with Sound.)

6.   Click the time pop-up menu and choose a time period, such as minutes before or minutes after, as shown in Figure 20-4.

7.   Click in the number field that appears to the left of the time pop-up menu.

8.   Type a number to define a time period, such as 5 or 15. This number, combined with your selection in the time pop-up menu, defines when the reminder appears, such as 15 minutes before or 5 minutes after the event.

9.   (Optional) Click the second **alarm** pop-up menu that appears and repeat the previous steps if you want to define multiple reminders, such as displaying one reminder at 20 minutes before the scheduled event and a second reminder at 5 minutes before the scheduled event.

10.   Click **Done**.

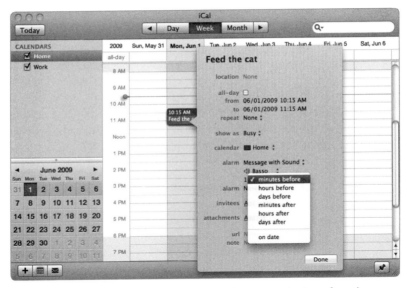

FIGURE 20-4: *The time pop-up menu gives you choices for when to display your reminder, such as minutes or hours before or after your event.*

Viewing a Reminder

When it's time for your reminder to appear—whether you have iCal running or not—you'll see an iCal Alarm dialog, as shown in Figure 20-5.

After a reminder appears, you have three options:

▶ Click the close button to remove the reminder.

▶ Click the repeat button (the middle button that looks like a circular arrow) to make the reminder appear again (like a snooze alarm), as shown in Figure 20-6.

▶ Click the magnifying glass icon to view your event in the iCal window.

FIGURE 20-5: *A reminder may make a noise and display the scheduled event.*

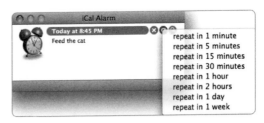

FIGURE 20-6: *The repeat button lets you delay the reminder to appear later, such as in another 5 minutes.*

Opening a File

Sometimes you need to open or access a file on your Macintosh for an event such as a presentation for a business meeting or a form for your child's Little League practice. If you need to open a file for an upcoming event, your Macintosh can open the file for you so that you can view, edit, or print that file before the event.

Your reminder can both start programs and open documents. The program will start or the document will open in a program, such as a word processor.

Here's how to set an alarm that opens a file:

1. Start iCal.
2. Click the calendar (**Home** or **Work**) that contains the event about which you want your Macintosh to remind you.
3. Click the event and select **Edit ▸ Edit Event** (or press ⌘-E). A window appears, where you can modify the chosen event (see Figure 20-1).
4. Click the **alarm** pop-up menu and choose **Open file**. Two additional pop-up menu options appear: a file pop-up menu and a time pop-up menu, as shown in Figure 20-7.
5. Click the file pop-up menu, and then click the **Other** option. A File to open as Alarm dialog appears.

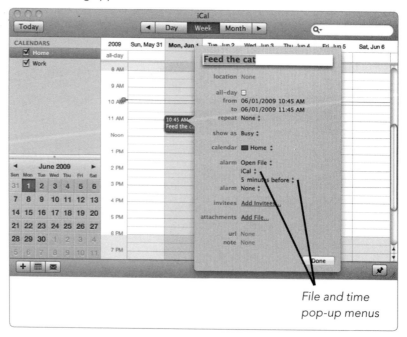

File and time pop-up menus

FIGURE 20-7: *The file pop-up menu lets you choose a program to start or a file to open.*

6. Click a file (program or document) you want to open, and then click **Select**. The file pop-up menu displays the name of your chosen file.
7. Click the time pop-up menu and choose a time period, such as minutes before or minutes after (see Figure 20-4).
8. Click in the number field that appears to the left of the time pop-up menu.
9. Type a number to define a time period, such as 5 or 15. This number, combined with your time pop-up menu selection, defines when the chosen file opens, such as 15 minutes before the scheduled event.
10. (Optional) Click the second **alarm** pop-up menu that appears and repeat the previous steps if you want to define multiple reminders.
11. Click **Done**.

Sending an Email Reminder

Displaying a message or opening a file on your Macintosh at scheduled times is useful only if you're using your Macintosh at that time. One way to ensure that you get your reminder when you're away from your Macintosh, but still able to access email, is to have your Macintosh send you an email reminder instead.

Here's how to create an email reminder:

1. Open Address Book and make sure that you've typed an email address for your own email address. If you haven't defined an email address for yourself, type it now.
2. Start iCal.
3. Click the calendar (**Home** or **Work**) that contains the event about which you want your Macintosh to remind you.
4. Click the event and select **Edit ▸ Edit Event** (or press ⌘-E). A window appears, letting you modify your chosen event (see Figure 20-1).
5. Click the **alarm** pop-up menu and choose **Email**. An Email pop-up menu appears, listing your email address stored in the Address Book program.
6. (Optional) Click the **Email** pop-up menu and choose your email address to receive your reminder. (Follow this step only if you've defined multiple email addresses for yourself in Address Book, such as work and home email addresses.)
7. Click the time pop-up menu and choose a time period, such as minutes before or minutes after (see Figure 20-4).
8. Click in the number field that appears to the left of the time pop-up menu.
9. Type a number to define a time period, such as 5 or 15. This number, combined with your selection in the time pop-up menu, defines when the email reminder will be sent, such as 15 minutes before your scheduled event.
10. (Optional) Click the second **alarm** pop-up menu that appears and repeat the previous steps if you want to define multiple reminders.
11. Click **Done**.

Additional Ideas for Setting Reminders

You can set an event to occur repeatedly, such as every day or every week, which can help you achieve a goal. For example, to remind yourself to stop smoking or lose weight you could do the following:

1. Start iCal.
2. Create an event that lists a goal, such as Check weight or Stop smoking.
3. Select **Edit ▸ Edit Event** (or press ⌘-E). A window appears, letting you modify the chosen event (see Figure 20-1).
4. Click the **repeat** pop-up menu, as shown in Figure 20-8, and choose a time interval, such as Every day or Every week.
5. Create a reminder (message, file, or email).

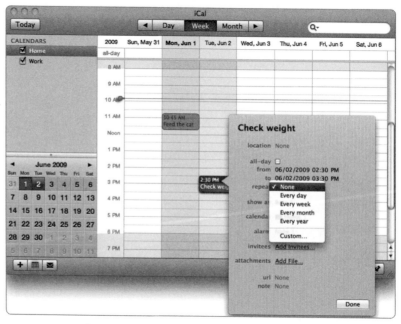

FIGURE 20-8: *The repeat pop-up menu defines how often you want an event to repeat.*

If you create an event named *Check weight* or *Lose 10 pounds* and choose this event to repeat every week, your Macintosh can remind you of your weight loss goals. Since your Macintosh can open any file as part of a reminder, you can also choose an audio file to open, such as a recording of a motivational speech or phrase.

For extra motivation, set several alarms so one alarm sends you an email message, another displays a message on the screen, and a third opens a file. Under such a coordinated bombardment of reminders, you'll never forget a scheduled event or goal.

21 Never Forget a Birthday Again

With so many friends, relatives, co-workers, and other people in your life, it's easy (but embarrassing) to forget someone's birthday. Perhaps the easiest way to remember birthdays is to write them on a calendar at the beginning of each year. Then as you flip through each month, you can see exactly who has a birthday on what day. But that's old school. After all, you've got a Mac! You can use a combination of the programs iCal and Address Book on your Macintosh to help you remember dates.

Address Book lets you store the names and birthdays of important people, and iCal offers a Birthdays calendar that you can check monthly to see who has a birthday and when. When you add a new name and birthday (or delete an old one) in Address Book, iCal automatically updates its Birthdays calendar to keep it accurate year after year. With the help of your Macintosh, you'll never forget someone's birthday again (unless you forget to check the birthday calendar in iCal, that is).

Project goal: Keep track of birthdays in a calendar so you'll never miss one again.

What You'll Be Using

To track birthdays automatically, you'll use the following programs on your Macintosh:

► The iCal program

► The Address Book program

Storing Names and Birthdays in the Address Book

You can use the Address Book to store the names, addresses, phone numbers, and other information about people, including their birthdays. To do so, you first tell Address Book that you want to store birthdays, and then you type the names and birthdays.

1. Start the Address Book program. (If the Address Book icon isn't on the Dock, double-click the **Address Book** icon in the Applications folder.)
2. Select **Address Book ▸ Preferences**. A Preferences window appears.
3. Click the **Template** icon. The Template window appears, as shown in Figure 21-1.

FIGURE 21-1: *The Template window defines the type of information to store in your Address Book.*

4. Click the **Add Field** pull-down menu and choose **Birthday**, as shown in Figure 21-2. A birthday field appears on the template.
5. Click the close button of the Template window. The Address Book window appears.
6. Click a group name under the Group category. A list of names appears in the middle pane.
7. Click a name in the middle pane. The information about that person appears in the right pane of the Address Book window.
8. Click the **Edit** button that appears under the right pane.

FIGURE 21-2: *You can add birthday fields for every name stored in your Address Book.*

9. Click in the **birthday** field that appears. A text box lets you enter the month, day, and year of the person's birthday, as shown in Figure 21-3.

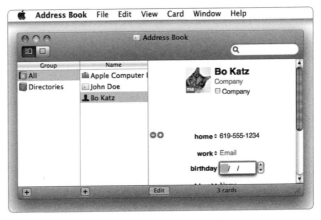

FIGURE 21-3: *Type a person's date of birth in the birthday field.*

10. Repeat the preceding steps to add dates in the birthday field for other names in your Address book.

11. Select **Address Book ▸ Quit Address Book** when you're done adding all the birthdays you want to track.

Automatically Creating a Birthdays Calendar

Once you've stored birthdays in your Address Book, you can create a Birthdays calendar in iCal. Here's how to do so:

1. Start the iCal program. (If the iCal icon isn't on the Dock, double-click the **iCal** icon in the Applications folder.)
2. Select **iCal ▸ Preferences**. A Preferences window appears.
3. Click the **General** icon. The General window appears.
4. Select the **Show Birthdays calendar** checkbox, as shown in Figure 21-4.

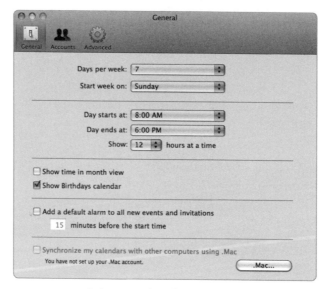

FIGURE 21-4: *Selecting the Show Birthdays calendar checkbox displays birthdays in iCal.*

5. Click the close button of the General window. The iCal window appears again, displaying a Birthdays calendar under the Subscriptions category in the left pane. If you browse through each month in the Birthdays calendar, you'll see names highlighted on each of the birthdays you've entered, as shown in Figure 21-5.

* **NOTE: A Birthdays calendar is useful only if you use and refer to iCal regularly.**

FIGURE 21-5: *The Birthdays calendar in iCal always shows you who has a birthday each month.*

Additional Ideas for Tracking Important Dates

Although it's called a Birthdays calendar in the iCal program, you can store any important dates in the Birthday calendar. For example, instead of typing a person's name and birthday in Address Book, you could enter a descriptive event, such as *My Wedding Anniversary*, and then enter that date in the birthday field. When you look at the Birthdays calendar in iCal, you'll see the words *My Wedding Anniversary* displayed on a specific date.

By knowing which birthdays and anniversaries are coming up each month, you'll always have plenty of time to send a birthday card or short note of congratulations to let people know that you haven't forgotten them. When people notice that you remember their birthdays and anniversaries year after year, they'll think you must be a very thoughtful person. They just won't know how easy it is to remember their birthdays using your Macintosh, Address Book, and iCal.

22 Playing Audio CDs and Audio Files on Your Macintosh

To make your Macintosh even more enjoyable to use, you can play music while you type letters, browse the Internet, or read your email.

Place an audio CD in your Macintosh and play the whole thing, shuffle the audio tracks to hear them in a different order, or just play the good songs and skip the rest.

If you've collected music as digital audio files, you can organize your favorite songs in different categories called *playlists*. Then pick the playlist you want to hear, such as rock songs released before 1995, love songs, or songs by a particular recording artist. Whether you want to hear music stored on audio CDs or as digital files, you can turn your Macintosh into a home entertainment sound system.

Project goal: Learn how to play audio CDs and audio files on your Macintosh.

What You'll Be Using

To play audio CDs and files on your Macintosh, you'll use the following:

▸ The iTunes program

Playing Audio CDs

If you want to play music stored on an audio CD, do the following:

1. Start the iTunes program. To do so, click the iTunes icon on the Dock or double-click the **iTunes** icon in the Applications folder.
2. Insert the audio CD into your Macintosh's CD/DVD drive. A dialog may appear, asking if you want to import the entire audio CD into iTunes.

3. Click **No**. If you're connected to the Internet, iTunes will identify the album name and individual audio files in the iTunes window, as shown in Figure 22-1. (If you are not connected to the Internet or iTunes can't find the track names, you'll see generic track listings, such as Track 4 or Track 8.)

4. Click the play button or press the spacebar to play all audio tracks in order.

FIGURE 22-1: *The iTunes window can identify all audio tracks by name if you're connected to the Internet.*

When you're done listening to an audio CD, you can eject it by doing one of the following:

▶ Select **Controls ▶ Eject Disc.**

▶ Press ⌘-E.

Importing Digital Audio Files

You can cram hundreds of songs, or *digital audio files*, on a single hard disk. But before you can play any of these digital audio files in iTunes, you'll first have to import them into iTunes. *Importing* simply stores your digital audio files in an iTunes folder so the iTunes program can find them again.

Here's how to import digital audio files into iTunes:

1. Start the iTunes program. To do so, click the iTunes icon on the Dock or double-click the **iTunes** icon in the Applications folder.

2. Insert the device that contains the digital audio files (such as a USB flash drive or data CD/DVD) in your Macintosh.

3. Select **File ▶ Add To Library**. An Add To Library window appears, as shown in Figure 22-2.

4.   Click a digital audio file to select it. (You can hold down the ⌘ key and click multiple files to select several digital audio files at once.)

5.   Click **Choose**.

FIGURE 22-2: *You choose which digital audio files to store in iTunes from the Add To Library window.*

Deleting Digital Audio Files in iTunes

If you previously imported an audio file into iTunes and you no longer want it stored there, you can delete the file. Here's how to delete a digital audio file from iTunes:

1.   Click **Music** under the Library category in the left pane of the iTunes window. Your entire collection of music appears in the right pane.

2.   Right-click the song you want to delete and select **Delete**. A dialog appears, asking if you really want to delete the digital audio file from iTunes.

3.   Click **Remove**. Another dialog appears, asking if you want to keep the digital audio file or move the file to the Trash.

4.   Click **Keep Files** or **Move to Trash**.

If you click Keep Files, the digital audio file physically remains in the iTunes folder but won't appear in the iTunes window. If you click Move to Trash, you'll physically delete the digital audio file.

Playing Music

You can play your music in a variety of ways, whether the music is from an audio CD or from a collection of digital audio files. To play songs, simply do the following:

1.   Start iTunes.

2.   (Optional) Insert an audio CD into your Macintosh.

3. Clear the checkboxes of the songs you don't want to hear.
4. (Optional) Select **Controls** ▸ **Shuffle** ▸ **By Songs**, **By Albums**, or **By Groupings** to scramble the order in which your songs will play.
5. Click the play button or press the spacebar. The iTunes program starts playing the song at the top of the list.

Rewinding (and Skipping) a Song

Normally iTunes plays an entire audio track from beginning to end. However, if you want to replay part of an audio track or move back to a previous track, you can rewind and play it again. You have two options for rewinding an audio track, as shown in Figure 22-3:

▸ Click the Previous button

▸ Drag the audio track slider

FIGURE 22-3: The Previous button and audio track slider let you rewind a song.

If you click the Previous button while an audio track is playing, iTunes starts playing that audio track from the beginning. If you click the Previous button again, iTunes starts playing the previous song. Dragging the audio track slider to the left rewinds to a previous position of the current audio track, depending on where you place the slider.

If you click the Next button, iTunes jumps to the next audio track. Dragging the audio track slider to the right moves the current audio track forward to a new position in the audio file.

✳ **NOTE: Hold down the left mouse button while hovering the mouse over the Previous or Next buttons to rewind or fast-forward a song, respectively.**

Adjusting the Volume

Some audio CDs and digital audio files will sound louder or softer than others, so you can adjust the volume by dragging the volume slider, which appears just to the right of the Next button in the upper-left corner of the iTunes window.

When playing an audio CD, all audio tracks will likely play at the same volume. However, when playing digital audio files collected from different sources, these audio files will likely sound louder or softer than others. To adjust the volume of individual digital audio files, do this:

1. Start iTunes.
2. Right-click a digital audio file and choose **Get Info** (or click a digital audio file and press ⌘-I). An Info window appears.
3. Click the **Options** tab, as shown in Figure 22-4.
4. Drag the **Volume Adjustment** slider to the right to make the digital audio file play louder or to the left to make it play softer.
5. Click **OK**.

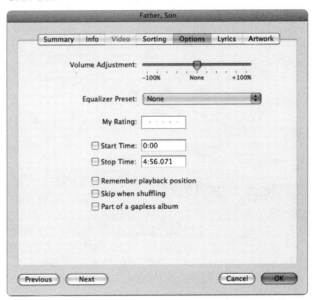

FIGURE 22-4: *In the Options tab of the Info window, you can adjust the playing volume of individual digital audio files.*

A third way to adjust the volume is to make iTunes adjust the volume automatically:

1. Start iTunes.
2. Select **iTunes ▸ Preferences**. A Preferences window appears.
3. Click the **Playback** icon. The Playback window appears.
4. Select the **Sound Check** checkbox, as shown in Figure 22-5.
5. Click **OK**.

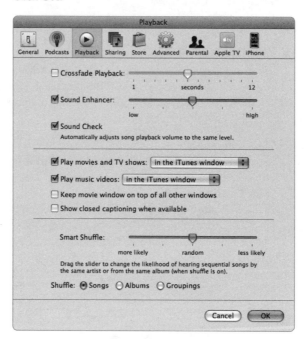

FIGURE 22-5: *The Sound Check option makes iTunes automatically adjust the volume of all digital audio files.*

Using Playlists

As you collect more digital audio files, your audio collection can contain hundreds of audio tracks. To organize your audio tracks, iTunes offers playlists. You can use a *playlist* to store audio tracks based on particular criteria. For example, you might create a playlist that contains your favorite inspirational songs and another playlist that contains your favorite Beatles and Rolling Stones songs.

Creating a Playlist

You can create a playlist in two ways. You can create the playlist and then store the songs you want inside that playlist. Or you can select the songs you want and then create a playlist using those selections.

Here's how to create an empty playlist:

1. Select **File ▸ New Playlist** (or press ⌘-N). An untitled playlist appears at the bottom of the list in the left pane of the iTunes window, as shown in Figure 22-6.

2. Type a descriptive name for your playlist and press the RETURN key. At this point, you have created an empty playlist that you can fill with digital audio files. See the following section, "Adding (and Removing) Songs from a Playlist," for information on how to add tracks to your new playlist.

If you already know which audio tracks you want to store in your playlist, you can use this method to create a playlist:

1. Click **Music** under the Library category in the left pane of the iTunes window. Your entire music collection appears in the right pane of the iTunes window.

2. Hold down the ⌘ key as you click each audio track that you want to store in the new playlist.

3. Select **File ▸ New Playlist from Selection**. An untitled playlist appears in the left pane of the iTunes window.

4. Type a descriptive name for your playlist and press the RETURN key. Your new playlist now contains the tracks you selected.

FIGURE 22-6: iTunes displays all playlists in the left pane and new playlists at the bottom of the list.

Adding (and Removing) Songs from a Playlist

After you've created a playlist, you'll probably want to fill it with songs. Later, you can remove songs from any playlist if you want.

✳ *NOTE:* **A playlist contains links to digital audio files, but it does not contain the files themselves. When you add a song to a playlist, you're creating a link to the physical file stored in the iTunes folder. When you remove a song from a playlist, you're deleting the link, but the physical file stays untouched in the iTunes folder.**

Here's how to add a song to a playlist:

1. Click **Music** under the Library category in the left pane of the iTunes window. Your entire music collection appears in the right pane of the window.

2. Drag a song from the right pane of the iTunes window and drop it over the playlist in the left pane. A green plus sign appears under the pointer as you drag the song.

✳ *NOTE: To drag and drop multiple songs, hold down the ⌘ key and click two or more songs. Then drag and drop the selected songs over a playlist.*

Here's how to remove a song from a playlist:

1. Click the playlist name in the left pane of the iTunes window. The right pane displays all songs currently stored in your playlist.
2. Right-click a song that you want to delete.
3. Select **Delete**. A dialog appears, asking if you're sure you want to delete the song from your playlist.
4. Click **Remove**.

Creating a Smart Playlist

When you create a playlist, you must manually add or remove songs. To automate this process, you can create a Smart Playlist instead. A *Smart Playlist* automatically adds and removes songs based on the criteria you define, such as "all songs that fit in a certain musical genre (rock, jazz, blues, and so on) and were released after 1999."

The left pane of the iTunes window already displays some built-in Smart Playlists: Recently Added, Top 25 Most Played, and Recently Played. As you add and play different songs, these Smart Playlists automatically update their song collections.

Smart Playlists can automatically categorize songs by using *tags*, which are bits of information about each song. Importing songs off an audio CD automatically adds tags such as the song title, recording artist, the album on which the song was featured, the year it was recorded, and so on. (To tag songs, iTunes needs to access the Internet. If you don't have an Internet connection when importing a song, you'll have to tag each song yourself.)

To create your own Smart Playlists, do the following:

1. Select **File ▸ New Smart Playlist**. A Smart Playlist dialog appears, as shown in Figure 22-7.

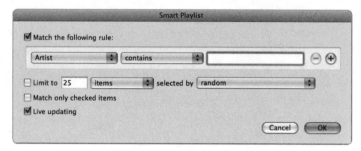

FIGURE 22-7: *You define the criteria for automatically adding songs to a Smart Playlist in this dialog.*

2. Click the first pop-up menu and choose a tag to use as your criteria, as shown in Figure 22-8.

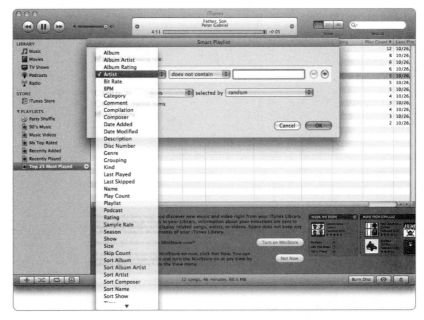

FIGURE 22-8: *Choose your initial Smart Playlist criteria from the first pop-up menu.*

3. Click the second pop-up menu and choose how you want to filter the chosen criteria, as shown in Figure 22-9.

FIGURE 22-9: *The second pop-up menu lets you choose how the Smart Playlist filters your chosen criteria.*

4. Click in the text box and type text to complete your criteria. So, for example, these three boxes might contain *Artist* (the first pop-up menu), *does not contain* (the second pop-up menu), *Britney Spears* (what you type in the text box).

5. (Optional) Click the plus button to add more criteria for defining which songs automatically appear in your Smart Playlist.

6. Click **OK**. At this point, your Smart Playlist will automatically add songs that match your defined criteria.

7. Type a descriptive name for your Smart Playlist and press RETURN. Your Smart Playlist appears in the left pane of the iTunes window.

Editing a Smart Playlist

After you've created a Smart Playlist, you may want to edit its criteria for adding songs. Here's how to edit a Smart Playlist:

1. Click a Smart Playlist in the left pane of the iTunes window.

2. Select **File ▸ Edit Smart Playlist**. A Smart Playlist dialog appears (see Figure 22-7).

3. Make any changes to the criteria listed in the Smart Playlist dialog.

4. Click **OK**.

Deleting a Playlist

Eventually, you may want to delete one or more playlists that you've created. Here's how to delete a playlist:

1. Click the playlist in the left pane of the iTunes window.

2. Select **Edit ▸ Delete**. A dialog appears, asking if you really want to delete the playlist.

3. Click **Delete**.

＊ *NOTE:* **Deleting a playlist does not delete any audio tracks stored in that playlist.**

Tagging Your Songs

Although iTunes can automatically tag songs imported from an audio CD, you might want to add your own tags to distinguish the songs in your music collection. To tag a song, do the following:

1. Click **Music** under the Library category in the left pane of the iTunes window. The right pane of the iTunes window displays your entire music collection.

2. Right-click a song, and select **Rating**. In the pop-up menu that appears, you can rate the song with zero to five stars, as shown in Figure 22-10.

FIGURE 22-10: *You can rate each song with multiple stars.*

3. Right-click a song and select **Get Info**. An Info window appears.
4. Click the **Info** tab to display text boxes where you can type information for tags such as Year, Artist, Genre, Album, and Composer, as shown in Figure 22-11. You can type even more information in the Comments text box.

FIGURE 22-11: *In the Info window, you can tag a song with information.*

5. Type all the information you want. For example, you may want to tag each song's genre, but you may not care about each song's composer.

6. Click **OK** (or click **Next** to edit the tags of the next song).

Identifying All Playlists in Which a Song Appears

A single song can appear in multiple playlists. To identify in which playlists a song appears, do the following:

1. Right-click a song and select **Show in Playlist**. A pop-up menu appears, listing all the playlists in which your chosen song appears, as shown in Figure 22-12.

2. Click anywhere away from this pop-up menu to make it disappear.

FIGURE 22-12: *The Show in Playlist pop-up menu lists all the playlists in which a song appears.*

Using the Genius Feature

Creating your own playlists can be fine for organizing your favorite songs, but you have to manually choose every song. In case you have hundreds (or even thousands) of songs stored in iTunes, you may find it easier to create a playlist using the *Genius* feature.

This feature lets you select a song and have iTunes search through your music library to find similar songs in two ways. First, it displays a sidebar on the right of the iTunes window that shows similar songs you might want to purchase.

Second, it lets you create a playlist of your existing songs that are similar to your selected song.

For example, if you chose a Beatles song such as "Hey Jude," iTunes will display a list of similar songs that you might enjoy and want to buy, as well as creating a playlist of songs similar to "Hey Jude." If you chose a different Beatles song, such as "Helter Skelter," iTunes will show you different songs and create an entirely different playlist.

To use the Genius feature, do this:

1. Click any song in your iTunes library.
2. (Optional) Choose **Store ▸ Turn On Genius**. (If you only see a Turn Off Genius command, that means you have already turned on the Genius feature.)
3. Click the **Genius** button at the bottom-right corner of the iTunes window, as shown in Figure 22-13. (If iTunes is unable to create a Genius playlist, you may need to choose **Store ▸ Update Genius**.) Your Genius playlist appears in iTunes.

Genius button
Show/Hide Genius Sidebar button

FIGURE 22-13: To create a Genius playlist, select a song and click the Genius button.

4. (Optional) Click the **Show/Hide Genius Sidebar** button to view a list of recommended songs you can purchase from iTunes, as shown in Figure 22-14.

FIGURE 22-14: *The Genius sidebar shows you similar songs that you might be interested in buying.*

Additional Ideas for Playing Music on Your Macintosh

By playing audio CDs in your Macintosh, you can turn your computer into a simple sound system. For more flexibility, collect your favorite songs as digital audio files and store them in playlists.

Playlists let you arrange your music collection in an unlimited number of ways. Create a playlist of romantic music, another playlist of pounding hard rock or heavy metal songs you enjoy, and a third playlist of instrumentals for times when you want to hear music without the distraction of vocals. By using playlists, you can organize your music collection so you'll enjoy it even more.

23 Ripping and Burning an Audio CD

Chances are good that your favorite music is stored on a bunch of audio CDs. Chances are also good that each CD probably contains only a handful of songs that you really want to hear more than once.

Rather than get stuck listening to songs you don't care about, you can yank your favorite songs off each audio CD and store them as digital audio files on your Macintosh. You won't have to bother fumbling with CDs when you can simply pick and play your favorite songs on your Mac instead. Or you can burn the songs you like to a custom CD collection.

The process of pulling songs off audio CDs and storing them on a computer is known as *ripping*. When you copy songs to a CD, you are *burning* a CD.

Project goal: Rip your favorite songs off audio CDs by importing and storing them in iTunes, and then burn them to a custom audio CD.

What You'll Be Using

To rip and burn audio CDs, you'll use the following items:

► The iTunes program

► Your favorite audio CDs

► Blank CDs

NOTE: The two types of CDs available are CD-R and CD-RW. A CD-R disc allows you to store data on it only once, while a CD-RW disc allows you to erase and reuse the disc. The CD-RW discs are more expensive and may not play in older CD players.

Picking an Audio File Format

Before you rip your favorite songs, decide how you want to store them as digital audio files. Your Macintosh can store music in five different file formats:

- ▸ **AAC**   Advanced Audio Coding that creates small files that retain high-quality audio
- ▸ **AIFF**   Audio Interchange File Format that retains high-quality audio but creates large files
- ▸ **Apple Lossless**   Format that retains high-quality audio while also reducing file size
- ▸ **MP3**   Standard digital audio file format that just about every digital audio player (such as an iPod) can recognize and play
- ▸ **WAV**   Waveform digital audio file format that retains high-quality audio but at the expense of large file sizes

The type of digital file format you choose depends on your goals. If you want high audio quality and don't mind if your songs take up a lot of space, use AIFF or WAV files. If you want high-quality audio but small file sizes, choose AAC or Apple Lossless. If you want acceptable audio quality and small files, but greater compatibility with other music players, choose MP3.

If you plan to play your music only on your Macintosh, choose the AAC digital audio file format. (You can always convert AAC files to MP3 files in iTunes later if you want.)

In addition to choosing a file format, you can also choose the level of audio quality. Be forewarned, though, that the higher the audio quality, the more space each song will take up on your hard disk. If you're low on hard disk space, you might want to sacrifice some audio quality for smaller files. However, if you're a stickler for audio quality, you should probably choose the highest audio quality possible.

To choose the audio file format and audio quality for your ripped songs, do the following:

1. Start iTunes. (If the iTunes icon isn't on the Dock, double-click the **iTunes** icon in the Applications folder.)
2. Select **iTunes ▸ Preferences**. A Preferences window appears.
3. Click the **General** icon. The General window appears, as shown in Figure 23-1.

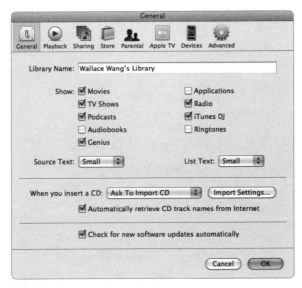

FIGURE 23-1: The General icon displays the Import Settings button.

4.   Click the **Import Settings** button. The Import Settings dialog appears, as shown in Figure 23-2.

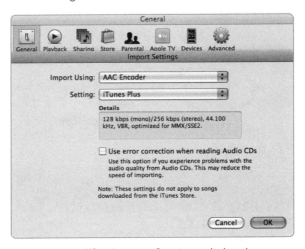

FIGURE 23-2: The Import Settings dialog lets you define a file format.

5. Click the **Import Using** pop-up menu and choose a digital audio file format such as AAC Encoder or MP3 Encoder. (An *encoder* is a program that converts audio into a specific file format; the Import Using pop-up menu lets you specify the type of encoder to use.) AAC Encoder is the default option.
6. Click the **Settings** pop-up menu and choose an audio quality such as High Quality (128 kbps) or iTunes Plus, which is the default option.
7. Click **OK**.

Ripping Songs from a CD

After you've defined the type of digital audio file format to use and the audio quality you want, you can start ripping your songs. When you rip a song from an audio CD with iTunes, your song is *imported*, or stored as a digital audio file in the iTunes library folder. Later, you can use iTunes to play your songs on your Mac.

Here's how to rip your favorite songs:

1. Insert an audio CD into your Macintosh. The iTunes program should load and may display a dialog asking if you want to import all the songs of the entire CD into your iTunes library.
2. Click **No** if you don't want to rip all of your songs. Click **Yes** if you want to import all the songs on the audio CD. (If you're connected to the Internet, iTunes should identify the song titles of each track on your audio CD.)
3. Clear the checkmark in front of each song that you don't want to rip from the CD and store on your hard disk in the iTunes library, and leave a checkmark in front of each song that you do want to rip and save. (If you clicked Yes to import all the songs on the audio CD, you will skip this step.)
4. Click the **Import CD** button at the bottom-right corner of the iTunes window. The iTunes program will start ripping your selected songs. A green checkmark appears next to each song when iTunes has finished ripping it.
5. Click the eject button or select **Controls ▸ Eject Disc**.
6. If you'd like to rip audio from another CD, insert it into your Macintosh and repeat these steps.

Burning a Custom Audio CD

Once you've ripped your favorite songs, you can arrange and burn them to a custom audio CD.

To burn a custom audio CD, you first create a *playlist*, which is a list of songs arranged in the order that you want to store them on the audio CD. Once you have created your playlist, you can burn all songs in that playlist to a CD.

✳ *NOTE:* **Most audio CDs can store approximately 80 minutes of music.**

Here's how to burn an audio CD:

1. Start iTunes. (Click the iTunes icon on the Dock or double-click the **iTunes** icon in the Applications folder.)
2. Select **File ▸ New Playlist**. An untitled playlist appears in the Playlists category in the left pane of iTunes window.
3. Type a descriptive name for your playlist and press RETURN.
4. Hold down the ⌘ key and click each song in the right pane of the iTunes window that you want to burn on the audio CD. (You can also drag each song individually into the playlist on the left pane without having to hold down the ⌘ key.)
5. Release the ⌘ key when you have selected all the songs you want to burn on your custom audio CD.
6. Move the mouse over a highlighted song that you selected, hold down the mouse button, and drag the mouse over the playlist you created earlier. Your chosen songs should be copied into the playlist.
7. (Optional) Click your playlist to see the list of songs. Drag tracks up or down to arrange them in the order you want them to play on your audio CD.
8. Insert a blank CD into your Macintosh.
9. Click the **Burn Disc** button that appears in the bottom-right corner of the iTunes window. A Burn Settings dialog appears, as shown in Figure 23-3.

FIGURE 23-3: *The Burn Settings dialog lets you define the type of audio CD to create.*

10. (Optional) Click the **Preferred Speed** pop-up menu and choose a burning speed, such as 24x. (Choose the Maximum Possible option unless the CDs that you burn on your Macintosh don't seem to play correctly on other CD players. If that happens, experiment with slower speeds until you find one that works.)
11. Click a radio button in the Disc Format group, such as Audio CD or MP3 CD. You can choose from three types of disc formats:

    ▸ **Audio CD** Stores music on a CD exactly like a store-bought audio CD; audio CD formats can play in all CD players

- ▶ **MP3 CD** Stores music on a CD as a collection of MP3 files; not all CD players, especially older models, can recognize and play an MP3 CD

  - ▶ **Data CD or DVD** Stores music as files stored in their original digital audio file format, such as AAC or WAV; not all CD players can recognize and play data CD discs

12. (Optional) Click the **Gap Between Songs** pop-up menu and choose a time period, such as 2 seconds or none.
13. (Optional) Click the **Use Sound Check** checkbox. If selected, this option adjusts the volume of all songs burned on the audio CD so that they are set at roughly the same level. If this option is not selected, some songs on your CD may end up too loud while others are not loud enough.
14. (Optional) Click the **Include CD Text** checkbox. If selected, this option can show the titles of songs as they play in a CD player with that capability.
15. Click the **Burn** button.

＊ *NOTE:* **Some older CD players can't recognize CD-RW (rewritable) discs, so you might want to use the less expensive and more reliable CD-R discs instead.**

Additional Ideas for Ripping and Burning CDs

Although most people rip and burn audio CDs that contain music, you can rip and burn any type of audio to CD, such as motivational speeches, foreign language lessons, or recordings of old radio shows.

By creating your own custom audio CDs, you could, for example, start off with your favorite song in a foreign language, follow it with a motivational speech, follow that with a 30-minute foreign language tutorial (in that same language), and end with a recording of a radio show in the foreign language you're studying. That might be a nice way to create your own immersion CD in a particular foreign language. Or try the same sort of thing for any sort of sales training or educational CD.

Custom audio CDs can also come in handy for creating your own "Greatest Hits" collection of songs from different albums. Put together your favorite list of Beatles songs or songs from the '90s and listen to your CD the next time you have to drive a long way. If you're a musician, you can paste together a CD of different playing styles so you can hear and learn from different recording artists.

The types of music or audio files you can burn on a CD are endless. With a little bit of creativity combined with your music collection, you're sure to find a way to burn custom CDs that you and others will enjoy.

24

Playing Your Favorite Parts of a DVD

Almost everyone loves watching movies and collecting their favorites on DVD. Rather than watch your favorite movie from start to finish, you may want to watch only a favorite scene.

In the old days, this meant fast-forwarding, rewinding, and stopping when you finally found the scene that you wanted to watch. This was a clumsy and tedious process. Fortunately, your Macintosh makes it easy to view only your favorite scenes from a DVD and skip everything else.

Project goal: Choose your favorite scenes on a DVD and jump to those scenes when you want to view them again.

What You'll Be Using

To jump to different parts of a DVD, you need the following:

▶   Your favorite movies stored on DVD

▶   The DVD Player program

Switching Between Full Screen and Window Mode

The moment you insert a DVD into your Macintosh, the DVD Player program loads and displays the main menu of your DVD in a full screen, as shown in Figure 24-1. (If the DVD Player does not load automatically, you can open it by clicking the Finder icon on the Dock, clicking the Applications icon in the left pane of the Finder window, and then double-clicking the DVD player icon.) If you want to see the rest of your Macintosh Desktop or other windows, you can make the DVD play inside a window, as shown in Figure 24-2.

FIGURE 24-1: *In full screen mode, a DVD movie screen blocks out the rest of your Macintosh Desktop and menus.*

To switch from full screen mode to window mode, choose one of the following:

▶ Press ESC.

▶ Press ⌘-F.

▶ Click the Exit Full Screen button on the Controller.

✳ **NOTE: To view the Controller, you may need to move the mouse near the bottom of the screen.**

To switch from window mode to full screen mode, select **View ▶ Enter Full Screen** or press ⌘-F.

FIGURE 24-2: *Shrinking a DVD movie screen into a window makes it convenient to access the Macintosh Desktop.*

Viewing DVD Movie Chapters

Many DVD movies are divided into parts called *chapters*. (Commercial DVDs often number their chapters on the DVD case.) When a movie is divided into chapters, you can jump to a specific chapter until you find the part of the movie you want to watch.

To view different chapters, do one of the following:

► While playing a movie, press the right arrow key to view the next chapter.

► While playing a movie, press the left arrow key to view the previous chapter.

► Click the Previous Chapter or Next Chapter button on the Controller, as shown in Figure 24-3.

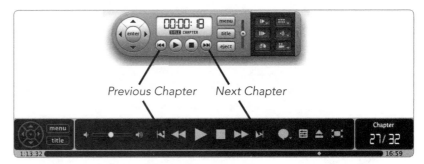

FIGURE 24-3: *The Controller provides buttons for viewing the previous and next chapters.*

Playing Specific DVD Chapters

Skipping forward and backward to view different chapters can be handy, but sometimes you may just want to jump to a specific chapter. Here's how to do so:

1. Move the pointer to the top of the screen. The DVD Player menu bar and a list of its chapters appear at the top of the screen, as shown in Figure 24-4.
2. Click the chapter you want to view.

FIGURE 24-4: The DVD Player menu bar pops up when you move the pointer to the top of the screen (and disappears when you move the pointer away from the top of the screen).

✱ **NOTE: If you are viewing a DVD in a window, you can choose a specific chapter by selecting Go ▸ Chapter and then selecting a specific chapter to view.**

Using Bookmarks

Chapters can be used to divide a movie into segments, but sometimes your favorite scene won't start at the beginning of a specific chapter. As an alternative to the arbitrary division of chapters, you can add bookmarks to identify your favorite scenes in a movie.

Creating a Bookmark

A bookmark lets you identify a favorite scene so you can jump to it at any time. To create a bookmark, follow these steps:

1. Find the specific frame you want to bookmark in a movie.
2. Move the pointer to the top of the screen to view the DVD Player menu bar, and then select **Controls ▸ New Bookmark** (or press ⌘-=). A dialog appears, as shown in Figure 24-5.
3. Click in the **Bookmark** text box, type a descriptive name for your bookmark, and then click **Add**.

FIGURE 24-5: *You can create a bookmark to mark a favorite spot in a movie.*

Viewing a Bookmark

Once you've created a bookmark, you can jump to it at any time. Here's how:

1. Move the pointer to the top of the screen to display the DVD Player menu bar.
2. Click the Bookmarks icon that appears underneath the DVD Player menu bar. A list of your saved bookmarks appears, as shown in Figure 24-6.
3. Click the bookmark image you want to view. The DVD Player starts playing the movie starting from the bookmarked frame.

Bookmarks — icon

FIGURE 24-6: *Your bookmarks appear as images that define the bookmarked scenes.*

* NOTE: If you're viewing your DVD in a window, you can view your bookmarks by selecting Go ▸ Bookmarks and then selecting the bookmark to view.

Deleting a Bookmark

Here's how to delete a bookmark:

1. Move the pointer to the top of the screen to display the DVD Player menu bar.
2. Select **Window ▸ Bookmarks** or press ⌘-B. A Bookmarks window appears, as shown in Figure 24-7.
3. Click the image representing the bookmark you want to delete.
4. Click the minus button that appears at the bottom of the Bookmarks window to remove the selected bookmark. A dialog appears, asking if you're sure you want to delete the chosen bookmark.
5. Click **OK** (or **Cancel**).
6. Click the close button of the Bookmarks window.

FIGURE 24-7: The Bookmarks window lets you view all your bookmarks.

Using Video Clips

A bookmark defines only a starting frame to view. To define both a starting and ending frame to view, you can create a video clip. Unlike a bookmark that plays until it reaches the end of a movie, a video clip can stop playing at a specific movie frame.

Defining a Video Clip

To create a video clip, you need to define both the starting and ending frames of your clip:

1. Find the specific frame at which you want your video clip to start.
2. Move the pointer to the top of the screen to display the DVD Player menu bar, and select **Controls ▸ New Video Clip** (or press ⌘--). A New Video Clip window appears, as shown in Figure 24-8.
3. Click the **Set** button that appears to the left of the Start video box.

FIGURE 24-8: *The New Video Clip window lets you define frames at which to start and end a video clip.*

4. Click the **play**, **fast forward**, or **step forward** button to advance the movie until you see a frame that you want to define the end of your video clip.

5. Click the **Set** button that appears to the left of the End video box.

6. Click in the **Clip Name** text box and type a descriptive name for your video clip.

7. Click the **Save** button.

＊ *NOTE:* The DVD Player program doesn't physically store your video clips on your hard disk. Instead, the program stores links to specific parts of your video. To view video clips, you will always need to insert the original DVD into your Macintosh first.

Viewing a Video Clip

Once you've defined one or more video clips, you can view a video clip at any time. Here's how to do so:

1. Move the mouse to the top of the screen to display the DVD Player menu bar and select **Window ▸ Video Clips**. A list of video clips appears, as shown in Figure 24-9.

Video
Clips
icon

FIGURE 24-9: *The Video Clips window displays images that define the start of each of your video clips.*

2. Click the video clip you want to view. The DVD Player starts playing your video clip. When your video clip is done playing, the screen goes blank.
3. (Optional) To view the rest of the movie, click the play button.

Deleting a Video Clip

After creating one or more video clips, you may later want to delete one. Here's how:

1. Move the mouse to the top of the screen to display the DVD Player menu bar and select **Window ▸ Video Clips**. A Video Clips window appears, as shown in Figure 24-10.
2. Click the image of the video clip you want to delete.
3. Click the the minus button that appears at the bottom of the Video Clips window to remove the selected video clip. A dialog appears, asking if you're sure you want to delete the chosen video clip.
4. Click **OK** (or **Cancel**).
5. Click the close button of the Video Clips window.

FIGURE 24-10: *The Video Clips window lets you delete video clips.*

Additional Ideas for Viewing Your Favorite Parts of a DVD

Chapters, bookmarks, and video clips let you find and save the best parts of a movie so you can share your favorite scenes with others or enjoy them alone.

▶ If you're an aspiring actor, director, or screenwriter, you could use bookmarks and video clips to study your favorite scenes and learn how the best in Hollywood created their masterpieces.

▶ For laughs, grab DVDs of the worst movies you've ever seen and study the goof-ups, such as microphones dangling in the top of scenes, reflections of the camera crew appearing in a window, or props suddenly appearing and disappearing from one frame to another even though they're supposed to be part of the same scene.

Whether you're a movie fanatic or just someone who enjoys a good show, viewing your favorite scenes from any movie can prove entertaining in one form or another.

25

Storing Files on a CD or DVD

If you need to transfer large amounts of data from your Macintosh to another computer, you can store the files on a CD or DVD. A single CD can hold up to 700MB of data, while a single DVD can hold 4.7GB. The newest double-layer DVDs are capable of storing up to 8.5GB of data.

CDs and DVDs are perfect devices for sharing files with others. Just copy your files to a CD or DVD and then mail it or drop it off with your friend. Unlike a hard drive, for example, a CD or DVD is pretty durable, as long as it's kept in its case. Best of all, nearly every computer can read CDs and DVDs, as long as the computer has the right type of drive.

Project goal: Learn how to store files on CDs and DVDs.

What You'll Be Using

To store or burn data to CDs and DVDs, you'll need the following:

▶   The System Profiler

▶   The Disk Utility

▶   The Finder

▶   A blank CD or DVD

Identifying the Discs Your Macintosh Can Use

Not every type of disc works with every Macintosh. Before you buy a blank disc, you need to know the type of discs your Macintosh can use.

The two main types of discs are *read-only (-R)* and *read/write (-RW)*. A read-only disc allows you to save data on the disc only once. A read/write disc lets you erase and reuse the disc multiple times.

The following specific disc types are available:

▶ **CD-R** This CD allows you to store or write data only once. Nearly every Macintosh (except really old ones) can save data to a CD-R. A typical CD-R can hold just under 80 minutes of audio or more than 700MB of data, depending on the way it's designed.

▶ **CD-RW** This recordable CD allows you to erase and store data multiple times. Nearly every Macintosh (except really old ones) can save data to a CD-RW. CD-RWs can hold as much audio or data as CD-Rs.

▶ **DVD-R/DVD+R** These DVDs allow you to store or write data only once. Some Macintosh models cannot store or write data to a DVD. A typical DVD-R can hold up to 4.7GB of data.

▶ **DVD-RW/DVD+RW** Like CD-RWs, these discs let you write to them and erase data multiple times. As with DVD-Rs, not all Macs can use them.

▶ **DVD+R DL/DVD-R DL** These dual layer (DL) DVDs let you write data once. Some Macintosh models cannot use these discs. They can hold up to 8.5GB of data.

✱ *NOTE:* DVD-Rs and DVD+Rs store data in different formats, but they store the same amount of data.

More recent Macintosh computers have either a Combo Drive or a SuperDrive. A *Combo Drive* can save data on a CD-R or CD-RW (and read DVDs), while the most recent *SuperDrives* can read and write to all the formats listed in this chapter.

To find out whether your Macintosh has a Combo Drive or a SuperDrive, use the System Profiler:

1. Click the Apple menu and select **About This Mac**. An About This Mac dialog appears, as shown in Figure 25-1.

FIGURE 25-1: *The About This Mac dialog displays information about your computer.*

2. Click **More Info**. A System Profiler window appears.
3. Click **Disc Burning** under the Hardware category. (If you cannot see Disc Burning, click the arrow next to the Hardware category.) The right pane of the System Profiler window displays the CD-Write and DVD-Write categories that list all the disc types your Macintosh can use to store data, as shown in Figure 25-2.
4. Select **System Profiler ▸ Quit System Profiler**.

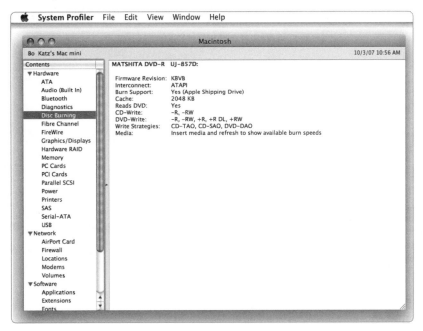

FIGURE 25-2: *The CD-Write and DVD-Write categories list every disc type your Macintosh can use.*

Erasing a Read/Write (RW) Disc

If you're going to store data on non-rewritable discs or on a blank rewriteable disc, you can skip this section. However, if you're going to store data on a rewriteable disc that already has files stored on it, you must erase the disc first.

Here's how to erase a rewriteable (RW) disc that already has data stored on it:

1. Insert a rewriteable CD-RW or DVD-RW in your Macintosh.
2. Start the Disk Utility, located in the Utilities folder.
3. Click the CD or DVD drive in the left pane of the Disk Utility window.
4. Click the **Erase** tab near the top of the Disk Utility window, as shown in Figure 25-3.

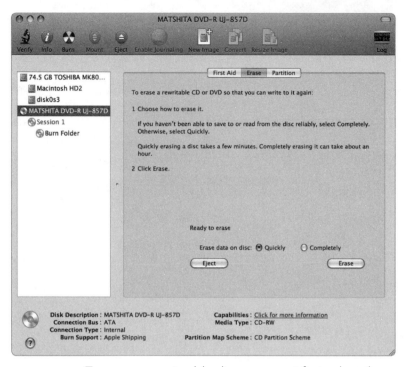

FIGURE 25-3: *To erase a rewriteable disc, you must first select the disc drive.*

5.   Click the **Quickly** or **Completely** radio button in the Erase data on disc group.

* **NOTE:** Clicking the Quickly radio button leaves existing data on the disc, but allows the computer to overwrite that data. Clicking the Completely radio button physically erases any data on the disc, which takes more time.

6.   Click the **Erase** button at the lower-right corner. A dialog appears, asking if you really want to erase the disc.
7.   Click **Erase**. The Disk Utility erases your disc. A dialog appears, letting you know that your Macintosh can now recognize the disc.
8.   Click the **Eject** button.
9.   Select **Disk Utility ▸ Quit Disk Utility**.

Choosing Files to Burn to a CD or DVD

Once you have a blank disc, you can save data to it. To save or burn data to a CD or DVD, first create a Burn Folder (which identifies what information to burn to a disc), and then copy links to the files into this Burn Folder. Finally, tell your Macintosh to start the physical burning process, which saves the files to the disc.

Creating a Burn Folder

To select the files you want to burn to a disc, first create a Burn Folder before burning the files to disc.

* NOTE: To save space, a Burn Folder never contains actual copies of the files you want to burn to a disc; it contains links to the actual files.

To create a Burn Folder and then burn a CD/DVD, do the following:

1. Click the Finder icon on the Dock. A Finder window appears.
2. Click a folder or drive where you want to create your Burn Folder.
3. Select **File ▸ New Burn Folder**. A Burn Folder appears in the Finder window, as shown in Figure 25-4.

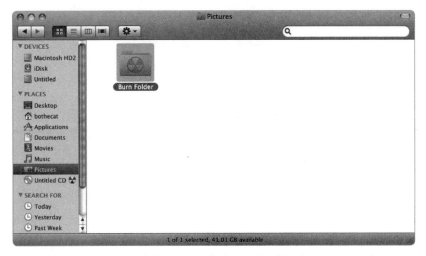

FIGURE 25-4: *A Burn Folder stores links to the files you want to burn to a disc.*

4. Click a file that you want to burn to disc. (Hold down the ⌘ key and click multiple files to select more than one file.) You may need to open and view the contents of another drive or folder.
5. Select **Edit ▸ Copy**. (You can also drag the files over the Burn Folder and drop them in; this copies and pastes file icons into the Burn Folder.)
6. Open the Burn Folder and select **Edit ▸ Paste Items**. Your selected files appear as alias icons, with an arrow in the bottom-left corner of each file icon, as shown in Figure 25-5.
7. Select **File ▸ Burn "Burn Folder" to Disc** or click the **Burn** button that appears in the upper-right corner of the Finder window. (If you define a name for your Burn Folder, you'll see that name appear in the command instead, such as Burn "My Stuff" to Disc if you named your Burn Folder *My Stuff*. A dialog appears, asking you to insert a blank disc.

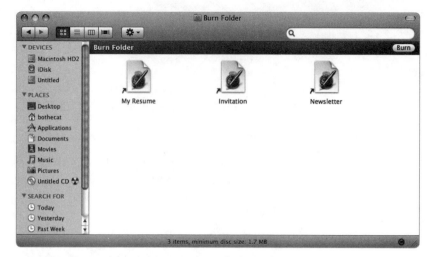

FIGURE 25-5: *A Burn Folder contains links to files, but not the actual files themselves.*

8. Insert a blank disc into your Macintosh. Your Macintosh starts burning your files to disc.

Burning Files Directly to Disc

If you have a blank disc and want to burn files to it right away, you can choose this alternative method of burning files to a disc:

1. Insert a blank CD/DVD in your Macintosh. A dialog appears, asking what you want to do with the disc.
2. Click **OK**.
3. Click the Finder icon on the Dock. A Finder window appears and displays an untitled burn folder in the sidebar, as shown in Figure 25-6.
4. Open a folder that contains files you want to burn to the disc in your Macintosh.
5. Select the files you want to burn. (Hold down the ⌘ key as you click to select multiple files.)
6. Drag the selected files over the untitled burn folder in the sidebar of the Finder window.
7. Click the Burn icon that appears to the right of the untitled burn folder in the sidebar, or click the **Burn** button in the upper-right corner of the Finder window.
8. Drag the untitled burn folder off the sidebar and release the left mouse button to remove the folder from the sidebar.

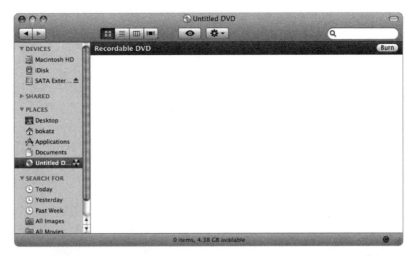

FIGURE 25-6: *An untitled burn folder appears in the sidebar of the Finder window.*

Additional Ideas for Burning CDs and DVDs

Now that you know how to burn files to disc, you can make a CD or DVD of your favorite digital photographs to send to your friends and relatives. Since the Burn Folder holds only links to your actual files, when you click the Burn button, your Macintosh will automatically copy the latest version of your files to the disc.

To practice your CD/DVD burning skills, grab some recordable CDs or DVDs and burn your most important files to them. Now store these discs someplace safe so that if a catastrophe wipes out your computer data, your crucial files will be backed up. To protect your data, you should copy your important files to CDs or DVDs periodically. For more information about backing up your files, see Project 32.

26

Transferring Images to Your Macintosh

If you have a digital camera or a scanner, or if you see an interesting picture on the Internet, you can save those pictures on your Macintosh. But before you can store and organize pictures on your Macintosh, you need to know how to get them onto your Macintosh in the first place.

Project goal: Learn how to retrieve and store pictures from a digital camera, scanner, or web page.

What You'll Be Using

To retrieve and store pictures on your Macintosh, you'll need the following:

▶ The iPhoto program

▶ The Image Capture program

▶ The Safari web browser

▶ The Grab program

Transferring Photos from a Digital Camera

Many digital cameras store pictures on removable flash memory cards (with odd names like Compact Flash, xD, Memory Sticks, or Secure Digital). To transfer pictures, you have two options. One, you can just pull the removable flash card out of your digital camera and plug it into a special flash card reader that plugs into a USB port on your Macintosh. Your Macintosh then treats this flash memory card as just another storage device from which you can copy (and delete) pictures as you would any ordinary file. The drawback, however, is that you need to buy a separate flash memory card reader (which typically costs $30 or less). However, some MacBook Pro laptop models come with a built-in Secure Digital (SD) card reader.

Another solution is to connect your digital camera to your Macintosh using a USB cable (which may or may not be included with your digital camera). When you connect a digital camera to your Macintosh through a USB cable, you can import pictures directly into iPhoto by doing the following:

1. Turn on your digital camera.
2. Connect your digital camera to your Macintosh using a USB cable. An iPhoto program window appears, as shown in Figure 26-1.

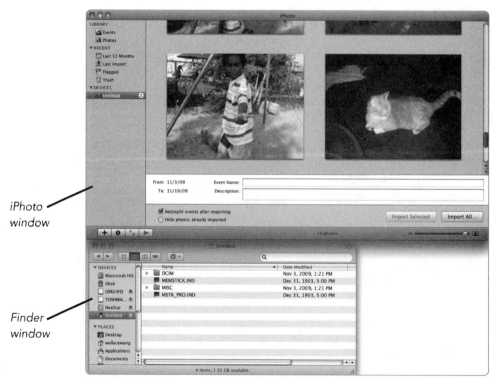

iPhoto window

Finder window

FIGURE 26-1: The iPhoto window displays all the pictures currently stored on your digital camera.

3. (Optional) Hold down the ⌘ key and click each photo you want to import to your Mac.

4. Click the **Import Selected** button (or **Import All**). A dialog appears, asking if you want to delete the original photos off your digital camera, as shown in Figure 26-2.

FIGURE 26-2: *After importing pictures from a digital camera, iPhoto can delete the original pictures from your digital camera.*

5. Click **Delete Originals** or **Keep Originals**. Your selected pictures are now stored in iPhoto.

6. Click the eject button to the right of the digital camera icon in the left pane of the iPhoto window. (Your digital camera will likely be called *Untitled* under the Devices category in the left pane of the iPhoto window.)

7. Turn off your digital camera and disconnect the USB cable.

Transferring Images from a Scanner

If you have a scanner, you can capture images from books, magazines, or old photographs and store them on your Macintosh. To use a scanner and save an image to your Macintosh, you need to use the Image Capture program by doing the following:

1. Turn on your scanner and place the item you want to scan on the scanner bed.

2. Click the Finder icon on the Dock. The Finder window appears.

3. Click the **Applications** folder. The contents of the Applications folder appear.

4. Double-click the **Image Capture** icon. The Image Capture window appears. (If a scanned image doesn't appear, click the **Overview** button.)

5. Drag the mouse to select the part of the image you want to capture, as shown in Figure 26-3.

FIGURE 26-3: *To scan an image, you must select the part of the image you want to save as a file.*

6. Click the **Scan To Folder** pop-up menu and choose a folder in which to store your scanned image (such as Pictures).

7. Click in the **Name** text box and type a descriptive name for your scanned image.

8. Click the **Format** pop-up menu and choose a file format, such as TIFF or JPEG.

9. Click the **Scan** button. Your selected image is saved to the folder you selected. The Preview program displays your saved image.

✳ **NOTE:** Until you drag the mouse to select the part of the image you want to save, the Scan button appears dimmed.

10. Select **Preview ▸ Quit Preview**.
11. Select **Image Capture ▸ Quit Image Capture**.

Copying Images from a Web Page

Many websites have interesting pictures that you might want to keep. To copy a picture off a web page, you can store the image as a file in a folder or in iPhoto, or you can copy it so you can paste it into a program without storing it as a separate file.

✳ *NOTE:* **Be careful copying pictures from websites since they may be copyrighted, which means you can't use them without permission.**

Saving an Image as a File

If you see a picture that you want to keep, you can save it as a file either in iPhoto or in a folder on your hard disk by doing the following:

1. Click the Safari icon on the Dock. (If the Safari icon is not visible, double-click the **Safari** icon in the Applications folder.)
2. Right-click a picture on any web page. A pop-up menu appears, as shown in Figure 26-4.

FIGURE 26-4: *A pop-up menu appears with image options.*

3. (Optional) Select **Save Image As** to save a picture in a folder, and when a dialog appears, click the drive and folder where you want to store your picture.
4. (Optional) Select **Add Image to iPhoto Library** to store a picture in iPhoto.

Copying and Pasting an Image into Another Program

If you don't need to save a picture as a separate file, you can copy a picture off a web page and then paste it directly into another program, such as an email program or word processor, by following these steps:

1. Click the Safari icon on the Dock. (If the Safari icon is not visible, double-click the **Safari** icon in the Applications folder.)
2. Right-click a picture on any web page. A pop-up menu appears (see Figure 26-4).
3. Select **Copy Image**.
4. Start or switch to the program in which you want to paste the picture, such as a graphics program or a word processor.
5. Select **Edit ▸ Paste** (or press ⌘-V) to paste your copied picture.

Capturing Screen Images

Sometimes you may run across a particularly interesting web page. You could save the entire web page as a file, but if you only want to save part of that web page, you might prefer to capture a screen image of the part you want to keep. Save this part as a separate file and then you can print this file or email it to someone so he or she can see the exact image that you saw on your screen.

To capture all or part of an image that appears on your screen, use the Grab program like so:

1. Run a program or open a web page to display a message or image on the screen that you want to capture in an image file.
2. Click the Finder icon on the Dock. The Finder window appears.
3. Select **Go ▸ Utilities**. The Utilities window appears.
4. Double-click the **Grab** icon. The Grab menu bar appears at the top of the screen.
5. Open the **Capture** menu and select one of four options: **Selection**, **Windows**, **Screen**, or **Timed Screen**, as shown in Figure 26-5.

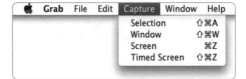

FIGURE 26-5: *The Capture menu offers four different ways to capture an image off the screen.*

6. (Optional) If you choose Selection, you'll need to drag the mouse over the area you want to save as a picture. If you select Windows, Grab captures the currently active window. If you select Screen or Timed Screen, Grab captures the entire screen. (Timed Screen gives you time to modify the screen appearance before Grab captures the screen.)

7. Select **File ▸ Save**. A dialog appears.

8. Type a descriptive name for your picture file, click the drive or folder in which to save your picture, and click the **Save** button.

9. Right-click the Grab icon on the Dock and select **Quit**.

Additional Ideas for Storing Images

Whether you capture pictures with a digital camera or snare them off the Internet using the Grab program, you can always find a way to store pictures on your Macintosh. The Grab program can be particularly handy to capture error messages so you can show people what problems you might be experiencing.

When you transfer pictures from a digital camera to your Macintosh, you have the option of deleting the pictures off of the digital camera, which can make room for more pictures.

With the Image Capture program and a scanner, you can convert old, faded, or torn photographs into digital versions that you can clean up with a photo editor. With the right printer, you can print your digital versions of scanned photographs so you can create an endless supply of precious memories.

By storing pictures on your Macintosh, you'll always be able to share, view, and print any type of picture, from digital photographs to scanned images of old photographs to images captured from your screen.

27 Organizing Digital Photographs in iPhoto

If you take pictures with a digital camera, you can store your images on your Macintosh using the iPhoto program. Using iPhoto, instead of dumping pictures in a shoebox and never seeing them again, you can browse and organize all your pictures so you can view them again and again.

Project goal: Learn how to store and organize pictures in iPhoto. (See Project 26 for information about moving pictures from your digital camera to your Macintosh.)

What You'll Be Using

To store and organize pictures on your Macintosh, you'll need the following:

▶   The iPhoto program

How iPhoto Works

iPhoto lets you store all your pictures in one place, called the iPhoto Library. iPhoto gives you five ways to view and organize the pictures in your library:

► Events

► Photos

► Albums

► Faces

► Places

Events represent a fixed period of time, such as one day. Using the date on which each picture was taken, iPhoto automatically organizes your pictures into events, where, for example, one event might represent all the pictures you took on July 24 and a second event might represent all the pictures you took on September 20, as shown in Figure 27-1.

FIGURE 27-1: Events organize your digital photographs into groups.

Think of events as iPhoto's way of storing your pictures into separate piles. When you want to view your pictures, you can double-click the event, and iPhoto shows you only the pictures stored in that event.

Much like laying out all your pictures on the living room floor so you can see them, iPhoto lets you view and scroll through your pictures onscreen, so you can see every picture you have stored. However, if you have stored a lot of pictures and you're looking for a particular shot, you'll have to browse through each picture, one by one, until you find the one you want.

Albums let you organize related pictures and store them together, regardless of the date on which you captured them. So, for example, one album might contain airplane pictures, a second album might contain pictures of your dog, and a third album might contain all your summer vacation pictures. Albums let you organize pictures based on your specific criteria.

Two additional ways iPhoto organizes pictures are *Faces* and *Places*. *Faces* organizes photos by the faces that appear in each picture. So if you have several pictures of your uncle or girlfriend, iPhoto can automatically identify and organize any picture that contains your uncle or girlfriend's face.

Places organizes pictures based on the location where you took them. So if you have pictures of a dog, a building, and a person that were all taken in San Francisco, iPhoto lumps those pictures together, even if your dog picture was taken in July 2008 and your building picture was taken in February 2009.

Working with Events

Events store pictures based on the time when you captured them. Initially, every event is untitled, but to make events easier to understand, you can give them descriptive names. For example, you might name one event *Summer Vacation* so that you know all the pictures stored in that event came from your summer vacation.

Viewing the Photos in an Event

To see pictures stored in an event, do the following:

1. Start iPhoto. (Click the iPhoto icon on the Dock or double-click the **iPhoto** icon in the Applications folder.) The iPhoto window appears.
2. Click **Events** under the Library category in the left pane of the iPhoto window. The right pane shows all your events (see Figure 27-1).

* **NOTE: For a quick way to view pictures stored in an event, slide the mouse pointer across the event from left to right. As you move the mouse pointer, a different picture from the event appears under the pointer.**

3. Double-click an event. The iPhoto window displays all the pictures stored in the chosen event, as shown in Figure 27-2.
4. Click the **All Events** button to return to viewing all your events as separate items.

Naming an Event

Initially, events are untitled. To give your events a descriptive name, do the following:

1. Click **Events** under the Library category in the left pane of the iPhoto window.
2. Move the mouse pointer over an event. The event's name, such as *untitled event*, appears directly underneath.
3. Click the event name. A text box appears, as shown in Figure 27-3.
4. Type a name for your event and press RETURN.

FIGURE 27-2: *Events can hold one or more pictures.*

Text box

FIGURE 27-3: *A text box appears under an event, where you can type a name for that event.*

Viewing All Your Photos

If you want to view all your pictures at once, do the following:

1. In iPhoto, click **Photos** under the Library category. The right pane of the iPhoto window displays all your pictures, grouped into events by a horizontal line, as shown in Figure 27-4.
2. Scroll through your pictures.

3. Drag the photo size slider in the bottom-right corner of the iPhoto window. By dragging this slider to the left, you can make each picture appear smaller so you can see more pictures on the screen, as shown in Figure 27-5.

4. Click **Events** under the Library category in the left pane to view your pictures grouped again into separate events.

FIGURE 27-4: *Clicking Photos, under the Library category, lets you view all your pictures at once.*

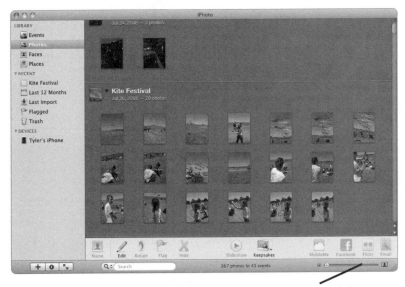

Photo size slider

FIGURE 27-5: *Changing the size of your displayed photos lets you see more of them at once.*

Working with Albums

You can use Events, Faces, and Places to view a selection of your stored photos. For example, if you have 504 total pictures in iPhoto, one event might store 35 pictures, and another might hold 4.

If you want to view all pictures stored in iPhoto, click the **Photos** category. This category lets you see every picture, grouped by events. Unlike clicking the Events category, clicking the Photos category lets you view pictures stored in multiple events at the same time—this would let you view all 504 pictures stored in iPhoto.

Albums let you create customized collections of photos no matter what the event or the location. So, for example, you can copy pictures from three different events and store those pictures in one album. (When you store pictures in an album, you can still view those pictures by clicking Events, Faces, Places, or Photos under the Library category.)

Creating an Album

The easiest way to create an album is to choose the pictures you want to store in the album, and then make iPhoto create the album. To select pictures and create an album automatically, do the following:

1. Click **Photos** under the Library category in the left pane of the iPhoto window. The right pane shows you all the pictures stored in iPhoto.
2. Hold down the ⌘ key as you click each picture you want to store in an album. A yellow border appears around each picture you select. You may need to scroll down to view all the pictures stored in iPhoto.
3. Select **File ▸ New Album From Selection**. A dialog appears, asking you to type a name for your album.
4. Type a descriptive name for your album and click **Create**. The name of your new album appears under the Albums category in the left pane of the iPhoto window, as shown in Figure 27-6.

Copying Photos to an Album

To add a picture to an album, do the following:

1. Click **Photos** under the Library category in the left pane of the iPhoto window. The right pane shows you all the pictures stored in iPhoto.
2. Click a picture you want to copy into an album. (Hold down the ⌘ key as you click to select multiple pictures.)
3. Drag and drop the selected picture over the album name under the Albums category in the left pane of the iPhoto window.

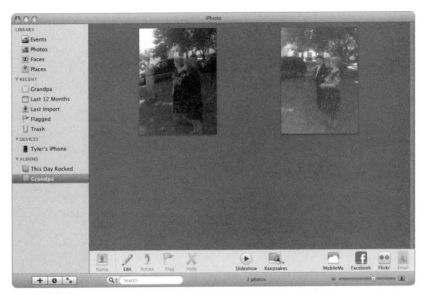

FIGURE 27-6: The name of your album appears in the left pane of the iPhoto window.

Removing Photos from an Album

To remove a picture from an album, do the following:

1. Click the album name under the Albums category in the left pane of the iPhoto window. The right pane shows all the pictures stored in your album.
2. Click a picture that you want to remove from the album. (Hold down the ⌘ key and click two or more pictures to remove several pictures from the album.)
3. Select **Photos ▸ Delete From Album**. Your selected picture disappears from the album (but still remains in the iPhoto Library).

Deleting Photos and Albums

If you no longer want to save some of your pictures, you can remove them from your iPhoto Library. If you have created albums that you no longer want, you can delete those, too.

Deleting Photos from iPhoto

Here's how to delete a picture from iPhoto:

1. Click **Photos** under the Library category in the left pane of the iPhoto window. The right pane shows you all the pictures stored in iPhoto.

2.   Click a picture that you want to delete. (Hold down the ⌘ key as you click two or more pictures to delete them.)

3.   Select **Photos ▸ Move To Trash** (or drag the selected pictures and drop them over the Trash icon in the left pane of the iPhoto window).

4.   (Optional) Right-click the Trash icon in the left pane and select **Empty Trash** to delete your pictures for good.

* **NOTE: If you don't empty the Trash, you can retrieve a picture from the Trash by dragging it back over Events or Photos under the Library category in the left pane of the iPhoto window.**

* **NOTE: Any pictures stored in the Trash still take up space on your hard disk, so empty the Trash to delete pictures you're sure you won't need.**

Deleting an Album

To delete an album, do the following:

1.   Click an album name under the Albums category in the left pane of the iPhoto window.

2.   Select **Photos ▸ Delete Album**. A dialog appears, letting you know that you won't delete any pictures stored in your album, just the album itself.

3.   Click **Delete**. Your chosen album disappears.

Working with Faces

By using facial recognition, iPhoto can identify a person in a picture and then automatically find any other pictures that contain that same person's face. Naturally, this face recognition feature isn't perfect, but it's remarkably useful for identifying multiple pictures of people.

Naming Faces in a Picture

To use the Faces feature, you must identify a face in a picture and type in that person's name by doing this:

1.   Click a category under the Library or Recent heading (such as Photos or Last Import) in the left pane of the iPhoto window. The right pane shows you all the pictures stored in iPhoto.

2.   Click a picture that contains the face of a person who appears in multiple pictures stored in iPhoto. The Name button appears near the bottom-left corner of the iPhoto window, as shown in Figure 27-7.

3.   Click the **Name** button. Your selected picture expands to fill the iPhoto window and an Add Missing Face button appears in the bottom-left corner of the iPhoto window, as shown in Figure 27-8.

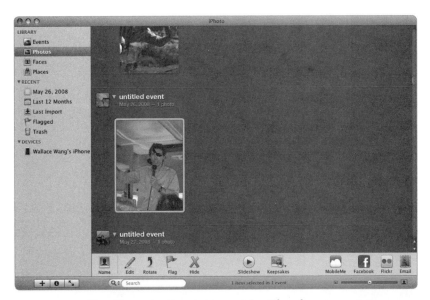

FIGURE 27-7: *The Name button lets you identify a face in a picture.*

FIGURE 27-8: *Click the Add Missing Face button to select a face for iPhoto to recognize.*

4. Click the **Add Missing Face** button. A rectangular box appears over your photo, as shown in Figure 27-9.

5. Drag the box corners to change the size of the box, or move the mouse pointer inside the box and drag to move the box over a face in the picture.

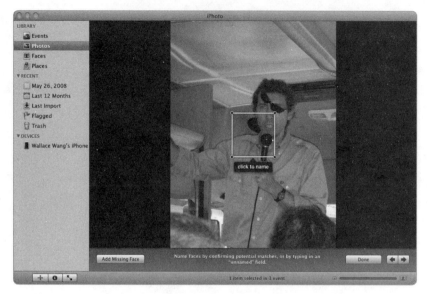

FIGURE 27-9: *You must highlight a face that you want iPhoto to recognize.*

6.   Click in the **click to name** text box, type the name of the person whose face is enclosed by the box, and press RETURN. An arrow in a circle appears to the right of the name you typed, as shown in Figure 27-10.

FIGURE 27-10: *After naming a face, you can search for additional photos that contain that same face.*

7.   Click the arrow to the right of the person's name. The iPhoto window shows other pictures that contain that same person's face, as shown in Figure 27-11.

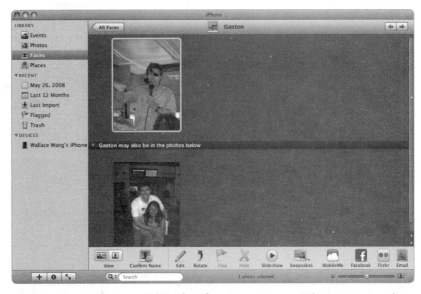

FIGURE 27-11: *After you identify a face in a picture, iPhoto tries to identify that face in all your other pictures.*

✳ *NOTE:* **If iPhoto fails to recognize a person in one or more of your pictures, you can repeat the above steps 2–6 to name that person's face.**

Finding Pictures Organized by Faces

After you've identified faces in your pictures, you can use the Faces category to find all pictures that contain the same person. To view all your pictures organized by a single person's face, do this:

1.   Start iPhoto. (Click the iPhoto icon on the Dock or double-click the **iPhoto** icon in the Applications folder.) The iPhoto window appears.
2.   Click **Faces** under the Library category in the left pane of the iPhoto window. Pictures of your defined faces appear against a corkboard image, as shown in Figure 27-12.
3.   Double-click a face to view all the pictures where you can see that same face.

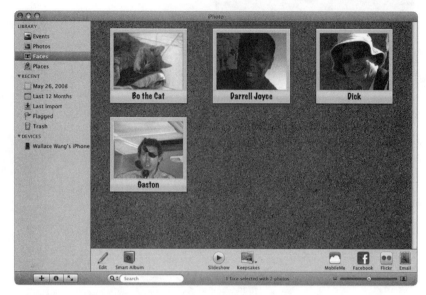

FIGURE 27-12: *The Faces category displays pictures of faces you've identified.*

Working with Places

Many digital cameras (including the one built in to the iPhone) contain GPS (Global Positioning System) information that identifies where that picture was captured. By using the GPS information stored in your pictures, iPhoto can identify pictures by the location where you captured them.

✳ **NOTE:** **If your camera does not insert GPS information, you can add location information manually. See the next section, "Editing Photo Locations."**

If you go on vacation to Europe, iPhoto can identify all the pictures taken in Paris, London, and Berlin. Because iPhoto organizes pictures by their location, it can help you find a picture if you know you captured it in a certain location, such as in downtown Los Angeles, or a suburb just outside of Los Angeles.

To view pictures organized by the location where they were captured, do this:

1. Start iPhoto. (Click the iPhoto icon on the Dock or double-click the **iPhoto** icon in the Applications folder.) The iPhoto window appears.
2. Click **Places** under the Library category in the left pane of the iPhoto window. A map appears with red pins marking the spots where you captured your pictures, as shown in Figure 27-13.
3. Click a red pin. The location of your pin appears with an arrow in a circle to the right of its location.
4. Click the arrow that appears to the right of the location name. iPhoto displays all pictures captured in that area.

FIGURE 27-13: The Places category displays a red pin on a map to identify where you captured a picture.

* NOTE: If you click the Satellite or Hybrid buttons, you can view a satellite image of your map with or without identifying street names, as shown in Figure 27-14.

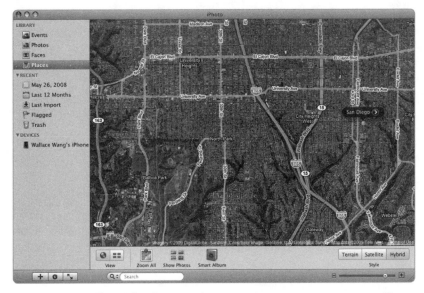

FIGURE 27-14: The Hybrid option lets you view your map as a satellite image with identifying street names.

Editing Photo Locations

The Places feature of iPhoto can identify where you captured certain pictures. However, if your camera didn't automatically include location information or if you scanned an image, your pictures may not have any location information. To fix this problem, you can manually add location information to any picture by doing this:

1. View a picture you want to add a location to. (To view a picture, click **Events** or **Photos** under the Library category in the left pane of the iPhoto window, or click an album under the Albums category.)
2. Right-click a picture. A pop-up menu appears.
3. Choose **Get Info**. An Info window appears, listing information about your chosen picture, as shown in Figure 27-15.
4. Click the photo place text box. A Find on map option appears, as shown in Figure 27-16.

FIGURE 27-15: *The Get Info window of a picture lets you define a location.*

FIGURE 27-16: *Clicking the photo place text box displays a Find on map option.*

5. At this point you can type a location or click the Find on map option to identify a location on a map. If you click **Find on map**, a map appears, as shown in Figure 27-17.
6. Click the **Drop Pin** button in the bottom-left corner of the Add New Place window. A pin appears on the map, which you can zoom in or out, as shown in Figure 27-18.

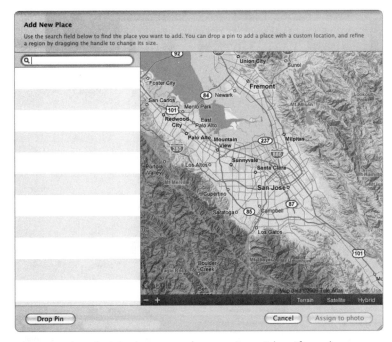

FIGURE 27-17: *A map lets you place a pin to identify a photograph's location.*

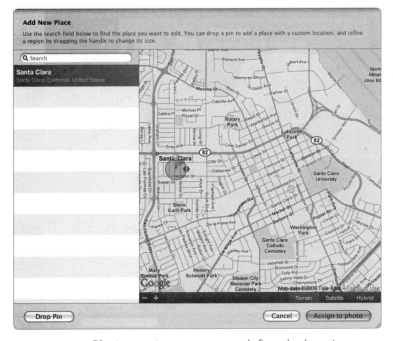

FIGURE 27-18: *Placing a pin on a map to define the location where you captured a picture*

7. Drag the pin on the map and then click the **Assign to photo** button when the pin accurately identifies the location where you captured your picture. The Get Info window appears again, displaying your map, as shown in Figure 27-19.

8. Click the **Done** button.

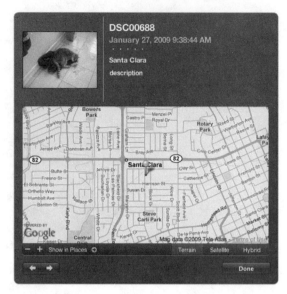

FIGURE 27-19: *The Get Info window displays a map to identify where you captured the picture.*

Additional Ideas for Organizing Digital Photographs in iPhoto

Events, Photos, Faces, and Places give you four different ways to store and view pictures in your iPhoto Library. When you want to organize pictures, you can store them in albums. You can even store the same picture in two or more albums, such as storing a picture of a ship in an album named *Ocean Trip* and in a second album named *Harbor Pictures*.

One practical way to use iPhoto is to store pictures of your house and possessions, such as big-screen TVs, stereos, and computers, and create albums named for different rooms in your house. By taking pictures of your house and possessions and storing them in separate albums, you'll have a photographic inventory of your home in case a disaster strikes and you need to file an insurance claim. (Just make sure you back up your iPhoto pictures or else any disaster wiping out your house will likely take out your Macintosh at the same time. To back up your pictures to a CD or DVD, see Project 25 for information on burning data to discs.)

28

Tagging and Sorting Digital Photographs in iPhoto

The iPhoto program is handy for storing and organizing pictures, but it can also sort pictures. You can tag images with titles, keywords, or ratings so you'll be able to search and find any image stored in your collection of digital photographs.

For example, you can tag a picture of your dog with the keyword *Rover* so whenever you want to find a picture of Rover, you can just search for the keyword. You can also rate your pictures from zero to five stars, so if you want to show off your best (five-star rated) pictures, iPhoto can help you find and display them in an instant.

Project goal: Learn how to tag and sort pictures in iPhoto.

What You'll Be Using

To tag and sort digital pictures on your Macintosh, you'll need the following:

▶ The iPhoto program

NOTE: If you need help getting your pictures onto your Macintosh, see Project 26.

Tagging Photos

You can tag each picture with a title (any name you want to give a picture), a rating (from one star to five stars), and a keyword (to identify a category for your picture). By tagging pictures with titles, ratings, or keywords, you can quickly find all your pictures displayed in alphabetical order by name, all your five-star pictures, or all pictures tagged with keywords, such as *Birthday* or *Vacation*.

After you load an image, your Macintosh uses the generic filename created by your digital camera, such as *DSC_048*. Since trying to find a picture based on a generic filename can be difficult, if not impossible, take time to rename picture titles, define a rating, and type keywords for each picture.

To view titles, ratings, and keywords, select the **View** menu, and then select **Titles**, **Rating**, or **Keywords** to place a checkmark next to the item, as shown in Figure 28-1. If a checkmark does not appear in front of Keywords, for example, iPhoto won't display keywords for any of your pictures.

FIGURE 28-1: *The View menu lets you choose to show or hide your pictures' titles, ratings, and keywords.*

Renaming a Photo

A picture's title can be any descriptive name you choose. A title can identify the subject of the picture, the location where the picture was taken, the event that the picture captured, or any arbitrary name you choose.

To change a picture's title, do the following:

1.   In iPhoto's View menu, make sure a checkmark appears in front of the Titles item.
2.   View a picture you want to rename. (To view a picture, click **Events** or **Photos** under the Library category in the left pane, or click an album under the Albums category.)
3.   Click the image title. A text box appears with the title highlighted.
4.   Type a new title or press the arrow and DELETE keys to edit the existing title.

Rating a Photo

To identify your best pictures, you can rate them with one to five stars. To rate a picture, do the following:

1. In iPhoto's View menu, make sure a checkmark appears in front of Rating.
2. View the picture you want to rename. (To view a picture, click **Events** or **Photos** under the Library category in the left pane, or click an album under the Albums category.)
3. (Optional) Hold down the ⌘ key as you click to select multiple pictures.
4. Right-click a picture, select **My Rating**, and then select a star rating from the submenu, as shown in Figure 28-2.

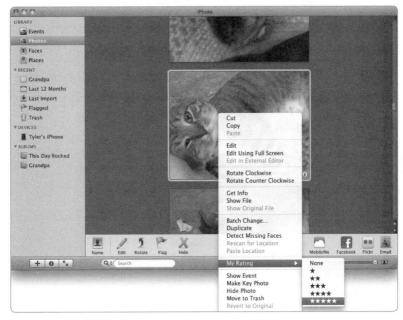

FIGURE 28-2: *The My Rating submenu lets you choose a rating for a picture.*

* **NOTE:** As a shortcut, you can click a picture and press ⌘-*Number*, where *Number* represents the number of stars you want to rate a picture. So if you click a picture and press ⌘-4, for example, you would give that picture a four-star rating.

Adding Keywords to a Photo

Keywords let you identify common types of pictures, such as vacation or birthday pictures. You can type keywords directly into the keywords text box, much like editing a picture's title. To avoid spelling typos, use the Keywords window.

The Keywords window displays a list of keywords that you can drag to the keyword text box of a picture. To tag a picture with a keyword, do the following:

1. In iPhoto's View menu, make sure a checkmark appears in front of Keywords.
2. View the picture that you want to tag with a keyword. (To view a picture, click **Events** or **Photos** under the Library category in the right pane, or click an album under the Albums category.)
3. Select **Window ▸ Show Keywords**. A Keywords window appears, as shown in Figure 28-3.

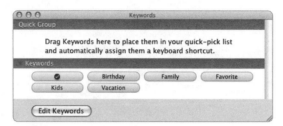

FIGURE 28-3: *The Keywords window lists key-words you can use to tag a picture.*

4. Click the picture that you want to tag with a keyword. (Hold down the ⌘ key as you click to select multiple pictures.)
5. Click a keyword in the Keywords window. Your chosen keyword appears under your selected picture.
6. Click the close button of the Keywords window.

Making Your Own Keywords

The iPhoto program comes with a list of keywords, such as *Kids* or *Vacation*, but you can add your own keywords to the Keywords window by doing the following:

1. In iPhoto, select **Window ▸ Show Keywords**. The Keywords window appears (see Figure 28-3).
2. Click **Edit Keywords**. The Edit Keywords window appears, as shown in Figure 28-4.
3. Click the plus button in the lower-left corner of the Edit Keywords window. A text box appears.

✳ **NOTE: If you click a keyword and then click the minus button, you can remove a keyword from the Keywords window.**

4. Type a new keyword and click **OK**. The Keywords window displays your newly added keyword.
5. Click the close button of the Keywords window.

FIGURE 28-4: *The Edit Keywords window lets you add (or remove) your own keywords.*

Sorting Photos

To help you find particular images, iPhoto can sort your pictures based on the following criteria:

▶ Date

▶ Keyword

▶ Title

▶ Rating

To sort pictures, make sure you tagged your pictures with keywords, titles, or ratings and then do the following:

1. In iPhoto's left pane, click **Events** or **Photos**, or click the album that contains the pictures you want to sort.
2. Select **View ▸ Sort Photos** and choose **By Date**, **By Keyword**, **By Title**, or **By Rating**. The iPhoto program sorts your pictures.
3. (Optional) Select **View ▸ Sort Photos** and choose either **Ascending** or **Descending**.

Additional Ideas for Sorting Digital Photographs in iPhoto

By tagging pictures with ratings, you can find all your five-star pictures to show off your photography skills to your friends.

For more flexibility in tagging and sorting pictures by keyword, make up your own keywords and tag a picture with multiple keywords so you can find it in different ways. For example, use keywords that evoke specific emotions, such as *Happy*, *Freedom*, or *Melancholy*. Then tag pictures using keywords that describe specific events or places, such as *Reunion* (to identify pictures involved with family reunions) or *Europe* (to identify pictures taken in Europe). By using multiple keywords for each picture, you'll always have multiple ways to find your pictures again—whether you want an image that evokes a certain emotion, captures a certain event, or shows a certain area or place.

Half of the fun of digital photography is the freedom to take pictures and keep only the good images. The other half of the fun is using iPhoto to organize and sort your pictures so you'll always be able to find them again.

29

Editing Digital Photographs in iPhoto

Even expert digital photographers sometimes capture images that are not quite
perfect—they're a shade too dark or slightly
overexposed. Rather than toss out less than
perfect digital photos, you can make them
better by editing them with iPhoto.

You can use iPhoto to rotate or straighten out images, remove blemishes,
lighten or darken images, or even add unique visual effects such as making a
photograph look old and faded like an antique.

Project goal: Learn how to modify photographs in iPhoto.

What You'll Be Using

To modify digital photos on your Macintosh, you'll need the following:

▶   The iPhoto program

NOTE: If you need help getting your pictures from your digital camera to your
Macintosh, see Project 26.

Rotating and Straightening Photos

Sometimes you'll need to tilt your camera sideways to capture an image, or you might have captured an image that's slightly crooked. You can straighten out both types of issues by doing the following:

1. In iPhoto, view the picture you want to edit. (To view a picture, click **Events**, **Photos**, **Faces**, or **Places** under the Library category in the left pane, or click an album under the Albums category.)
2. Click a picture you want to edit and click the **Edit** button at the bottom of the iPhoto window. The iPhoto window displays editing tools along the bottom, as shown in Figure 29-1.

FIGURE 29-1: *The iPhoto window displays editing tools.*

3. If an image appears sideways, click the **Rotate** button to rotate the image counter-clockwise. (Hold down the OPTION key while clicking the **Rotate** button to make the image rotate clockwise.)
4. If an image appears slightly cockeyed, click the **Straighten** button. A yellow grid and a horizontal slider appear over the image, as shown in Figure 29-2.
5. Drag the horizontal slider left or right to tilt the image.

✳ **NOTE: If you don't like your changes, press ⌘-Z to return the image to its original appearance. You can undo changes only before you click the Done button.**

6. Click the **Done** button when you're finished rotating or straightening out the image.

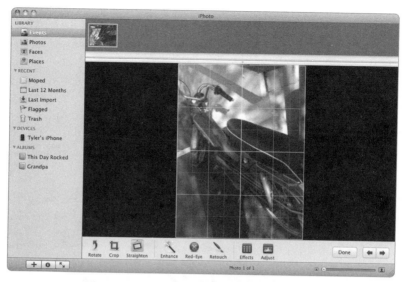

FIGURE 29-2: The yellow grid helps you align the image while using the horizontal slider to tilt the image.

Cropping a Photo

You might capture a great image that contains a bit too much of the background. To make it easier to see the subject of your photo, you can *crop* it, which means selecting just the part of the picture you want to keep and deleting everything else around it.

To crop a picture, do the following:

1. In iPhoto, view the picture you want to rename. (To view a picture, click **Events** or **Photos** under the Library category in the right pane, or click an album under the Albums category.)
2. Click a picture to edit, and click the **Edit** button at the bottom of the iPhoto window so that editing tools appear (see Figure 29-1).
3. Click the **Crop** button. A white rectangle appears around the center of the image, as shown in Figure 29-3.
4. Move the mouse pointer over the edge of the white rectangle until it turns into a two-way pointing arrow. Then drag the mouse to adjust the size of the rectangle.
5. (Optional) Click the **Constrain** checkbox and click the **Constrain** pop-up menu to define a size ratio for your picture, such as a postcard size.
6. Click **Apply**. Your image now appears as cropped.

* *NOTE:* **If you don't like your changes, press ⌘-Z to return the image to its original appearance. You can undo changes only before you click the Done button.**

7. Click **Done**.

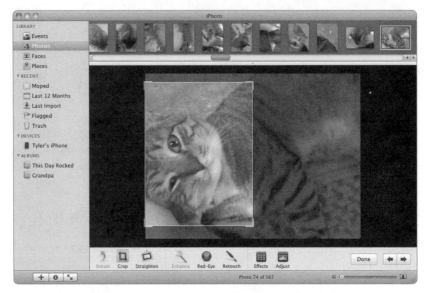

FIGURE 29-3: *To crop a picture, adjust the size and position of the white rectangle.*

Touching Up a Photo

Some photographs may look perfect except for a few minor blemishes, such as red-eye caused by the camera's flash or a pimple on a person's nose. To erase these types of problems, do the following:

1. In iPhoto, view the picture that you want to touch up. (To view a picture, click **Events** or **Photos** under the Library category in the right pane, or click an album under the Albums category.)
2. Click an image to edit, and click the **Edit** button at the bottom of the iPhoto window to display editing tools (see Figure 29-1).
3. (Optional) Click the **Enhance** button. The iPhoto program tries to enhance the colors in your image automatically by making them appear brighter and sharper.
4. (Optional) Click the **Red-Eye** button and click the red color in the subject's eye. The iPhoto program replaces the red color with a dark color.
5. (Optional) Click the **Retouch** button and drag the mouse over a blemish you want to erase. The iPhoto program tries to erase the blemish by blending nearby colors over the area where you dragged the mouse.

✳ **NOTE:** If you don't like your changes, press ⌘-Z to return the image to its original appearance. You can undo changes only before you click the Done button.

6. Click **Done**.

Creating Unusual Visual Effects

For fun, you can turn ordinary digital pictures into unique images—make a color picture appear in black-and-white or fade colors to make the image look older. To modify the appearance of a picture, do the following:

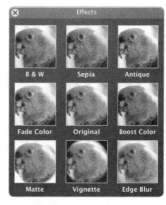

1. In iPhoto, click a picture to edit, and click the **Edit** button at the bottom of the iPhoto window to display editing tools (see Figure 29-1).
2. Click the **Effects** button. An Effects window appears, displaying the effects from which you can choose (see Figure 29-4).
3. Click an effect in the Effects window. Your image changes according to the effect you chose.

FIGURE 29-4: *The Effects window shows how your image will appear if you choose a particular effect.*

∗ *NOTE:* **If you don't like your changes, press ⌘-Z to return the image to its original appearance. You can undo changes only before you click the Done button.**

4. Click **Done**.

Adjust a Photo Manually

Although you can use the Enhance button to fix many images automatically, you might want more control over parts of your picture. To adjust an image manually, do the following:

1. In iPhoto, click a picture to edit and click the **Edit** button at the bottom of the iPhoto window to display editing tools (see Figure 29-1).
2. Click the **Adjust** button. An Adjust window appears, displaying different sliders you can move to modify the appearance of the image, as shown in Figure 29-5.
3. (Optional) Drag the **Exposure** slider to lighten or darken the image.
4. (Optional) Drag the **Contrast** slider to emphasize differences between dark and light areas of the picture.
5. (Optional) Drag the **Saturation** slider to modify the intensity of colors in a picture.
6. (Optional) Drag the **Definition** slider to make your picture fuzzier or sharper.
7. (Optional) Drag the **Highlights** slider to lighten or darken the lightest parts of a picture.

8. (Optional) Drag the **Shadows** slider to lighten or darken the shadows (darker portions) of a picture.

9. (Optional) Drag the **Sharpness** slider to adjust the focus of a picture.

10. (Optional) Drag the **De-noise** slider to adjust the graininess of a picture.

11. (Optional) Drag the **Temperature** slider to change the coldness/ warmth appearance of a picture.

12. (Optional) Drag the **Tint** slider to lighten or darken the red/green colors in a picture.

✳ *NOTE:* **If you don't like your changes, press ⌘-Z to return the image to its original appearance. You can undo changes only before you click the Done button.**

13. Click **Done**.

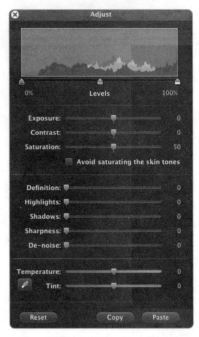

FIGURE 29-5: *The Adjust window provides sliders so you can adjust individual parts of an image.*

Additional Ideas for Editing Digital Photographs in iPhoto

Nobody takes perfect photos all the time (including professional photographers), so iPhoto's editing features let you rescue marginally acceptable pictures and turn them into perfect ones. Take the time to fix your pictures and people will think you're a better photographer than you really might be.

For fun, experiment with visual effects and turn a photo of your newest car into a faded, black-and-white image that looks like it was taken in another era. Play with other visual effects and turn ordinary portraits of people into more interesting images with blurred edges and other unique touches. With digital photography and iPhoto, you can make practically any picture worth saving, even those containing people you don't like.

30

Turning Your Macintosh into an Electronic Picture Frame

Most people display pictures on their desk inside picture frames or hung on the wall as posters. The problem is that an ordinary picture frame or poster can get boring after a while—it always shows the same picture until you replace it with another one.

Rather than force yourself to deal with such archaic display technology, you can store and display pictures on your Macintosh screen. By turning your Macintosh into an electronic picture frame, you can display the same image or multiple images one after another in a slideshow. If you don't yet have any pictures you want to display, you can take pictures of yourself or others using your Macintosh computer's built-in iSight digital camera.

Project goal: Turn your Macintosh into an electronic picture frame that displays pictures in a slideshow on your screen.

What You'll Be Using

To turn your Macintosh into an electronic picture frame, you'll need to use the following items:

▶   The Finder

▶   The System Preferences program

▶   One or more digital photographs

▶   (Optional) The built-in iSight digital camera

▶   (Optional) The Photo Booth program

Creating a Slideshow Folder

Before you can turn your Macintosh into an electronic picture frame, you must first collect all the pictures you want to display. Normally, you should store all pictures in the Pictures folder. However, the more pictures you place in the Pictures folder, the more difficult it can be to find the pictures you want. To solve this problem, you can create a new folder that stores only those pictures you want to display (and not those embarrassing pictures of you that you don't want other people to see). You can store this folder in the Pictures folder or anywhere else that you find convenient.

To create a slideshow folder for customizing your screensaver or Desktop, follow these steps:

1. Click the Finder icon on the Dock. The Finder window appears (if it doesn't appear, select **File ▸ New Finder Window**).
2. Click the **Pictures** folder in the left pane of the Finder window. The Finder window displays the contents of the Pictures folder.
3. Select **File ▸ New Folder**. An untitled folder icon appears in the Finder window.
4. Type a descriptive name for your folder, such as *My Slideshow*.
5. Your new folder appears, ready to store any digital photographs you want to display on your Macintosh.

Storing Pictures in Your Slideshow Folder

Once you've created a slideshow folder, you can start storing your pictures in it. Any pictures stored in this folder will appear in your slideshow. If you want to display existing pictures, just copy them into this folder. If you don't yet have any pictures, you can take pictures using the iSight camera and store them in the folder.

Copying Existing Pictures into Your Slideshow Folder

To display existing digital photographs, first copy them into your slideshow folder:

1. Click the Finder icon on the Dock. The Finder window appears.
2. Click the storage device that contains the pictures you want to use. (If your pictures are stored on a compact flash card or flash drive, click the icon that represents that storage device.)
3. Open the folder that contains the pictures you want to use.
4. Hold down the ⌘ key and click each picture you want to use. (If you want to select all the pictures in that folder, press ⌘-A.)
5. Select **Edit ▸ Copy**. (Depending on the exact number of pictures you copied, the command will read *Copy X Items*.) This copies your selected pictures (although nothing seems to happen).
6. Click the **Pictures** folder in the left pane of the Finder window and double-click your slideshow folder.

7. Select **Edit ▸ Paste Items**. Your chosen pictures appear inside the slideshow folder. (Repeat these steps for any additional pictures you want to use in your slideshow.)

Copying Existing Pictures from iPhoto into Your Slideshow Folder

If you have existing digital photographs stored in iPhoto, you can copy pictures and store them into your slideshow folder:

1. Click the iPhoto icon on the Dock. The iPhoto window appears. (If you can't find the iPhoto icon on the Dock, look for the iPhoto icon inside the Applications folder in the Finder window.)
2. Hold down the ⌘ key and click the pictures you want to store in your slideshow folder.
3. Select **File ▸ Export**. An Export Photos dialog appears.
4. Choose any options (such as defining the size of the images) and click **Export**. A second Export Photos dialog appears.
5. Click your slideshow folder and click **OK**.

Capturing Pictures with iSight and Photo Booth

Most new Macintosh computers include an iSight digital camera that's built into the top of the computer screen, like a cyclops' eye, watching your every move. To take pictures with iSight, you can use the Photo Booth program.

The Photo Booth program icon looks a lot like the curtain you would close in a coin-operated photo booth, and that's the idea. No quarters are required for these photos, though—you've already spent many hundreds of quarters to buy your Mac. You can take pictures with Photo Booth and store these images in your slideshow folder:

1. Click the Photo Booth icon on the Dock. (If you can't find the Photo Booth icon on the Dock, look for the icon in the Applications folder in the Finder window.) The Photo Booth window appears, as shown in Figure 30-1—and look, there you are, staring back at yourself. (Better fix your hair first.)
2. Click the Capture button. Photo Booth displays a countdown (3, 2, 1) before capturing your picture, which then appears at the bottom of the Photo Booth window. (If you hold down the OPTION key while clicking the Capture button, Photo Booth will take your picture immediately without the countdown.)
3. Capture as many pictures as you want. Make strange faces, angle or raise your Macintosh to take pictures of other people across the room, or hold your dog up to the camera lens and take his picture. This is the time to let your creativity go wild without losing inhibitions completely, even if it could mean doing something you might be embarrassed about later.

Capture button

FIGURE 30-1: *The Photo Booth program immediately shows the image from the iSight camera lens.*

4.   Select **Photo Booth ▸ Quit Photo Booth**.
5.   Click the Finder icon on the Dock. The Finder window appears.
6.   Click **Pictures** in the left pane of the Finder window. The contents of the Pictures folder appears.
7.   Double-click the **Photo Booth** folder. All the pictures you captured with Photo Booth appear.
8.   Hold down the ⌘ key and click each picture you want to use in your slide-show. (If you want to select all the pictures in that folder, press ⌘-A.)
9.   Select **Edit ▸ Copy X Images**. This copies your selected pictures (although nothing seems to happen).
10. Click **Pictures** in the left pane of the Finder window and double-click your slideshow folder.
11. Select **Edit ▸ Paste Items**. Your chosen pictures appear inside the slideshow folder.

Creating a Slideshow

After you've stored pictures in your slideshow folder, you can decide how to display your pictures: on the Desktop or as a screensaver.

Displaying pictures on the Desktop means your images will always appear on the Desktop screen. Displaying pictures as a screensaver means your pictures will be displayed only when you stop using your computer and your screensaver starts. If you want to be able to look at your pictures at any time, display them on the Desktop. If you want others to look at your pictures while you're away from your computer, display them as a screensaver.

You can get really creative and have a slideshow appear on both your Desktop and screensaver. You can even display one set of pictures as a slideshow on your Desktop and a second set of pictures as a slideshow on your screensaver, so that way if you walk away from your computer, your screensaver can show pictures of you making faces to your boss, co-workers, spouse, kids, and anyone else who wanders by and stares at your computer.

Displaying a Desktop Slideshow

When you create a slideshow on your Desktop, you must specify how often you want your pictures to change and how you want them to appear on the screen.

Pictures can change as often as every five seconds or as infrequently as every day. You can also choose to change pictures only when you log in to your account (so a different picture greets you every morning) or when your computer wakes up from going to sleep (so a different picture greets you every time you return to your computer).

In addition to defining how often your Desktop will display different pictures, you can also define how your pictures appear. You have five choices:

▶ **Fit to Screen** or **Fill Screen**   Both choices enlarge pictures to fill the entire screen, but small pictures may appear grainy.

▶ **Stretch to Fill Screen**   This option distorts pictures to fill the entire screen, which can warp small pictures.

▶ **Center**   This option displays each picture in the middle of the screen at its original size.

▶ **Tile**   This choice fills the entire screen with multiple copies of the same picture.

To create a Desktop slideshow, follow these steps:

1. Click the Apple menu and select **System Preferences**. The System Preferences window appears.
2. Click the **Desktop & Screen Saver** icon under the Personal category. The Desktop & Screen Saver window appears.

3. Click the **Desktop** tab as shown in Figure 30-2.

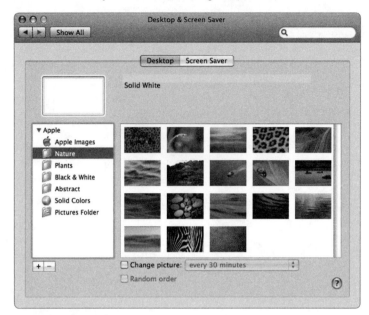

FIGURE 30-2: *The Desktop & Screen Saver window allows you to define which pictures to display and how to display them.*

4. If you can't see the slideshow folder that you created inside the Pictures folder, click the plus button just below the left pane of the Desktop & Screen Saver window. The Finder window appears, as shown in Figure 30-3.
5. Click **Pictures** in the left pane of the Finder window. The contents of the Pictures folder appears in the right pane.
6. Click your slideshow folder and click the **Choose** button. The Desktop & Screen Saver window displays thumbnail images of your pictures, as shown in Figure 30-4.

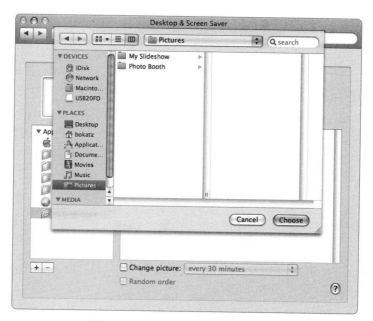

FIGURE 30-3: The Finder window appears so you can choose your slideshow folder.

FIGURE 30-4: Thumbnail images of your pictures appear when you choose your slideshow folder of images.

7. Click the picture display pop-up menu, which appears just under the Desktop and Screen Saver tabs, and choose an option: **Fit to Screen**, **Fill Screen**, **Stretch to Fill Screen**, **Center**, or **Tile**, as shown in Figure 30-5.

FIGURE 30-5: *The picture display list box lets you choose how to display your pictures.*

8. Check the **Change picture** checkbox. (If a checkmark already appears, skip this step.)
9. Click the **Change picture** pop-up menu and choose a time duration, as shown in Figure 30-6.
10. (Optional) Check the **Random order** checkbox so your Macintosh displays pictures in a different order each time instead of alphabetically by filename.
11. From the Apple menu, select **System Preferences ▸ Quit System Preferences**. One of your pictures will appear on the Desktop and will change based on the time interval you chose.

FIGURE 30-6: *The Change picture pop-up menu lets you define how often a new picture appears.*

Displaying a Screensaver Slideshow

One problem with creating a slideshow directly on your Desktop is that the changing pictures can be distracting. As an alternative, you might want to create a slideshow as a screensaver; that way, your slideshow won't begin until you stop using your computer for a while.

When creating a slideshow as a screensaver, you can define how long your computer waits before the screensaver starts and in what style you want to display your pictures. You can use three different types of display styles:

▶ **Slideshow** Displays pictures one at a time

▶ **Collage** Displays multiple pictures on the screen, mimicking dropping a picture on a tabletop one at a time

▶ **Mosaic** Displays pictures as multiple thumbnail images that fill the screen in patterns

To create a Desktop slideshow, follow these steps:

1. Click the Apple menu and select **System Preferences**. The System Preferences window appears.
2. Click the **Desktop & Screen Saver** icon under the Personal category. The Desktop & Screen Saver window appears.
3. Click the **Screen Saver** tab as shown in Figure 30-7.

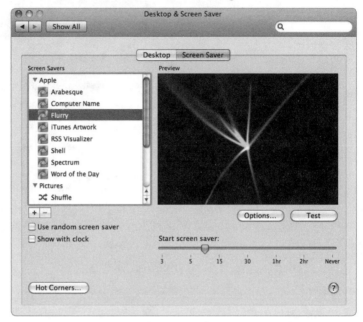

FIGURE 30-7: The Desktop & Screen Saver window allows you to define a time for the screensaver to start and a style in which to display your slideshow.

4. Click the plus sign that appears directly above the Use random screen saver checkbox. A pop-up menu appears, as shown in Figure 30-8.
5. Click **Add Folder of Pictures**. A dialog appears, letting you select a folder.
6. Click the folder that contains the pictures you want to use for your slideshow and click **Choose**. The Desktop Screen Saver window displays one of the pictures from the chosen folder.
7. Click the Slideshow, Collage, or Mosaic icon in the Display Style group, as shown in Figure 30-9. The Preview window shows how your screensaver will look.
8. (Optional) Click **Options**. A dialog appears, offering additional ways to modify the appearance of pictures depending on which display style you chose.
9. (Optional) Click **Test**. Your screensaver fills up the screen so you can preview it. Click the mouse when you're done testing your screensaver.

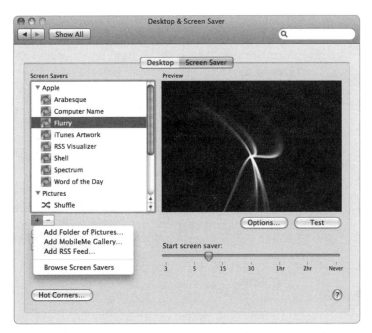

FIGURE 30-8: *A pop-up menu lets you select a folder that contains your pictures.*

FIGURE 30-9: *The Desktop & Screen Saver window lets you preview the images of your slideshow.*

10. Drag the **Start screen saver** slider to specify how much time to wait before starting the screensaver.

11. From the Apple menu, select **System Preferences ▸ Quit System Preferences**.

More Ideas for Displaying Slideshows

Most people are likely to display pictures of the family dog or their spouse and children, and be happy with that. If this sounds too tame for you, you can get more creative and try some of the following ideas.

Gather some pictures of other people and store those pictures as your screensaver. That way, whenever you walk away from your desk and your Macintosh's screensaver kicks in, your boss, co-workers, spouse, roommate, or kids can watch themselves flashing across the screen. (Just make sure those pictures aren't embarrassing, or you could find yourself being blackmailed by the people in them, instead!)

Take some pictures of yourself, and then surprise a friend or relative by displaying those pictures on his or her Macintosh, either on the Desktop or as a screensaver. The next time that person uses his or her Macintosh, they'll see you staring or waving right back at them.

Instead of storing ordinary digital pictures in your slideshow folder, put together your own pictures of useful information using a digital editing program such as the free Seashore program (*http://seashore.sourceforge.net/*) or Paintbrush program (*http://paintbrush.sourceforge.net/*).

If you're studying a foreign language, gather pictures of different items and type the English word and its equivalent foreign word for each picture. When your Macintosh starts running the slideshow, you can use these digital flash cards to help you study and review.

The same principle can be used for work as well. You can create graphical images of tasks you need to complete that day or goals you want to achieve. When your slideshow starts, your Macintosh can remind you of your to-do list or help you review your goals so you'll remember them and stay focused and motivated.

By turning your slideshow into more than just a picture frame, you can use your Macintosh as a learning tool, limited only by your own imagination and sense of humor.

31

Sharing Files Wirelessly with Bluetooth

If you'd like to transfer a file stored on your laptop Macintosh computer to another Macintosh, you could connect both computers using a FireWire or Ethernet cable, but few people carry these cables with them (and even fewer people know what a FireWire or Ethernet cable is). If you have a blank CD or DVD, you could save a file on the disc and then pop the disc into the other Macintosh computer—but how often do you have a blank CD or DVD on hand?

Rather than fiddle with cables or discs, you can use *Bluetooth*, a wireless connection standard used by all new Macintosh computers. By using Bluetooth, you can swap files between Macintosh computers without using cables, CDs, or DVDs.

Project goal: Learn to share files wirelessly using Bluetooth.

What You'll Be Using

To swap files wirelessly, you'll be using the following:

▶ The Bluetooth File Exchange program

▶ The Finder

Checking for Bluetooth Capability

All new Macintosh computers have Bluetooth capability, but older Macintosh computers do not. To add Bluetooth capability to an older Mac, you can buy a Bluetooth adapter that plugs into your Macintosh.

Before you can swap files using Bluetooth, you must be sure that both computers have Bluetooth capability. Here's how to check:

1. Click the Apple menu and select **System Preferences**. A System Preferences window appears.
2. Look for a Bluetooth icon under the Internet & Wireless category. If you see a Bluetooth icon, your Macintosh has Bluetooth capability. If you don't see a Bluetooth icon, your Macintosh does not have Bluetooth capability.
3. Click the close button of the System Preferences window.

Turning On Bluetooth

Before you can use Bluetooth on your Macintosh, you might need to turn on Bluetooth capability:

1. Click the Apple menu and select **System Preferences**. A System Preferences window appears.
2. Click **Bluetooth** under the Internet & Wireless category. The Bluetooth window appears, as shown in Figure 31-1.
3. Select the **On** checkbox to turn on Bluetooth. (Clearing this checkbox turns off Bluetooth.)

FIGURE 31-1: *The Bluetooth window lets you configure how Bluetooth works on your Macintosh.*

4. Select the **Discoverable** checkbox so your Macintosh can accept files from other Bluetooth-enabled devices, such as another Macintosh or a mobile phone. (Clearing this checkbox keeps other Bluetooth-enabled devices from connecting to your Macintosh.)

5. Click the close button of the System Preferences window.

Sharing Files with Bluetooth

Once you've turned on Bluetooth, you can receive files from other Macintosh computers or handheld devices such as personal digital assistants (PDAs) or mobile phones.

Sharing Files Between Macintosh Computers

If you have a Macintosh laptop, you can share files wirelessly with other Macintosh computers in a classroom, coffeehouse, or anywhere you take your Macintosh laptop. Here's how to share files:

1. Make sure both Macintosh computers have Bluetooth capability, that Bluetooth is turned on, and that the other Macintosh has selected its Discoverable checkbox. (See "Turning On Bluetooth" on page 286.)

2. Click the Finder icon on the Dock. The Finder window appears.

3. Select **Go ▸ Utilities**. The right pane of the Finder window displays the contents of the Utilities folder, as shown in Figure 31-2.

FIGURE 31-2: *The Bluetooth File Exchange program is stored inside the Utilities folder.*

4.   Double-click the **Bluetooth File Exchange** program icon. The Bluetooth File Exchange pull-down menu appears at the top of the screen.

5.   Choose **File ▸ Send File**. A Select File to Send dialog appears, as shown in Figure 31-3.

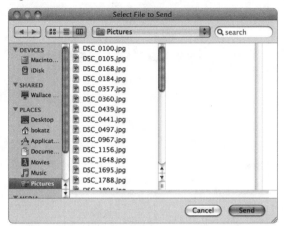

FIGURE 31-3: *The Select File to Send dialog lets you choose one or more files to send wirelessly to another Macintosh.*

✳ *NOTE:* **If Bluetooth is turned off, a dialog appears asking if you want to turn on Bluetooth. Click Turn Bluetooth On.**

6.   Click a file that you want to send to another Macintosh.

7.   Click **Send**. A Send dialog appears, where you can choose to which Bluetooth-capable Macintosh you want to send your files, as shown in Figure 31-4.

FIGURE 31-4: *The Send dialog lets you choose a Bluetooth-capable Macintosh to receive your files.*

✳ *NOTE:* If you don't see the other computer listed, that computer may not have Bluetooth turned on or may have cleared its Discoverable checkbox. (See "Turning On Bluetooth" on page 286.)

8. Click the Macintosh that you want to receive your files, and click **Send**. An Incoming File Transfer dialog appears on the screen of the other Macintosh, offering a chance to accept or decline the files being sent, as shown in Figure 31-5.

9. Click **Accept** (or select the **Accept all** checkbox). Your files start transferring from one Macintosh to the other.

10. Click the close button of the Incoming File Transfer dialog. Your transferred files appear in the Documents folder.

11. Select **Bluetooth File Exchange ▶ Quit Bluetooth File Exchange**.

FIGURE 31-5: *You must accept or decline a file transfer from another Macintosh.*

✳ *NOTE:* You can also transfer files between your Macintosh and computers running Windows or Linux, just as long as those other computers offer Bluetooth.

Additional Ideas for Transferring Files Wirelessly

If you're in a classroom with your laptop Macintosh, you can swap files with your classmates if you get bored. Take your laptop Macintosh to a friend's house and pass along some interesting pictures and files you downloaded off the Internet, such as news stories or funny pictures of celebrities or politicians you can't stand. If you have two or more Bluetooth-enabled computers at home or in an office (even if they're not Macs), use Bluetooth as a simple network for swapping files back and forth.

If you need to share small files, such as word processor documents or digital images, Bluetooth makes sharing files simple and effortless. (If you need to share large files, such as video or collections of your favorite songs, you may still want to copy and transfer files through cables, flash drives, CDs, or DVDs.)

32 Retrieving Files Back in Time

If you accidentally delete a file or if your hard disk crashes, you could lose your data for good. To back up your crucial files, your Macintosh comes with a program called *Time Machine*.

By attaching an external hard disk to your Macintosh, you can use Time Machine to back up your files automatically. If you lose a file, you can use Time Machine to retrieve it again. You'll never again risk losing a critical file.

Project goal: Learn how to back up and retrieve deleted or lost files.

What You'll Be Using

To back up and retrieve files on your Macintosh, you'll need the following:

▶   The Time Machine program

▶   An external hard disk or Apple's Time Capsule

Retrieving Files from the Trash

The simplest way to retrieve deleted files is to look for them in the Trash. Every time you delete a file, your Macintosh stores it in the Trash. To retrieve files stored in the Trash, do the following:

1.   Right-click the Trash icon on the Dock and select **Open**. A Finder window appears, displaying the contents of the Trash.
2.   Right-click any file stored in the Trash window. A pop-up menu appears.
3.   Choose **Put Back**. Your chosen file returns back to the folder where it was stored before you deleted it. (You can also drag a file out of the Trash window and drop it in any folder you want.)

✴ *NOTE:* If you empty the Trash and accidentally throw out any files you might really need, you can buy a special utility program that can recover deleted files. Three popular disk utility programs that can recover deleted files are DiskWarrior (*http://www.alsoft.com/*), TechTool Pro (*http://www.micromat.com/*), and Drive Genius (*http://www.prosofteng.com/*).

If you're sure you want to delete files for good, empty the Trash, which frees up space on your hard disk. To empty the Trash, right-click the Trash icon on the Dock and select **Empty Trash**.

✴ *NOTE:* If you point to the Trash icon on the Dock and hold down the left mouse button (or the trackpad button on a laptop Macintosh) for a few seconds, a pop-up menu appears that's the same as if you right-clicked the Trash icon.

Backing Up and Retrieving Files with Time Machine

If you've deleted files and emptied the Trash, or if your hard disk crashes or corrupts your files, your data may be gone for good unless you've been using Time Machine. To use Time Machine, you first need to connect an external hard disk (or Apple's Time Capsule) to your Macintosh and then set up Time Machine. As you use your Macintosh, Time Machine backs up your files hourly, daily, and weekly. The amount of backups that Time Machine can save depends on the amount of space available on your external hard disk.

Before you can use Time Machine, you must set it up. After that, Time Machine will start backing up your files automatically. You won't have to do a thing.

Setting Up Time Machine

To set up Time Machine with your Macintosh, do the following:

1. Connect an external hard disk (or Apple's Time Capsule) to your Macintosh. (If you connect an external hard disk or Time Capsule unit that already contains data, a dialog appears, asking if you want to delete all data currently stored on the hard disk. If the data isn't important, go ahead and choose to delete all data on that hard disk. Otherwise, you will need to use another hard disk.)
2. Click the Apple menu and select **System Preferences**. A System Preferences window appears.
3. Click the **Time Machine** icon under the System category. The Time Machine window appears.
4. Click the **On** switch, as shown in Figure 32-1.

FIGURE 32-1: *The Time Machine window lets you turn on Time Machine and choose an external hard disk to use.*

5. Click the **Select Backup Disk** button. A dialog appears, as shown in Figure 32-2, letting you click the external hard disk that you want to use. (If you have Apple's Time Capsule, click the **Set Up Time Capsule** button.)

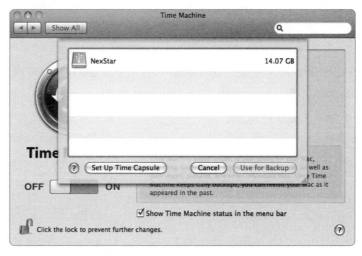

FIGURE 32-2: *To use Time Machine, you must select an external hard disk.*

6. Click the icon that represents the hard disk you want to use and click the **Use for Backup** button. The Time Machine dialog shows that Time Machine is now turned on, as shown in Figure 32-3.

7. Click the close button of the Time Machine window.

FIGURE 32-3: *The Time Machine dialog displays information about your external hard disk.*

Retrieving Files with Time Machine

After you've connected an external hard disk to your Macintosh and turned on Time Machine, you can retrieve any lost files that have been backed up to the hard disk. The size of your external hard disk determines how far back in time the Time Machine program will save backed up files. If you have a large external hard disk (such as 200GB or more), you may be able to retrieve files from the past year or two. If you have a smaller external hard disk (such as 80GB or less), you may be able to retrieve files only from a few months back in time. When your external hard disk runs out of room, Time Machine wipes out the oldest files to make room for newer files.

To retrieve a backed up file using Time Machine, do the following:

1. Click the Time Machine icon on the Dock. (If the Time Machine icon is not visible, double-click the **Time Machine** icon in the Applications folder.) The Time Machine window appears, displaying a single Finder window, as shown in Figure 32-4.

2. (Optional) You can change which folders appear in the Finder window displayed by Time Machine. For example, you might need to find a file stored in the Applications folder instead of the Documents folder.

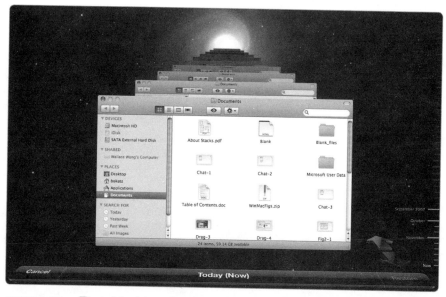

FIGURE 32-4: *Time Machine shows multiple saved states of your Macintosh.*

3. Click the back and forward arrows in the bottom-right corner of the Time Machine window, or click the timeline along the right side of the window to retrieve a backed up file. For example, if you want to retrieve a file that you last saw on December 5, click the back arrow or click the timeline to find the December 5 date.

4. Click the file or folder you want to retrieve, and then click the **Restore** button in the bottom-right corner of the Time Machine window. Time Machine exits, retrieves your chosen file or folder, and stores it back on your hard disk in the location where you last stored it.

Additional Ideas for Backing Up Files

By using Time Machine as a safety net, you can freely experiment with your Macintosh, knowing that even if you make a horrendous mistake and delete a crucial file, you'll always be able to retrieve it again using Time Machine (provided, of course, that you backed up the file using Time Machine first).

Time Machine is great for backing up files, but for even more protection, consider a program such as SuperDuper! (*http://www.shirt-pocket.com/*), which can "clone" your entire hard disk and store it on a DVD. If you store the DVD in a safe place away from your Macintosh (such as in another building), you'll protect your data in case a disaster (such as a fire or flood) wipes out your Macintosh and your external hard disk. With a DVD containing your "cloned" Macintosh data, you'll be able to copy the data onto a new Macintosh, and your new Macintosh will contain all your files, programs, and settings from your old Macintosh.

For maximum security, use offsite storage. Some free offsite storage providers are ADrive (*http://www.adrive.com/*) or HugeDrive (*http://www.hugedrive.com/*).

If your data is important, back it up now. The time most people think about backing up their files is after they've lost them. You can protect yourself by backing up your files today before it's too late.

33 Typing Foreign Languages

Since people read and write in different languages, you may need to write in languages as diverse as Arabic and Vietnamese (or dozens of other languages) on your Macintosh. While languages such as French and Italian use some of the same characters used in English, languages such as Japanese and Korean do not.

Fortunately, your Macintosh lets you type special characters, such as é or ë, or completely foreign characters, such as 中文. Best of all, you can type these characters and words in practically any text-based program.

Project goal: Learn how to type foreign characters and words in any Macintosh program.

What You'll Be Using

To type foreign characters and words on your Macintosh, you'll need the following:

▶   The System Preferences program

Typing Foreign Characters

Many languages share the English alphabet but use accents over or under some characters to indicate specific pronunciations. Although most keyboards don't display these accented characters, you can still type them by pressing keyboard combinations, such as those shown in Table 33-1.

Table 33-1: Common Foreign Language Characters and Keyboard Combinations

Character	Keys to Press
Acute	
á or Á	OPTION-E, then type *a* or *A*
é or É	OPTION-E, then type *e* or *E*
í or Í	OPTION-E, then type *i* or *I*
ó or Ó	OPTION-E, then type *o* or *O*
ú or Ú	OPTION-E, then type *u* or *U*
Circumflex	
â or Â	OPTION-I, then type *a* or *A*
ê or Ê	OPTION-I, then type *e* or *E*
î or Î	OPTION-I, then type *i* or *I*
ô or Ô	OPTION-I, then type *o* or *O*
û or Û	OPTION-I, then type *u* or *U*
Grave	
à or À	OPTION-` (grave, appears on the same key as the ~ symbol), then type *a* or *A*
è or È	OPTION-` (grave, appears on the same key as the ~ symbol), then type *e* or *E*
ì or Ì	OPTION-` (grave, appears on the same key as the ~ symbol), then type *i* or *I*
ò or Ò	OPTION-` (grave, appears on the same key as the ~ symbol), then type *o* or *O*
ù or Ù	OPTION-` (grave, appears on the same key as the ~ symbol), then type *u* or *U*
Tilde	
ñ or Ñ	OPTION-N, then type *n* or *N*
õ or Õ	OPTION-N, then type *o* or *O*
ã or Ã	OPTION-N, then type *a* or *A*

Character	Keys to Press
Umlaut	
ä or Ä	OPTION-U, then type *a* or *A*
ë or Ë	OPTION-U, then type *e* or *E*
ï or Ï	OPTION-U, then type *i* or *I*
ö or Ö	OPTION-U, then type *o* or *O*
ü or Ü	OPTION-U, then type *u* or *U*
Miscellaneous	
¡	OPTION-1
¿	SHIFT-OPTION -?
ç	OPTION-C
Ç	SHIFT-OPTION-C
œ	OPTION-Q
Œ	SHIFT-OPTION-Q
ß	OPTION-S
ø	OPTION-O
Ø	SHIFT-OPTION-O
å	OPTION-A
Å	SHIFT-OPTION-A
æ	OPTION-' (apostrophe key)
Æ	SHIFT-OPTION-' (apostrophe key)

Clicking to Choose Foreign Characters

Another way to add special characters to text is to view a list of characters and click the one you want. If you need to type characters in a language based on the Roman alphabet (such as French, Spanish, or Italian), for example, you need to display and use the *Character Viewer*.

Adding the Character Viewer to the Language & Text Menulet

To make the Character Viewer visible, you first enable it so that it appears on the Language & Text menulet on the right side of the menu bar by doing this:

1. Click the Apple menu and select **System Preferences**. A System Preferences window appears.
2. Click the **Language & Text** icon under the Personal category. The Language & Text window appears.
3. Click the **Input Sources** tab.

4. Select the **Keyboard & Character Viewer** checkbox, as shown in Figure 33-1.

5. Click the close button of the Language & Text window.

FIGURE 33-1: *The Language & Text window lets you choose a language and lets you display the Character Viewer.*

Opening the Character Viewer

After you've added the Keyboard & Character menulet, you can open or display the Character Viewer by doing the following:

1. Move the cursor where you want to insert the character (in a word processor document, for example).

2. Click the Keyboard & Character menulet on the right side of the menu bar and select **Show Character Viewer**, as shown in Figure 33-2. The Character Viewer appears, as shown in Figure 33-3.

3. Click **Accented Latin** in the left pane. The right pane displays all accented Latin characters based on the Roman alphabet.

4. Double-click the character you want to use to insert it at the current location of the cursor.

5. Click the close button of the Character Viewer.

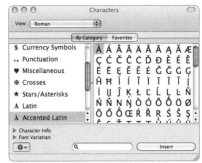

FIGURE 33-2: *The Keyboard & Character menulet appears on the menu bar.*

FIGURE 33-3: *The Character Viewer window displays characters you can choose by clicking them.*

Typing on a Foreign Language Keyboard Layout

Pressing keyboard shortcuts or clicking characters in the Character Viewer can be useful for occasionally adding foreign characters to text. However, if you need to type multiple foreign language characters, a *foreign language keyboard layout* may offer a much simpler solution.

A foreign language keyboard layout assigns foreign characters to ordinary keys on the keyboard. By using the Keyboard Viewer, you can see which keys on the keyboard can be used to type foreign language characters, as shown in Figure 33-4.

Choosing a Foreign Language

Before you can type foreign language characters using the foreign language keyboard, you need to tell your Macintosh which foreign language you want to use:

1. Click the Apple menu and select **System Preferences**. A System Preferences window appears.
2. Click the **Language & Text** icon under the Personal category. The Language & Text window appears.
3. Click the **Input Sources** tab.
4. Select the **Keyboard & Character Viewer** checkbox, as shown in Figure 33-5.
5. Select the checkboxes of each foreign language you want to use.
6. Click the close button of the Language & Text window.

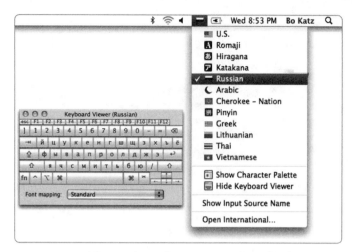

FIGURE 33-4: *The Keyboard Viewer window displays a variety of foreign characters.*

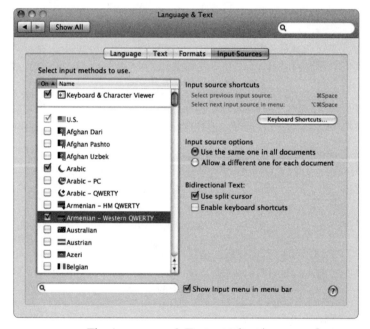

FIGURE 33-5: *The Language & Text window lets you choose a language and display the Keyboard Viewer window.*

Typing in a Foreign Language

After you've defined one or more foreign languages to use on your Macintosh, you can type in those languages in any Macintosh program, such as a word processor.

Here's how you switch to and type in a foreign language:

1. Start any program that can accept text, such as the TextEdit program. The program window appears.
2. Click the Language & Text menulet that appears on the right side of the menu bar. A pull-down menu of available languages appears, as shown in Figure 33-6.

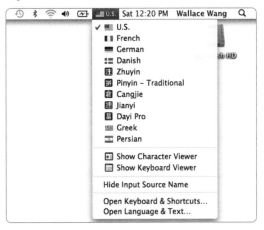

FIGURE 33-6: *The Language & Text menulet displays all your selected foreign languages.*

3. Click one of the languages listed in the pull-down, such as French or German.
4. (Optional) Click the Language & Text menulet and click **Show Keyboard Viewer**. The Keyboard Viewer window appears (see Figure 33-4) to show you which keys to press to type certain characters. (You can also click the characters in the Keyboard Viewer window to "type" the characters as well.)
5. Use the keyboard to type the corresponding foreign characters displayed in the Keyboard Viewer window.

Typing in Foreign (Non-Roman) Characters

To type in languages that use non-Roman characters, such as many Asian languages like Chinese or Japanese, you must choose an input method that lets you type a Chinese or Japanese word using the Roman alphabet on a typical keyboard. After you've chosen an input method, you need to know how to type the words that your chosen input method recognizes.

For example, the Pinyin input method is common for representing traditional Chinese words as Western alphabet characters, such as typing *wo* to represent the Chinese character 我.

Choosing an Input Method

Asian languages often use multiple input methods, so you must choose the one with which you're most familiar, such as Pinyin for typing traditional Chinese characters. Here's how to choose an input method:

1. Click the Apple menu and select **System Preferences**. A System Preferences window appears.
2. Click the **Language & Text** icon under the Personal category. The Language & Text window appears.
3. Click the **Input Sources** tab.
4. Select the checkbox of the language you want to use (such as Simplified Chinese, Traditional Chinese, or Japanese).
5. Click the close button of the Language & Text window.

Typing Using a Foreign Language Input Method

After you've chosen an input method for a language, you will use that input method to start typing the foreign language characters by doing the following:

1. Start a text program, such as a word processor document, and move the cursor where you want to type the foreign characters.
2. Click the Language & Text menulet and choose the input method for your foreign language, such as Pinyin for Traditional Chinese.
3. Type a word, using ordinary Western alphabet characters, that represents the foreign language word you want to choose.
4. Press the spacebar. A menu appears, listing possible characters from which you can choose. Figure 33-7 shows the Chinese character that appears when you type *wo*, which is the Western equivalent for representing several characters.
5. Click the character you want to "type" into the document or press the arrow and spacebar (or press the RETURN key) to choose a character.

FIGURE 33-7: *Typing in many Asian languages often requires typing equivalent words on a standard keyboard and choosing the actual symbol from a pull-down menu.*

Typing Chinese, Japanese, and Korean Characters

At first glance, Chinese, Japanese, and Korean words look like a random jumble of lines, but once you get familiar with one of the languages, you'll notice that Asian language characters often use similar lines and patterns, which are called *radicals*. By identifying a particular type of radical, you can choose from a list of common characters that use that same radical.

To type an Asian character using radicals, do this:

1. Move the cursor where you want to type an Asian character, such as in a word processor document.
2. Click the **Language & Text** menulet and choose **Show Character Viewer**. The Character Viewer window appears.
3. Click the **View** pop-up menu and choose Korean, Japanese, Traditional Chinese, or Simplified Chinese, as shown in Figure 33-8.
4. Click the **By Radical** tab to view the list of radicals in the left pane, as shown in Figure 33-9.
5. Click a radical in the left pane. The right pane displays common characters.
6. Click a character in the right pane.
7. Click the **Insert** button in the bottom-right corner.
8. Click the close button of the Character Viewer window.

FIGURE 33-8: *The Character Viewer window lets you select an Asian language.*

FIGURE 33-9: *Radicals let you select common Asian characters.*

Additional Ideas for Typing Foreign Characters

Many people are familiar with languages that are written left to right. However, many other languages are normally written from right to left, such as Arabic and Hebrew. To type in these languages, you may need a special word processor such as Nisus Writer (*http://www.nisus.com/*) or Mellel (*http://www.redlers.com/*) that allows right-to-left typing.

As an alternative, you can configure the free TextEdit program that comes with your Macintosh to type right to left. Here's how to use TextEdit to type right to left:

1. Click the Finder icon on the Dock. The Finder window appears.
2. Click **Applications** in the sidebar of the Finder window. The contents of the Applications folder appear in the right pane of the Finder window.
3. Double-click the **TextEdit** icon. The TextEdit window appears.
4. Select **Format ▸ Text ▸ Writing Direction ▸ Right to Left**.

Now that you know how to type in different languages, try writing and sending an email message to a friend or relative overseas. Writing in a foreign language can be easy and fun, and that's what using the Macintosh is all about.

PART 4

Touching the World Through the Internet

34

Getting on the Internet and Sharing Folders

Your Macintosh may be great for playing games, drawing pictures, listening to music, or watching movies. However, at some point, you'll probably want to browse the Internet, send email, or download programs and updates. To do this, you need to get on the Internet.

Two common ways to get on the Internet include plugging a cable into your Macintosh or connecting through a *wireless (WiFi)* network. As a general rule, shoving a cable into your Macintosh will be faster and more reliable, but connecting to a wireless network is far more convenient. In this chapter, you'll learn how to use both methods.

Project goal: Learn how to connect your Macintosh to the Internet.

What You'll Be Using

To connect to the Internet and share your folders, you'll be using:

▶   The System Preferences program

▶   The Network Diagnostics program

▶   The Safari web browser

Plugging Your Macintosh into the Internet

Every Macintosh comes with a special plug called an *Ethernet port*, which looks like an oversized telephone jack. Ethernet is a standard originally used to connect computers in a network.

To connect your Macintosh to the Internet using Ethernet, you'll need a high-speed Internet connection through your cable or telephone company, such as a *Digital Subscriber Line (DSL)*. Next, you'll need a cable or DSL modem, which plugs into the cable or DSL line. Finally, you need an Ethernet cable that connects your modem to your Macintosh, as shown in Figure 34-1.

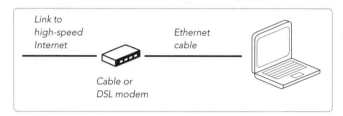

FIGURE 34-1: *Connecting your Macintosh to the Internet using Ethernet*

If you have multiple computers, you can use a device called a *router*, which plugs into your modem and provides multiple Ethernet ports so several computers can share the same cable or DSL connection, as shown in Figure 34-2.

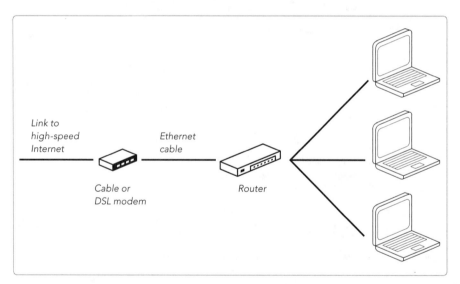

FIGURE 34-2: *A router lets multiple computers share a single Internet connection.*

After you have plugged in and turned on your modem and router, you'll be able to connect to the Internet by doing this:

1. Click the Apple menu and choose **System Preferences**. The System Preferences window appears.
2. Click the **Network** icon under the Internet & Wireless category. The Network dialog appears.
3. Click the **Ethernet** icon in the left pane. The right pane displays various options, as shown in Figure 34-3.

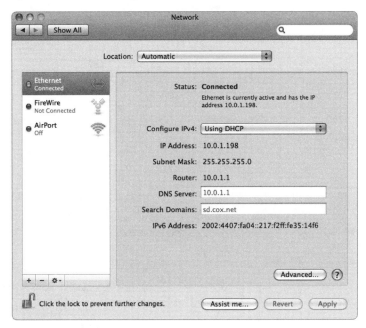

FIGURE 34-3: *The Network dialog lets you configure your Ethernet connection.*

4. Click the **Configure IPv4** pop-up menu and choose **Using DHCP**. (Dynamic Host Configuration Protocol is a fancy standard that lets your Macintosh automatically configure your Ethernet connection, so you don't have to worry about doing it manually—although you can if you really want to.)
5. Click the **Apply** button.
6. Click the close button in the Network dialog to make it go away.

7. Click the Safari icon on the Dock. You should see a web page. If you cannot see a web page, there is a problem with your Ethernet connection and you'll see an error message, as shown in Figure 34-4.

FIGURE 34-4: *The Network Diagnostics button appears when you cannot connect to the Internet.*

8. Click the **Network Diagnostics** button. This opens a Network Diagnostics dialog, as shown in Figure 34-5.

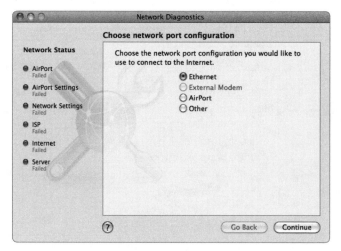

FIGURE 34-5: *The Network Diagnostics dialog can help you troubleshoot your Internet connection.*

9. Click the **Ethernet** radio button and click the **Continue** button. Follow the directions on the Network Diagnostics dialog, which will guide you through troubleshooting the problem with your Internet connection.

* *NOTE:* **Make sure all cables are connected and your modem and router are turned on.**

Connecting to a Wireless Internet Connection

Plugging an Ethernet cable into your Macintosh is the old-fashioned way of connecting to the Internet. If you don't like the idea of stringing Ethernet cables all over the floor, or if you're constantly on the move, you'll probably prefer to connect to a wireless or WiFi Internet connection instead. A WiFi connection essentially replaces a physical Ethernet cable with a radio signal between a WiFi router and your computer.

Many public wireless connections are open to anyone. However, for security reasons, many other wireless Internet connections require a password before you can connect to them. To connect to a wireless Internet connection, do this:

1. Click the Apple menu and choose **System Preferences**. The System Preferences window appears.
2. Click the **Network** icon under the Internet & Wireless category. The Network dialog appears.
3. Click the **AirPort** icon in the left pane. The right pane displays various options, as shown in Figure 34-6.
4. (Optional) Click the **Turn Airport On** button. The Status line to the left of the Turn Airport On button should now read *Connected*.
5. Click the **Network Name** pop-up menu and choose the name of the WiFi network you want to use. If the WiFi network requires a password, a dialog will appear, letting you type the password.
6. Click the close button on the Network dialog.
7. Click the Safari icon on the Dock. You should see a web page. If you cannot see a web page, there is a problem with your WiFi connection and you'll see an error message (see Figure 34-4). You'll need to click the Network Diagnostics button and then follow the instructions to troubleshoot your WiFi connection.

Sharing Folders over a Network

If you have a bunch of Macintosh computers hooked up to the same router, you have a simple network. When you have such a network connected together, either physically through Ethernet cables or wirelessly through a WiFi router, you can freely share files between your computers.

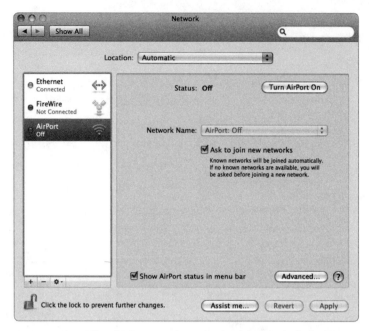

FIGURE 34-6: *The AirPort options in the Network dialog*

To make your Macintosh share files with other Macintosh computers on the same network, you need to do the following:

▸ Turn on File Sharing

▸ Define which folders you want to share from your Macintosh

These two steps simply make your folders visible to other Macintosh computers on your network. Those other computers can then access files in those specified folders through the Finder window, essentially treating the folders on another computer as if they were physically part of that particular Macintosh.

To share folders from your Macintosh, do this:

1. Click the Apple menu and choose **System Preferences**. The System Preferences window appears.
2. Click the **Sharing** icon under the Internet & Wireless category. The Sharing dialog appears, as shown in Figure 34-7.
3. Select (or clear) the **File Sharing** checkbox in the left pane of the Sharing dialog to turn File Sharing on (or off). Under the Shared Folders group, your Macintosh automatically includes a folder called *Public Folder*.

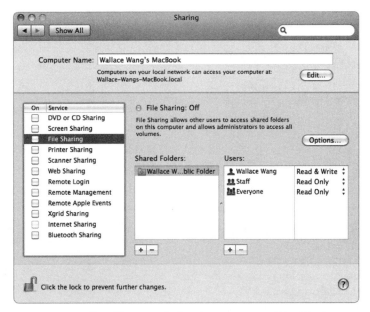

FIGURE 34-7: The Sharing dialog lets you turn File Sharing on or off.

4. (Optional) If you want to make other folders visible to the network, click the plus sign icon under the Shared Folders group. A dialog appears letting you click another folder you want to share. Click a folder and click the **Add** button. (Repeat for each additional folder you want to share.)

5. (Optional) If you wish to change the permissions on your shared folders, click the **Users** pane. The settings here determine whether remote users will only be able to read files (Read Only), only place new files (Write Only), or both read files and place new files (Read & Write) in that folder. You can set different permissions on each shared folder.

6. (Optional) If you also want to share your folders with Windows computers on your network, click **Options** and then click the checkbox marked **Share Files and Folders Using SMB (Windows)**.

* **NOTE:** To stop sharing a folder, click a folder that you want to hide, click the minus sign icon under the Shared Folders group, and click the OK button when a dialog asks if you really want to stop sharing your selected folder.

7. Click the close button to make the Sharing dialog go away. Your selected folders are now visible in the Finder of every Macintosh connected to the same network, as shown in Figure 34-8.

FIGURE 34-8: The Shared category in the Finder window treats shared folders on other computers as additional storage devices.

✳ **NOTE:** If you share folders and connect to a WiFi network, your shared folders will be accessible to anyone also connected to that WiFi network. That means if you connect your laptop to a public WiFi network at a coffeehouse or a library, anyone else using that WiFi connection will be able to access your shared folders.

Additional Ideas for Connecting to the Internet

Most of the time, connecting to the Internet through an Ethernet cable is as simple as plugging the cable into your Macintosh and accessing the Internet. Likewise, after you turn AirPort on, you can often latch onto a WiFi network just by loading a program like Safari.

As a shortcut, you can also click the WiFi menulet on the right side of the menu bar. This displays a list of available WiFi networks that you can choose, as shown in Figure 34-9.

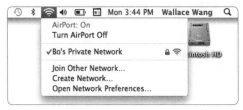

FIGURE 34-9: The WiFi menulet lets you choose from available WiFi networks.

After you connect to the Internet, you can use Safari to browse websites, Mail to send and receive messages, and iChat to chat with your friends in real time. Some of Dashboard's widgets rely on a live Internet connection to retrieve information like stock prices and weather forecasts.

Other ways to connect to the Internet include using a *USB cellular modem*. This device plugs into a USB port and lets you access the Internet through a cellular phone network. Naturally, you'll need to pay for this privilege, but if you need Internet access at all times, this can get you on the Internet wherever you can find cellular phone coverage from your phone company.

A similar method relies on *tethering*, which essentially means connecting your mobile phone to your Macintosh and connecting to the Internet through your mobile phone. This will also cost you extra, but if you regularly travel with a mobile phone and a laptop Macintosh, it's another option to ensure you can get on the Internet practically anywhere you receive a cellular signal.

Finally, you can always buy an antiquated telephone modem that plugs into your computer's USB port. These old-fashioned modems then plug into an ordinary telephone line and let you access the Internet through a telephone line and an account with an Internet provider that offers dial-up access.

With so many options for getting on the Internet, there's no reason why your Macintosh cannot get connected to the rest of the world. If you don't feel like paying for monthly Internet access, just take your laptop to the nearest public library and latch onto their free public WiFi network.

With a little creativity (or money), there's no reason you can't get on the Internet today. Now you just have to figure out what you want to do on the Internet once you get your Macintosh hooked up to it.

35

Remembering Your Favorite Websites

To visit a website, you can either type the website address (such as *http://www.nostarch .com/*) into a browser or use a search engine (such as Google) to find a list of websites

that you can try. Unfortunately, both methods can be time-consuming. To save time, you can use Safari's bookmarks and history list to help you find and visit websites that you visited at some earlier point in time.

Bookmarks let you store your favorite website addresses as descriptive names that you can click to open the sites. The history list keeps track of all the websites you've visited recently so you can easily find a previously viewed website.

Project goal: Learn to use bookmarks and the history list to view previously visited websites.

What You'll Be Using

To keep track of websites you've visited, you'll use the following:

▸ The Safari web browser

▸ An Internet connection

Using Bookmarks

You can use bookmarks to save website addresses so that they can be easily accessed again and again. Safari can save website addresses in two places (as shown in Figure 35-1):

▶ The Bookmarks Bar

▶ The Bookmarks menu

FIGURE 35-1: *Bookmarks can appear in the Bookmarks Bar or Bookmarks menu.*

The Bookmarks Bar adds your favorite website names to the top of the Safari window so you can access any website with the click of the mouse. The Bookmarks menu tucks your favorite websites out of sight until you click the menu to view them.

Bookmarking a Favorite Website

Bookmarks are useful for saving websites that you plan to visit frequently, such as a favorite news site. To save a bookmark in either the Bookmarks Bar or Bookmarks menu, do the following:

1. Start Safari.
2. Go to a website that you know you'll want to visit again, such as *http://www.cnn.com/* or *http://www.yahoo.com/*.
3. Click the plus button at the top of the Safari window, or select **Bookmarks ▶ Add Bookmark**. A dialog appears, where you can type a name for your bookmark and a location at which to store it, as shown in Figure 35-2.

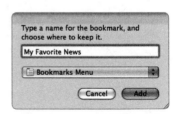

FIGURE 35-2: *A dialog appears, where you can type a bookmark name and location.*

4. Type a descriptive name for your bookmark (or edit the existing name displayed in the text box).
5. Click the pop-up menu and choose a location at which to store your bookmark, such as Bookmarks Bar or Bookmarks Menu.
6. Click **Add**. Safari adds your bookmark to your chosen location.

For a quick way to store bookmarks in the Bookmarks Bar, you can drag a website address over the Bookmarks Bar as follows:

1. Start Safari.
2. Visit a website that you know you'll want to visit again, such as *http://www .cnn.com/* or *http://www.yahoo.com/*.
3. Move the mouse pointer over the icon that appears to the left of the website address.
4. Drag the website icon and address over the Bookmarks Bar and release the left mouse button. A dialog appears, where you can type a name for your bookmark.
5. Type a descriptive name, or edit the existing displayed name, and then click **OK**.

Moving and Copying a Bookmark

When you first create a bookmark, you must define where you want to store it. After you've stored a bookmark, you may want to move or copy it to another location. Here's how you can do this:

1. Click the Open Bookmarks icon on the far left of the Bookmarks Bar (the icon looks like an open book), or select **Bookmarks ▸ Show All Bookmarks**. The Bookmarks window appears.
2. Click **Bookmarks Bar** or **Bookmarks Menu** under the Collections category in the left pane of the Bookmarks window. The top-right pane displays all your bookmarked websites as thumbnail images, similar to the Cover Flow appearance of album covers in iTunes. The bottom-right pane displays the names of the bookmarks stored in the selected location, as shown in Figure 35-3.
3. Click a website thumbnail image in the top-right pane or a bookmark name in the bottom-right pane that you want to copy or move.
4. Select **Edit ▸ Cut** (to remove the bookmark from the present location) or **Edit ▸ Copy** (to copy the bookmark from the present location).
5. Click a collection in the left pane (such as Bookmarks Bar or Bookmarks Menu) or a folder where you want to move or copy your chosen bookmark.
6. Click the bottom-right pane where you want to paste your bookmark.
7. Select **Edit ▸ Paste**.

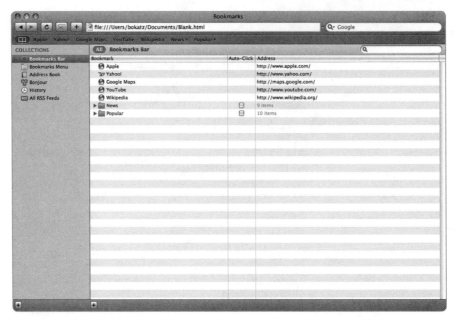

FIGURE 35-3: *The Bookmarks window lets you view all your stored bookmarks.*

Editing a Bookmark

After you create a bookmark, you might later want to change its name or edit its stored website address. Here's how to edit a bookmark name or address:

1. Click the Open Bookmarks icon on the far left of the Bookmarks Bar, or select **Bookmarks ▸ Show All Bookmarks**. The Bookmarks window appears.
2. Click **Bookmarks Bar** or **Bookmarks Menu** under the Collections category in the left pane of the Bookmarks window. The right pane displays all the bookmarks stored in the selection (see Figure 35-3).
3. Right-click a bookmark and select **Edit Name** or **Edit Address**. Your chosen bookmark's name or address appears highlighted.
4. Use the arrow and DELETE keys to edit the existing name, or type a new name or address for your bookmark and press RETURN.

Deleting a Bookmark

You can delete a bookmark you no longer want. Here's how:

1. Click the Open Bookmarks icon on the far left of the Bookmarks Bar, or select **Bookmarks ▸ Show All Bookmarks**. The Bookmarks window appears.

2. Click **Bookmarks Bar** or **Bookmarks Menu** under the Collections category in the left pane of the Bookmarks window. The right pane displays all the bookmarks stored in the selection (see Figure 35-3).

3. Right-click a bookmark and select **Delete**. Alternatively, you can drag the bookmark over the Trash icon on the Dock.

✳ *NOTE:* **If you delete a bookmark by mistake, press ⌘-Z to retrieve it.**

Organizing Bookmarks in Folders

The more bookmarks you add to the Bookmarks Bar or Bookmarks menu, the more crowded your bookmarks lists can get, and the harder it can be to find the one bookmark you want. To avoid this problem, you can store related bookmarks in a folder.

Creating a Bookmark Folder

The Bookmarks Bar can display bookmarks and folders. When you click a bookmark, Safari displays the appropriate website. When you click a folder, a menu of bookmarks appears, as shown in Figure 35-4. You can identify folders easily because they display a downward-pointing arrow to the right of the folder name.

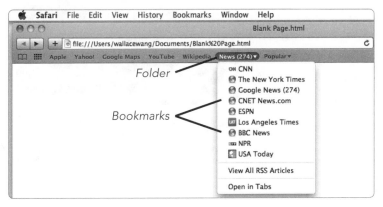

FIGURE 35-4: *A folder acts like a pull-down menu on the Bookmarks Bar.*

On the Bookmarks menu, bookmark names appear with icons, while each folder name appears with a folder icon and an arrow pointing to the right. Moving the pointer over a folder on the Bookmarks menu displays a submenu that lists the bookmarks stored in the folder, as shown in Figure 35-5.

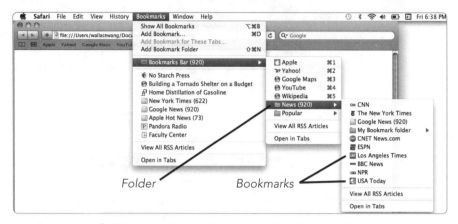

FIGURE 35-5: *A folder acts like a submenu on the Bookmarks menu.*

Here's how to create a bookmark folder:

1. Select **Bookmarks ▸ Add Bookmark Folder**. A Bookmarks window appears, displaying an untitled bookmark folder in the left pane, as shown in Figure 35-6.

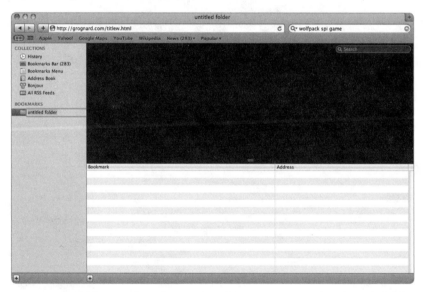

FIGURE 35-6: *The Bookmarks window lets you name a bookmark folder and fill it with bookmarks.*

2.   Type a descriptive name for your bookmark folder and press RETURN. At this point, your newly created and named bookmark folder is empty and ready to store bookmarks.

Adding Bookmarks to a Folder

After you've created a folder, you need to store bookmarks in it. Here's how to copy bookmarks into a folder:

1.   Select **Bookmarks ▶ Show All Bookmarks**. The Bookmarks window appears. (Skip this step if the Bookmarks window is already in view.)
2.   Click **Bookmarks Bar** or **Bookmarks Menu** under the Collections category in the left pane of the Bookmark window to view all the bookmarks stored in that location (see Figure 35-3).
3.   Drag and drop a bookmark from the right pane over the bookmark folder in the left pane. (Dragging a bookmark moves it from its current location into your bookmark folder. If you want to copy a bookmark, hold down the OPTION key as you drag and drop the bookmark.)
4.   Repeat this step for each bookmark you want to store in your bookmark folder.

Moving a Bookmark Folder

After you've filled a bookmark folder with bookmarks, you need to move the folder off the left pane and on to the Bookmarks Bar or Bookmarks menu. Here's how:

1.   Select **Bookmarks ▶ Show All Bookmarks**. A Bookmarks window appears. (Skip this step if the Bookmarks window is already in view.)
2.   Click **Bookmarks Bar** or **Bookmarks Menu** under the Collections category in the left pane of the Bookmarks window. You'll see all your bookmarks in the right pane (see Figure 35-3).
3.   Drag your bookmark folder from the left pane to a spot in the right pane. A horizontal line appears where your bookmark folder will appear if you release the left mouse button, as shown in Figure 35-7.

✳ *NOTE:* **The contents of existing folders appear indented so you can see which bookmarks appear directly on the Bookmarks Bar or Bookmarks menu and which ones appear inside a folder. It's even possible to drag and drop a folder inside another folder.**

4.   Drop (release the left mouse button) your bookmark when the horizontal line appears at the place where you want to store your bookmark folder.

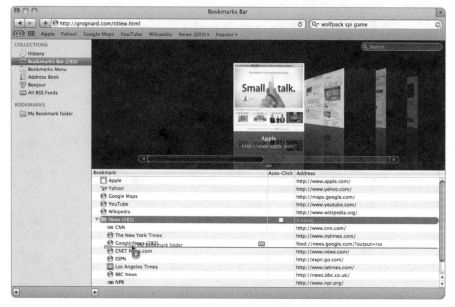

FIGURE 35-7: *A horizontal line appears when you drag a bookmark folder into the right pane of the Bookmarks window.*

Rearranging Bookmarks and Folders

You can move bookmarks and folders on both the Bookmarks Bar and Bookmarks menu, like so:

1. Select **Bookmarks ▸ Show All Bookmarks**. The Bookmarks window appears. (Skip this step if the Bookmarks window is already in view.)
2. Click **Bookmarks Bar** or **Bookmarks Menu** under the Collections category in the left pane of the Bookmarks window. The right pane contains all the bookmarks stored in the location (see Figure 35-3).
3. Drag a bookmark or folder in the right pane up or down. A horizontal line appears where your bookmark or folder will appear when you release the left mouse button.
4. Drop (release the left mouse button) your bookmark or folder when the horizontal line appears in the place where you want the bookmark or folder to appear.

Saving and Sharing Bookmarks

As your collection of bookmarks grows, you might want to make a backup copy and store this copy in a safe place; this protects your bookmarks from corruption or loss. Another reason for saving your bookmarks is to share them with others so they can visit your favorite websites.

Here's how to save your bookmarks:

1. Select **File ▸ Export Bookmarks**. An Export Bookmarks dialog appears, where you can type a name for your saved bookmarks and a location at which to store them, as shown in Figure 35-8.

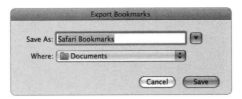

FIGURE 35-8: The Export Bookmarks command displays a dialog where you can type a name for your book- mark and save it in a new location.

2. Click in the **Save As** text box and type a descriptive name for your bookmark file.
3. Click the **Where** pop-up menu and choose a folder in which to store your bookmarks.
4. Click **Save**.

✳ *NOTE:* **If somebody gives you a saved list of bookmarks, you can add the bookmarks to your own collection by selecting File ▸ Import Bookmarks. After you import bookmarks, you'll probably want to rearrange the newly imported bookmarks to organize them to fit within your own bookmarks.**

Using the History Menu

As you're browsing websites, you might want to go back and revisit a website you viewed a few minutes (or days) ago. If you didn't bookmark that website, you can still easily find it by using Safari's history menu.

The history menu stores all websites you've visited in the past month. To view the history menu, do this:

1. Click the **History** menu, and you'll see a list of all the websites you've visited today.
2. Click a website in the list, or click a day to view a submenu of websites you visited on that day, as shown in Figure 35-9.

FIGURE 35-9: *The History menu displays a submenu of websites you visited on a particular day.*

Creating a List of Top Sites

Chances are good that you'll want to visit the same handful of websites every day, such as your favorite news sites. You could store your favorite sites as bookmarks, but Safari offers a feature called *Top Sites*.

The idea behind Top Sites is to let Safari automatically track which websites you visit most often and save those websites as thumbnail images that you can view and click to visit those sites again.

Viewing the Top Sites List

The Top Sites list displays the websites you've visited most often. To view the Top Sites list, do this:

1. Click the Top Sites icon that appears to next to the Bookmark icon. Your frequently visited websites appear as a list of thumbnail images, as shown in Figure 35-10. A star in the upper-right corner of a website thumbnail means that the site has new information since the last time you looked at it.
2. Click the thumbnail image of the website you want to view.

Editing the Top Sites List

Your Top Sites list changes over time as you visit different websites and stop visiting other sites. If you want, you can define a website to always appear on the Top Sites list. On the other hand, you can also define a website to never appear on the Top Sites list.

Top Sites
icon

FIGURE 35-10: *The Top Sites list displays websites as thumbnail images.*

To define a website on your Top Sites list, do this:

1. Click the Top Sites icon that appears to next to the Bookmark icon. Your frequently visited websites appear as a list of thumbnail images (see Figure 35-10).
2. Click the **Edit** button that appears in the bottom-left corner of the Top Sites window. An X and a pushpin icon appear in the upper-left corner of each thumbnail, as shown in Figure 35-11.
3. (Optional) Click the X icon in the upper-left corner of any website that you do not want to appear in your Top Sites list anymore.
4. (Optional) Click the pushpin icon in the upper-left corner of any website that you always want to appear in your Top Sites list.
5. (Optional) Drag the icon in the Address text box, which displays the website address (such as *http://www.nostarch.com/*) over the Top Sites icon in the upper-left corner of the Safari window to add a website to the Top Sites list.
6. (Optional) Click the **Small**, **Medium**, or **Large** tab in the lower-right corner of the Top Sites window to change the number and size of the thumbnail images displayed.
7. Click the **Done** button in the lower-left corner of the Top Sites window.

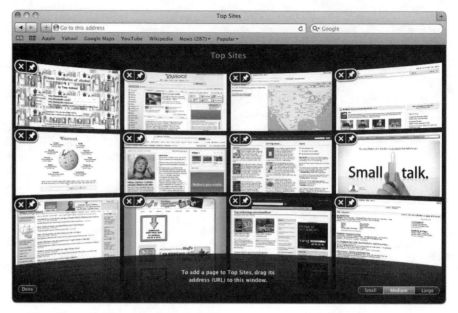

FIGURE 35-11: *Editing the Top Sites list*

Searching the Top Sites List

If you want to find a particular website in your Top Sites list, you can search for it manually or let Safari search for it much faster. To search through your Top Sites list, do this:

1. Click the Top Sites icon that appears to next to the Bookmark icon. Your frequently visited websites appear as a list of thumbnail images (see Figure 35-10).
2. Click in the **Search History** text box in the lower-right corner of the Top Sites window. The Top Sites window displays all your websites as Cover Flow images, as shown in Figure 35-12.
3. Type a word or phrase that appears on the website that you want to find. The Top Sites window displays only those website images that contain the word or phrase you typed.
4. Click the horizontal scrollbar at the bottom of the window to scroll through the list of websites that match the text you want to find.
5. Click the thumbnail image of the website that you want to view.

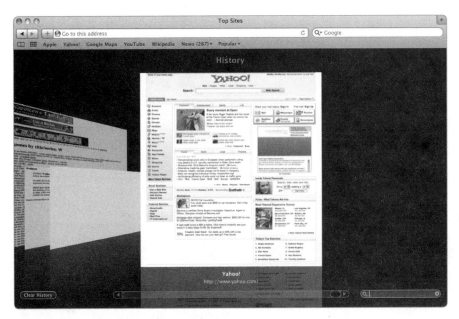

FIGURE 35-12: *Searching for a website*

Additional Ideas for Using Bookmarks and the History Menu

By peeking at someone else's history menu, you can see the websites they've visited recently; this is a simple way to check up on the websites your children (or spouse) have viewed. For yourself, the history menu acts like a virtual trail of bread-crumbs that leads you back to an interesting website you recently viewed.

Bookmarks can help you organize your web browsing habits and keep your favorite websites handy. Bookmark all your favorite shopping websites in one folder and recipe websites in another. Then export your bookmarks and share them with friends so they can visit your favorite websites with a single click. With bookmarks (and the history menu), you should never lose track of another website again (unless, of course, you lose track of your computer).

36

Getting the Latest News Using RSS

Everyone has a favorite website. To see the latest changes to a website, you could visit it periodically, but it's much easier to use RSS feeds instead. (*RSS* stands for *Rich Site Summary* or *Really Simple Syndication*.)

RSS feeds can let you know when your friend writes a new post on her blog, or when your favorite newspaper releases a new story. If RSS sounds complicated, just think of it as something like subscribing to a website, just as you might subscribe to a magazine. Instead of manually checking many different news sites, you'll have the news delivered straight to you. RSS feeds let you know exactly when your favorite website has new material for you.

Project goal: Learn to use RSS feeds to receive the latest news from your favorite websites.

What You'll Be Using

To receive and read RSS feeds, you'll need the following:

▶ The Safari web browser

▶ The Mail program

Using RSS Feeds

To read RSS feeds, you need to define how to access RSS feeds, identify which websites offer RSS feeds, and then bookmark the RSS feeds so you can view them later.

Configuring Safari

Before you read any RSS feeds, take time to configure the way the Safari browser works with them, such as defining how often Safari checks a website for updates. Here's how to configure Safari:

1. Start Safari.
2. Select **Safari ▸ Preferences**. A Preferences window appears.
3. Click the **RSS** icon. The RSS window appears.
4. Select the **Bookmarks bar** and **Bookmarks menu** checkboxes under the Automatically update articles in category, as shown in Figure 36-1. Safari will display the name of a bookmarked RSS feed along with the number of new articles in parentheses, such as (12).

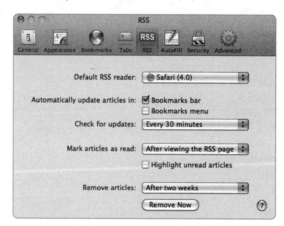

FIGURE 36-1: *The RSS window lets you customize how Safari displays RSS feeds.*

5. Click the arrow button in the **Check for updates** pop-up menu and choose a time, such as **Never, Every day, Every hour,** or **Every 30 minutes**.
6. Click the arrow button in the **Mark articles as read** pop-up menu and choose an option such as **After viewing the RSS page** or **After clicking them**. This option identifies which articles on an RSS feed you've already seen.

7. Click the arrow button in the **Remove articles** pop-up menu and choose an option such as **After two weeks** or **After one day**. This option automatically removes old RSS articles after a fixed period of time, whether you've read them or not. (You can click the **Remove Now** button to remove all RSS articles immediately.)

8. Click the close button of the RSS window.

Identifying and Bookmarking RSS Feeds

To identify which websites offer RSS feeds, do this:

1. Start Safari.

2. Visit your favorite websites and look for the RSS icon in the address box, as shown in Figure 36-2. (If you don't see an RSS icon, then that particular website doesn't offer RSS feeds.)

RSS icon

FIGURE 36-2: *The RSS icon identifies a website that offers RSS feeds.*

3. Click the **RSS** icon. The RSS feed appears as a web page listing different articles, as shown in Figure 36-3.

Articles

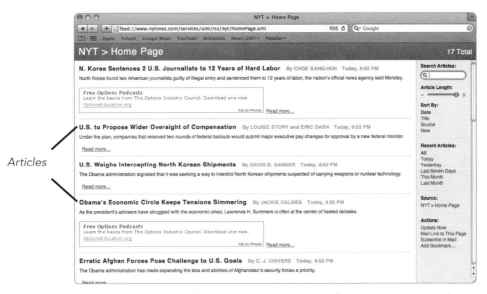

FIGURE 36-3: *An RSS feed displays its latest information organized as articles on a web page.*

4. Click the plus button or select **Book-marks ▸ Add Bookmark**. A dialog appears, as shown in Figure 36-4.

5. Click in the **RSS Bookmark Name** text box and type a descriptive name for your bookmarked RSS web page.

6. (Optional) Click the **Safari** pop-up menu and choose a location to store your bookmark, such as Bookmarks Bar or Bookmarks Menu.

7. (Optional) Click the **Mail** checkbox if you want to read RSS web pages using the Mail program.

8. Click **Add**.

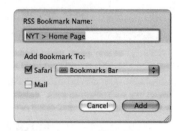

FIGURE 36-4: *A dialog lets you choose a name for your bookmarked RSS feed.*

Many larger websites, such as the *New York Times*, offer two or more RSS feeds so you can keep track of different information, such as the latest financial, entertainment, or international news. That way you only need to subscribe to the RSS feeds that interest you and ignore the ones you don't care about.

Viewing RSS Feeds

After you've bookmarked RSS feeds of your favorite websites, you can check your bookmarked RSS feeds for the number of updates or articles available. These appear as a number in parentheses, such as (6), next to the website's name on the Bookmarks Bar or Bookmarks menu.

To check and view a bookmarked RSS feed, do this:

1. Click your RSS feed bookmark either on the Bookmarks Bar or in the Bookmarks menu. Figure 36-5 shows an RSS feed bookmark on the Bookmarks menu.

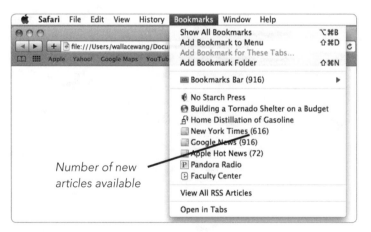

FIGURE 36-5: *A bookmarked RSS web page tells you how many new articles are available.*

2. Click the bookmarked RSS feed that you want to read. Safari displays the RSS feed as a web page.
3. Click an article to begin reading.

＊ **NOTE:** **On websites that offer RSS feeds, the Safari address box displays a Show/Hide RSS icon. When you're viewing the normal website, this RSS icon appears in white letters on a blue square (the Show RSS icon). Clicking this RSS icon displays the list of RSS feeds and displays the RSS icon as blue letters against a white background (the Hide RSS icon). Clicking this RSS icon toggles between viewing the normal website and the RSS feed web page.**

Reading RSS Feeds by Email

If you selected the Mail checkbox when you bookmarked an RSS feed, you can read RSS feeds in the Mail program. To read RSS feeds, you must first bookmark RSS feeds (see "Identifying and Bookmarking RSS Feeds" on page 335) and then specify which of those bookmarked RSS feeds you want to read.

Selecting RSS Feeds

The Mail program displays RSS feeds in the left pane under the RSS category. To add (or remove) RSS feeds to this category in the left pane, do the following:

1. Start the Mail program.
2. Select **File ▸ Add RSS Feeds**. An Add RSS Feeds dialog appears, letting you choose from a list of bookmarked RSS feeds, as shown in Figure 36-6.
3. Select the checkboxes of the RSS feeds you want to view and click **Add**. Your chosen RSS feeds appear under the RSS category of the left pane of the Mail program.

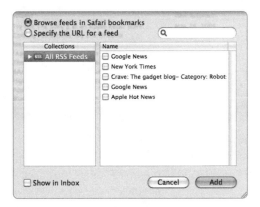

FIGURE 36-6: *The Add RSS Feeds dialog displays a list of RSS feeds you can display within the Mail program.*

Viewing and Reading RSS Feeds

After you've chosen which RSS feeds to list in the Mail program, you can choose which ones to view and which articles to read:

1. Start the Mail program. An RSS category appears in the left pane of the Mail window.
2. Click the triangle that appears to the left of the RSS category. A list of all RSS feeds appears along with a number to identify all new articles on each website.
3. Click an RSS feed. A list of RSS articles appears.
4. Click the RSS article you want to read, as shown in Figure 36-7.
5. Click the hyperlink in the RSS feed to read more.

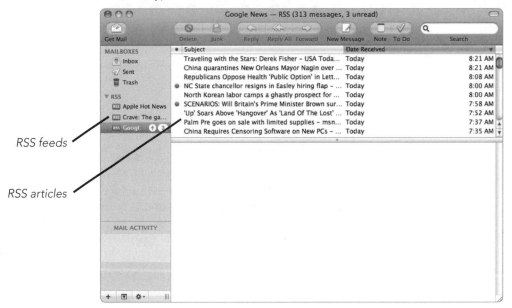

FIGURE 36-7: *The Mail program lets you read articles stored in different RSS feeds.*

Additional Ideas for RSS Feeds

Visit your favorite news sites and bookmark their RSS feeds in Safari or Mail, or try both to determine which program you find most convenient. In addition, bookmark RSS feeds from blogs, online stores (to learn about the latest sales), or movie trailer websites (so you can get a glimpse of the latest movies). If you like the idea of RSS feeds, but don't care for Safari or Mail, you should try a Web-based RSS reader, such as Netvibes (*http://www.netvibes.com/*), Google Reader (*http://www.google.com/reader*), Bloglines (*http://www.bloglines.com/*), or Pageflakes (*http://www.pageflakes.com/*).

Your time is valuable, so use RSS feeds to spend less time browsing and more time reading information on the Internet at your convenience.

37

Keeping Your Internet Activities Private

Every time you use the Internet, you risk losing your privacy. If you visit malicious websites, you risk losing your credit card number or other sensitive information to thieves. In addition, if others use your Macintosh, they can see which websites you've visited.

To protect your privacy on the Internet, you need to keep private information and your activities to yourself. Your Macintosh can help you avoid malicious websites that may trick you into giving away sensitive information and mask the websites you've browsed.

Project goals: Identify when it's safe to send credit card numbers and other sensitive information over the Internet. Wipe out all data that could show others which websites you've visited.

What You'll Be Using

To protect your Internet privacy you'll need the following:

▶   An Internet connection

▶   The Safari web browser

Identifying Safe Websites

When buying products or services over the Internet, you usually need to enter your credit card number. Unfortunately, typing anything on an Internet web page is never completely secure due to the way the Internet works.

When you connect to a website, your computer actually connects to half a dozen other computers that pass the data gathered from your input from one computer to another until the data reaches its destination. This means that anything you type can be seen and intercepted by multiple computers between you and the final destination computer that hosts the website. Think of reciting your credit card numbers to six total strangers, who then relay those numbers to a store. How safe do you think your credit card numbers might be?

When using the Internet, you should assume that anything you type can be intercepted and read by strangers unless the site that you're visiting is a secure site that uses *encryption*.

Encryption scrambles any data you type or send so that only the final receiving computer (such as a shopping website) can decipher that information. Anyone else reading encrypted data along the way will see random gibberish.

To determine whether a website uses encryption, you can do the following:

1. Click the Safari icon on the Dock. (If the Safari icon does not appear on the Dock, double-click the **Safari** icon inside the Applications folder.) The Safari window appears.
2. Visit a web page of an online shopping site, such as Amazon.com or OmahaSteaks.com. Pick an item to buy and place your order. As soon as the website asks you to enter a credit card number, look for the lock icon, as shown in Figure 37-1.

https:// identifies a secure, encrypted connection.

A descriptive website address name identifies the site that's receiving your encrypted data.

The lock (encryption) icon identifies a secure website that uses encryption.

FIGURE 37-1: *Before typing credit card numbers or other sensitive information, look at the website address and look for the lock icon to determine whether it is secure.*

3. Look at the Address text box in Safari that shows the site's complete web address. If the site is secure, the Address box should contain the URL (the *uniform resource locator*, or address) of the website itself, beginning with the characters *https://*, which stand for HyperText Transfer Protocol over SSL (Secure Socket Layer—the part that makes the site secure). If the URL

consists of random letters and numbers, as shown in Figure 37-2, you may be visiting a fraudulent website masquerading as a legitimate site. If you don't see the *https://*, the website is probably not secure and you should not enter credit card numbers or other personal information here.

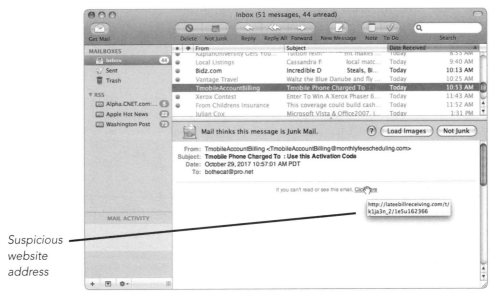

Suspicious website address

FIGURE 37-2: *Moving the pointer over a link can often reveal the actual website address, which may consist of different letters and numbers instead of a simple descriptive address.*

* **NOTE:** The larger online shopping company websites process their own credit card transactions, which means you should see the name of the company as part of the website address. Smaller online shopping websites often pay another company to process their credit card transactions. In this case, you'll see the name of a credit card processing company (such as PayPal or *www .paypal.com*) instead of the online shopping website name as part of the website address.

4. Look for the lock (encryption) icon in the upper-right corner of the Safari window. This lock icon identifies that you're connected to a secure site.
5. You are safe entering your credit card number only if you see a recognizable name in the website URL, the letters *https://* in front of the address, and the lock (encryption) icon in the upper-right corner of the Safari window.

* **NOTE:** If any one of these three items is missing, you may still be connected to a secure site, but beware. You might play it safe and shop elsewhere, research the reputation of the online shopping website, or place your order by telephone instead.

Clearing Your Internet Tracks

Every time you browse the Internet, the Safari browser stores three types of information. First, Safari tracks all websites you've visited so you can return to any previously viewed sites, as shown in Figure 37-3.

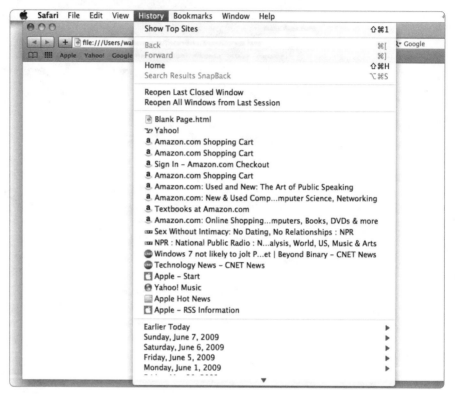

FIGURE 37-3: *Safari's History menu lists all the websites you've visited recently.*

Second, Safari stores every visited web page in a storage area called a *cache*. The cache speeds up your web browsing by retrieving web pages from its local storage, which is faster than downloading web pages off the Internet.

Finally, Safari stores any text you type into the Google search text box. For example, if you search Google for information about Apple, you might want to find all websites offering this information again a day or two later. Rather than retype the word *apple* every time you want to search, you can view a list of your past Google searches and click the *apple* search to repeat it, as shown in Figure 37-4.

FIGURE 37-4: *Safari keeps track of all your past Google searches.*

Storing your browsing history, web pages in a cache, and Google searches can make browsing faster and easier. Unfortunately, anyone with access to your Macintosh can view Safari's history to see which web pages you visited, examine its cache to see which web pages you saw, and skim through Safari's list of Google searches to see what you tried to find. If this information might prove embarrassing or just plain annoying, flush this information out of your Macintosh.

Resetting Safari

To clear this data in Safari that could reveal your behavior on the Internet, you'll need to do the following:

1. Start the Safari program. The Safari window appears.
2. Select **Safari ▸ Reset Safari**. A Reset Safari window appears, as shown in Figure 37-5.

FIGURE 37-5: *The Reset Safari window lets you reset Safari back to its original, unused state.*

3. Make sure the **Clear history**, **Empty the cache**, and **Remove all cookies** checkboxes are selected. (You can clear or leave selected the other checkboxes.)
4. Click **Reset**.

Avoiding Fraudulent Websites and Phishing Scams

Online con artists often design fake websites that look exactly like well-known sites such as sites for Apple or eBay. To avoid visiting such fraudulent websites, never visit any website address links sent to you by email unless you trust the person sending you the link. (Of course, sometimes even trusted friends can be fooled into sending you a link to a fraudulent website, so be very careful.)

Instead of clicking a link sent to you in email to open a website, type the website address yourself into the Address text box and then visit the site, or search for the site first through Google. Typing a website address yourself ensures that you're visiting the legitimate website and not a fraudulent one whose address may be spelled nearly the same (such as *www.amozon.com* instead of *www.amazon.com*). When you search for websites through Google, Google can often identify and alert you to suspicious website addresses.

Hiding Your Browsing from Others

To guard your privacy from others, lock your Macintosh away. If that's not possible, create separate accounts (see Project 16) to isolate your information from that of others. After clearing out Safari's history and cache, turn on Private Browsing to keep Safari from saving your browsing history. Here's how to turn on Private Browsing:

1. Start Safari.
2. Select **Safari ▸ Private Browsing**. A message appears, informing you that private browsing will keep Safari from maintaining its web page history, cache, or Google searches.
3. Click **OK** (or **Cancel**).

Remember that privacy may not seem important until you lose it. By taking steps to protect yourself now, you'll stay on the safe side.

38 Saving Research Information from a Web Page

Almost everyone uses the Internet to research topics for work, for school, or just for fun (so you can avoid doing anything for work or school). Of course, it's easy to find information on the Internet. The hard part is finding a way to store that information so you can find, share, and use it again.

You can print out a web page or save the page as a file to view and print out at your leisure. Both methods work, but they can be clumsy, because they often save (or print) ads or web page links that you may not want.

You can also send the information on a web page to someone else. Rather than printing the page and mailing it, or saving the page as a file and sending it as an attachment to an email message, your Macintosh lets you email web pages in one easy step.

Project goal: Make Internet research easier by saving information on web pages as separate files, web pages, or notes that you can read or listen to at your convenience.

What You'll Be Using

To save web page information and email it to someone, you'll use the following tools included with your Macintosh (assuming that you're already on the Internet):

▶   The Safari web browser

▶   The Mail program

▶   The Stickies program

Saving a Web Page as a File

You can save an interesting web page in one of the following file formats:

▸ **Page Source** Saves a web page in standard HyperText Markup Language (HTML) format that any browser can open

▸ **Web Archive** Saves a web page in a format that only Safari can open

▸ **PDF** Saves a web page in the Portable Document Format, also known as Adobe Acrobat format, which can be viewed by most computers

Saving a Web Page in Page Source (HTML) or Web Archive Format

Saving a web page as a Page Source file can be useful if you want to view a page's HTML tags to see how the web page is constructed, or if you want to share web pages with people who don't use a Macintosh. The drawback to the Page Source format is that it doesn't always save all parts or formatting of a web page; it sometimes omits certain graphics or skews the formatting so that text appears scattered instead of neatly aligned.

The Web Archive format creates a file larger than an equivalent Page Source file, but it retains a web page's formatting more accurately than Page Source. The drawback to the Web Archive format is that it displays correctly only when the Safari web browser is used to access it. If you plan to share web pages with someone who also uses Safari, the Web Archive format will display the web page more accurately than Page Source.

Here's how you save a web page in the Page Source or Web Archive format:

1. Click the Safari icon on the Dock or double-click it in the Applications folder. The Safari window appears.

2. Go to a web page that you want to save and select **File ▸ Save As**. A dialog appears, as shown in Figure 38-1.

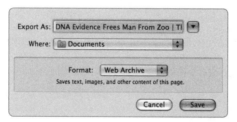

FIGURE 38-1: *The Save As dialog lets you save a web page in the Page Source or Web Archive format.*

3. (Optional) Click in the **Export As** text box and type a name for your saved web page.

4. (Optional) Click the **Where** pop-up menu arrow and choose a folder in which to store your web page.
5. (Optional) To create a folder for storing a web page, follow these additional steps:

   a. Click the arrow button that appears to the right of the **Export As** text box to expand the Save As dialog, as shown in Figure 38-2.

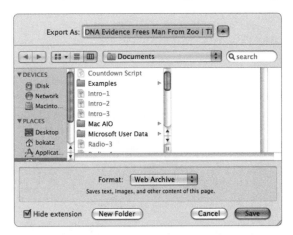

FIGURE 38-2: *Expanding the Save As dialog displays the New Folder button.*

   b. Click the folder pop-up menu at the top of the dialog and choose a location for your new folder.
   c. Click **New Folder**. A New Folder dialog appears.
   d. Type a name for your new folder and click **Create**.
6. Click the Format list box and choose **Page Source** or **Web Archive**.
7. Click **Save**.

Saving a Web Page as a PDF File

When you save web pages as PDF files, you can share them with just about anyone. The PDF files preserve the exact appearance of a web page. Here's how to save a web page as a PDF file:

1. Click the Safari icon on the Dock or double-click it in the Applications folder. The Safari window appears.
2. Go to a web page that you want to save, and select **File ▸ Print**. A Print dialog appears, as shown in Figure 38-3.
3. Click the **PDF** button in the bottom-left corner of the Print dialog. A menu appears, as shown in Figure 38-4.

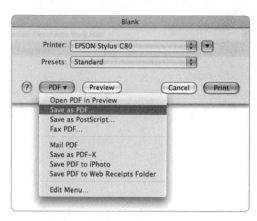

FIGURE 38-3: *The Print dialog gives you a choice of printing a web page or saving it as a PDF file.*

FIGURE 38-4: *Clicking the PDF button displays a menu of additional options.*

4. Select **Save as PDF**. A Save dialog appears, as shown in Figure 38-5.
5. (Optional) Click in the **Save As** text box and type a name for your web page.
6. (Optional) Click the **Where** pop-up menu and choose a folder in which to store your PDF file.
7. (Optional) Click in the **Title**, **Author**, **Subject**, and **Keywords** text boxes and type any information you want to save in those text boxes.
8. Click **Save**.

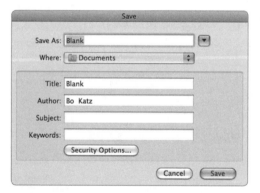

FIGURE 38-5: *The Save dialog displays text boxes for identifying your PDF file.*

※ **NOTE:** Did you notice the Security Options button in the Save dialog? If you click this button, a Security Options dialog appears. Enter a password here to protect your PDF file so that it can be opened only with a password. This feature can be handy to protect sensitive documents from prying eyes.

Emailing a Web Page

After you save a web page as a file, you can send that file as an attachment to an email message. You can also email a web page via the Mail program directly from Safari, without saving it first. When you email a web page, you can send it as a link or embed it into your email message.

✱ **NOTE: If you haven't set up Mail yet, or don't use Mail to manage your email, this will not work. For instructions on configuring Mail, see Project 43.**

The disadvantage of sending a page as a link is that websites often change, which could break the link (that is, the address of the link to the page you are trying to send may change). So if someone tries to view a broken link, he or she will see an error message instead of the intended web page.

The disadvantage of sending an entire web page embedded as part of your message is that it increases the size of your message. In addition, some people filter their email to block messages that contain graphics (to avoid junk email), which means your message may not get through the filter.

Emailing an Entire Web Page

Here's how to email a web page:

1. Click the Safari icon on the Dock or double-click it in the Applications folder. The Safari window appears.
2. Go to a web page that you want to send.
3. Select **File ▸ Mail Contents of This Page**. The Mail window appears and displays the web page as part of your message, as shown in Figure 38-6.

FIGURE 38-6: *Embedding a web page into a message ensures that the recipient will see the web page you're sending.*

4. Click in the **To** text box and type an email address.
5. Click **Send**.

Emailing a Link to a Web Page

Here's how to email a link to a web page:

1. Click the Safari icon on the Dock or double-click it in the Applications folder. The Safari window appears.
2. Go to a web page that you want to share.
3. Select **File ▸ Mail Link to This Page**. The Mail window appears and displays the link to the web page.
4. Click in the **To** text box and type an email address.
5. Click **Send**.

Saving a Web Page as a Note

When you save a web page, you also save all graphics displayed on that page, including borders, ads, and pictures. To save only the text on the web page, without all of the extra stuff, you have two options:

▸ Save the web page text as a note in the Mail program.

▸ Save the web page text as a sticky note using the Stickies program.

Saving a Web Page as a Note in the Mail Program

Besides letting you send and receive messages, the Mail program also lets you store notes. To save a web page as a note in the Mail program:

1. Click the Safari icon on the Dock or double-click it in the Applications folder. The Safari window appears.
2. Go to a web page that contains text you want to save.
3. Select the text that you want to save.
4. Select **Safari ▸ Services ▸ Make New Mail Note**, as shown in Figure 38-7. Your selected text appears as a note in the Mail program.

FIGURE 38-7: *You can choose to save selected text as a Mail note.*

Saving Web Page Text as a Sticky Note

Since we typically read only part of a web page, why not save just part of a page rather than the entire text? You could, of course, copy and paste the text from a page into your favorite word processor, but it's much cooler to copy and paste text directly into the Stickies program that comes with your Macintosh.

The advantage to storing and viewing text using sticky notes is that the text appears in a tiny window that makes it easy to see without covering up the rest of your screen, as shown in Figure 38-8. That way, you can see your sticky note at the same time you are using any program, such as a word processor, web browser, or spreadsheet.

FIGURE 38-8: *Sticky notes can remain on the screen even while you use another program.*

To save text as a sticky note, do the following:

1. Click the Safari icon on the Dock or double-click it in the Applications folder. The Safari window appears.
2. Go to a web page and select the text you want to save.
3. Select **Safari ▸ Services ▸ Make New Sticky Note**. The selected text appears in a sticky note window, as shown in Figure 38-9.
4. (Optional) Select **Note ▸ Floating Window** to add a checkmark and keep your sticky note visible on the screen at all times.
5. (Optional) Select **Note ▸ Translucent Window** to make your sticky note translucent so you can see programs running underneath it, as shown in Figure 38-9. (Keep in mind that this may make the text on your sticky note difficult to read.)

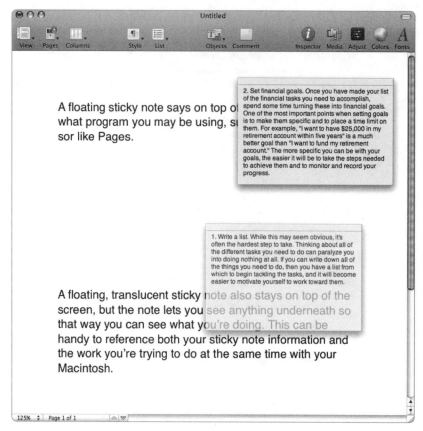

FIGURE 38-9: Floating sticky notes stay visible at all times. Floating, translucent sticky notes stay visible but let you see through them.

＊ **NOTE:** To remove sticky notes from view, select Stickies ▸ Quit Stickies, or click a floating sticky note and choose Note ▸ Floating Window to remove the checkmark from the Floating Window option.

Listening to Text on a Web Page

The Internet can contain a vast amount of information, but all of it will be useless if you can't read it due to poor vision or eyestrain. Rather than force yourself to read a computer screen, you might choose to have your Macintosh read an article to you instead. Here's how to hear your Macintosh read text:

1. Click the Safari icon on the Dock or double-click it in the Applications folder. The Safari window appears.
2. Go to a web page and select the text you want your Macintosh to read.
3. Select **Safari ▸ Services ▸ Speech ▸ Add to iTunes as Spoken Track**.

After you have saved text as a spoken track, you can listen to it by doing this:

1. Load iTunes.
2. Click the Spoken Text playlist under the Playlists category.
3. Click the track (generically titled *Text to Speech*) and click the **Play** button to hear iTunes read your selected text.

Your Mac will use the default voice to read your selected text. If you want to choose a different voice, do this:

1. Click the Apple menu and choose **System Preferences**. The System Preferences window appears.
2. Click the **Speech** icon under the System category. The Speech window appears.
3. Click the **Text to Speech** tab, as shown in Figure 38-10.
4. Click the **System Voice** pop-up menu and select a different default voice.
5. Click the close button on the Speech window to make it disappear.

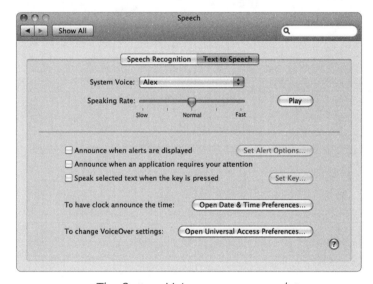

FIGURE 38-10: *The System Voice pop-up menu lets you select a different default voice.*

Additional Ideas for Researching on the Internet

With so many ways to save information off the Internet, you'll always be able to organize information to access it again and again. For maximum flexibility, you can combine several features.

For example, if you like to skim the latest news, visit your favorite web pages and save text from web pages as notes in the Mail or Stickies programs. Then select **Add to iTunes as Spoken Track**. Now you'll be able to read along while hearing your Mac read the text back to you. This can be especially fun to do with young children to help them learn to read, or it can be helpful as a way to read text and then refresh your memory later by listening to the text read aloud.

By saving your research as audio files or as sticky notes, you'll never lose a valuable tidbit of Internet information again. With a Macintosh, you'll not only have fun doing research on the Internet, but you'll always have the information you've dug up at your fingertips when you need it.

39

Creating an Electronic Clipping Service for Web Pages

In the old days, we suffered from information overload from the flood of newspapers and magazines that we never had time to finish reading. Rather than having to wade through all of those publications ourselves, we could hire clipping services that would scan newspapers and magazines for articles on specific topics and then send those clippings to us for a fee. Such services filtered out news so we could focus only on the information we wanted.

Nowadays, information overload comes not only from newspapers and magazines, but from Internet sites as well. With the Internet, you can retrieve information almost in real time—including stock market data, sports scores, traffic updates, and headline news flashes.

One way to keep up with rapidly changing information is to load various web pages and glance at them periodically, at your convenience. But you may want to view only part of a web page and not the entire thing—for example, if you're tracking baseball scores, you may want to watch only the scores of the New York Yankees or the Los Angeles Dodgers, but not the scores of any other teams.

To view only the part of a web page that contains the information you want, you can use Web Clips. *Web Clips* let you select a part of a web page that displays rapidly changing information so you can view it periodically while you're busy working on your computer. Instead of having to view an entire web page to look for the information you want, you can use Web Clips to see only the parts of a page that interest you.

Project goal: Create an electronic clipping service to display information that changes frequently on web pages and show you only the information that interests you.

What You'll Be Using

To clip web pages and view those Web Clips, you'll use the following on your Macintosh:

▶ An Internet connection

▶ The Safari web browser

▶ Dashboard

Clipping a Web Page

Your first step is to find a web page that displays interesting information that will likely change, such as a news site. Once you clip part of a web page, you can later view your Web Clip using Dashboard.

To create a Web Clip, follow these steps:

1. Click the Safari icon on the Dock. (If the Safari icon does not appear on the Dock, you can double-click the icon in the Applications folder.) The Safari window appears.
2. Find a web page that displays frequently changing information, such as sports scores or headline news.
3. Select **File ▸ Open in Dashboard** or click the Web Clip button. (The Web Clip button displays scissors and a dotted rectangle icon in the upper-left corner of the Safari window.) The entire web page darkens, except for a rectangular area, as shown in Figure 39-1.

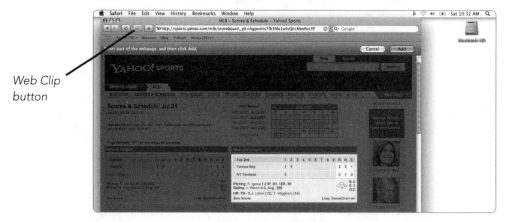

Web Clip button

FIGURE 39-1: *Web Clips highlight different parts of a web page based on where you move the mouse pointer.*

4.   Move the mouse pointer over the part of the web page you want to view, and click the mouse button. Handles appear around your selection, as shown in Figure 39-2.

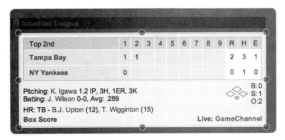

FIGURE 39-2: *Handles let you select the exact portion of a web page you want to save as a Web Clip.*

5.   (Optional) To expand or shrink the area of the Web Clip, move the mouse pointer over a handle, hold down the mouse button, and drag (move) the mouse.

6.   Click the **Add** button near the upper-right corner of the Safari window. After a few seconds, Dashboard displays your Web Clip in a tiny window, called a *widget*, as shown in Figure 39-3.

FIGURE 39-3: *Web Clips appear as Dashboard widgets.*

7.   (Optional) To move a Web Clip, move the mouse pointer over the Web Clip, hold down the mouse button, and drag (move) the mouse to move the Web Clip to wherever you want it to appear on the screen.

8. Press F12, click the Dashboard icon on the Dock, or click any open space on the screen (not on any Dashboard widget). This will hide all Dashboard widgets (including your Web Clips) from view.

Viewing a Web Clip

You can create as many Web Clips as you want. After you've created one or more Web Clips, you can periodically view all Dashboard widgets (including your Web Clips) by doing one of the following:

1. Press F12.
2. Click the Dashboard icon on the Dock.

Changing the Appearance of a Web Clip

Just for fun, you can make the border of your Web Clip appear in different styles or themes, such as a Pegboard or Deckled Edge. Changing the theme of a Web Clip doesn't change its contents, but it can make the Web Clip more visually interesting and satisfy your own aesthetic.

To change the theme of a Web Clip, follow these steps:

1. Press F12 (or click the Dashboard icon on the Dock) to open Dashboard and display your Web Clips.
2. Click the Inspector button (which looks like a letter *i* in the bottom-right corner of the Web Clip widget). The Web Clip widget twirls around to show you the themes available, as shown in Figure 39-4.
3. Click a theme (such as Deckled Edge) and click **Done**. Your Web Clip now appears in your chosen theme.

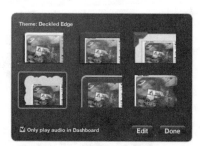

FIGURE 39-4: *You can customize the appearance of a Web Clip by choosing a different theme.*

Deleting a Web Clip

Most Web Clips will display information that you want to view only temporarily, such as the latest game scores of your favorite sport. Once a particular game is over, you'll probably want to delete this Web Clip since you won't need to keep staring at the same information. When you want to get rid of a Web Clip, follow these steps:

1. Press F12 (or click the Dashboard icon on the Dock) to open Dashboard and display your Web Clips.
2. Click the cross inside the circle button that appears in the bottom-left corner of the screen. Dashboard displays a close button—a little *X* inside a circle—in the upper-left corner of every Dashboard widget, including your Web Clips, as shown in Figure 39-5.
3. Click the close button of the Web Clip you no longer want to see. The Web Clip disappears.

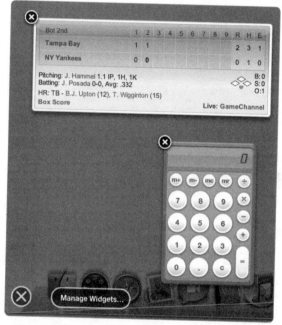

FIGURE 39-5: *Close icons appear on every Dashboard widget, including your Web Clips.*

Additional Ideas for Web Clips

Web Clips can be used to track any type of information that changes on a web page. Create a Web Clip of game scores so you can track your favorite team. Make a Web Clip of an eBay auction to keep track of bids as a deadline approaches. Visit a traffic route website and use a Web Clip to keep you informed on which highways may be the least congested when you want to find the fastest route somewhere, like going back home from work.

To save space, many news sites such as AOL (*http://www.aol.com/*) display a handful of top news stories as a constantly changing slideshow of pictures and links. By capturing this slideshow portion of the top headline news, you can keep up with the latest events and click a link in a Web Clip to open Safari and view the complete web page if you want.

Capture your favorite blog in a Web Clip so you can see updates as a Dash-board widget. If you're expecting a friend or relative to visit, you can capture a Web Clip of a flight's estimated arrival time from the airline's website so you can tell at a glance whether the flight is on time, late, or cancelled.

If you're a hard-core Macintosh fanatic, you can even visit a Macintosh rumor site, such as MacRumors (*http://www.macrumors.com/*), which often provides live coverage of conferences when Apple announces a new product. This live coverage provides up-to-the-minute updates as the conference occurs, so you can keep track of the latest iPhone or iMac announcements if you can't attend the conference in person.

Think of Web Clips as a way to turn your Macintosh into a personal news clipping service. As shown in Figure 39-6, Web Clips let you choose and view only the information that's most important to you from any number of websites.

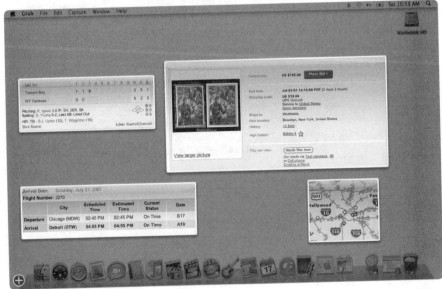

FIGURE 39-6: *Web Clips can show you multiple clips from completely different websites at a glance.*

40 | Watching Video on Any Website

Many websites offer video that you can watch on your computer. Unfortunately, every website offers video stored in different file formats. To view video stored in different file formats, you need to download and install special video player programs that know how to play particular video files.

Four types of video file formats are most commonly used on websites:

► Flash

► QuickTime

► RealVideo

► Windows Media

The Macintosh can recognize and play videos stored in Flash or QuickTime formats. However, some websites store video in RealVideo or Windows Media formats, which means you can't view those videos until you download and install a player that can recognize and play RealVideo or Windows Media files.

Project goal: Download and install video player programs so you can view any videos on any website.

What You'll Be Using

To view all types of videos on the Internet, you'll be using the following:

► The Safari web browser

► An Internet connection

Downloading and Installing RealPlayer

To add sound and video to websites, a company called RealNetworks created its own audio and video file formats called *RealAudio* and *RealVideo*, respectively. Like nearly all audio and video files available over the Internet, both RealAudio and RealVideo file formats compress large files with little noticeable loss in audio or video quality. By compressing large audio and video files into smaller files, Real-Audio and RealVideo allow web pages to download audio and video files quickly onto your computer. Since RealAudio and RealVideo were two of the first popular audio/video file formats available over the Internet, a handful of websites still offer only RealAudio and RealVideo files.

To play these files, you need to download the RealPlayer program. Here's how to download and install the RealPlayer program for playing audio and video files stored in RealAudio and RealVideo file formats:

1. Start Safari and visit the RealNetworks website at *http://www.real.com/*. The RealNetworks website appears.
2. Click the **Get RealPlayer Free** button.

∗ **NOTE:** Make sure you click the Free button. You'll also see a version of Real-Player that offers more features, but it costs money, so click the Free button to download and install the free version. You can install a trial version of the not-free program, but you'll be able to use it only for a limited time; then you'll have to pay for it.

3. Click **Download**. The Down-loads window appears.
4. Double-click the **RealPlayer** icon in the Downloads window. A dialog appears, asking if you want to configure RealPlayer.
5. Click **Configure**.

After you've installed RealPlayer on your Macintosh, you can view any video and audio files stored in RealVideo and RealAudio file formats, as shown in Figure 40-1.

FIGURE 40-1: RealPlayer lets you view videos on the Internet.

Downloading and Installing Flip4Mac

Every Macintosh comes with a copy of the QuickTime player, which is meant to play QuickTime, MPEG, AVI, and many other types of video file formats, but not Windows Media files. To watch video stored in the Windows Media format, you have two choices: You can download and install a free program called Flip4Mac, or you can download and install an old version of Windows Media Player for Mac.

To make the QuickTime Player play Windows Media files, you need to download and install Flip4Mac, shown in Figure 40-2.

Here's how to download and install Flip4Mac:

FIGURE 40-2: *The Flip4Mac program lets the QuickTime player view Windows Media Videos (WMVs).*

1. Start Safari and visit Microsoft's website at *http://www.telestream.net/ flip4mac-wmv/overview.htm*. The Flip4Mac website appears.
2. Click the **Free download** button. Another web page appears, explaining all the details about the Flip4Mac program.
3. Click the **Download** button. A Downloads window appears.
4. Double-click the **Flip4Mac** icon in the Downloads window to install the program.

Downloading and Installing Windows Media Player for Mac

Occasionally, a website may not recognize Flip4Mac when playing WMV files. If you have installed Flip4Mac and still can't view WMVs, you may have to resort to installing the Windows Media Player for Mac.

✻ **NOTE:** **Microsoft has stopped developing the Windows Media Player for Mac, so you will still need the Flip4Mac video player to view newer versions of WMVs.**

Here's how to download and install Windows Media Player for Mac:

1. Start Safari and visit Microsoft's website at *http://www.microsoft.com/windows/windowsmedia/player/mac/mp9/default.aspx*. The Windows Media Player for Mac OS website appears.
2. Click the **Download Now** button.

The Windows Media Player for Mac appears in your Downloads folder as a *.sitx* compressed file. To uncompress this *.sitx* file, you need to download and install the free StuffIt Expander program (if you haven't done so already) at *http://my.smithmicro.com/mac/stuffit/expander.html*. Then double-click the .sitx file to uncompress and install the Windows Media Player for Mac program.

Additional Ideas for Watching Videos on the Internet

After you have installed RealPlayer and Flip4Mac (or RealPlayer, Flip4Mac, and Windows Media Player for Mac), you'll be able to view video on any website in the world. To ensure that you will be able to view any video on your Macintosh, you might also want to download the free VLC Media Player (*http://www.videolan.org/*).

Some popular video sites include YouTube (*http://www.youtube.com/*), AOL Video (*http://video.aol.com/*), and Yahoo! Video (*http://video.search.yahoo.com/*), all of which store video in the Flash file format. By browsing through these video sites, you can see unusual events (such as a man juggling while surfing), comedy skits (such as people parodying Britney Spears or Paris Hilton), or interesting clips that people have captured (such as a lion fighting an alligator over a gazelle).

Most news websites offer video clips of the latest stories. To view these videos, visit your favorite news network such as CNN (*http://www.cnn.com/*), FoxNews (*http://www.foxnews.com/*), CBS News (*http://www.cbsnews.com/*), MSNBC (*http://www.msnbc.msn.com/*), or ABC News (*http://abcnews.go.com/*).

To watch international news broadcasts, visit the following sites:

▶   Voice of America (*http://www.voanews.com/*)

▶   BBC News (*http://news.bbc.co.uk/*)

▶   MTA International (*http://www.mta.tv/*)

▶   Channel NewsAsia (*http://www.channelnewsasia.com/*)

▶   TV5Monde (*http://www.tv5.org/*)

▶   Deutsche Welle (*http://www.dw-world.de/*)

▶   RTR-Planetra (*http://www.rtrplaneta.com/*)

▶   CCTV (*http://www.cctv.com/*)

▶   RAI International (*http://www.international.rai.it/*)

▶   NHK (*http://www.nhk.or.jp/*)

International news websites tend to offer video in a variety of file formats, including Flash, RealVideo, and Windows Media, so you'll need to make sure you have RealPlayer, Flip4Mac, or Windows Media Player for Mac installed on your computer before you can watch the videos stored on these websites.

With so many videos to watch from all over the world, you can see something interesting, educational, or entertaining without once having to turn on the TV. Using your Macintosh and an Internet connection, you can peek into the world around you from the safety of your home and your Macintosh computer.

41

Expanding Your Mind by Listening to Free College Lectures

Sometimes listening to the same tunes in your music collection can get old. For variety, you could listen to Internet radio stations, but even that can get tiresome after a while. Rather than use iTunes to listen to music, you might want to expand your mind by using iTunes to listen to college lectures.

Normally, the only way to listen to college lectures is to attend classes, which can be both expensive and time consuming. Fortunately, with your Macintosh and a copy of the iTunes program, both of these barriers no longer exist, because iTunes lets you listen to recordings of college lectures on a variety of topics from different universities. Want to learn about biology, sociology, computer science, or business management? Just run iTunes and listen to lectures from such well-known universities as the Massachusetts Institute of Technology (MIT), Texas A&M, Stanford University, and the University of California, Berkeley, through a free service called iTunes U.

Universities voluntarily record and store audio and video recordings of lectures on specific subjects and post these audio and video recordings in the iTunes Store for anyone to download, copy, and listen to or watch for free. While you won't get any college credit or earn a degree, you just might get a little bit smarter, and you won't have to take final exams or pay tuition. The two basic steps required for getting a free college education are:

1. Find and download a lecture from iTunes U.
2. Listen to your chosen lectures with iTunes.

Project goal: Use iTunes U to expand your mind by listening to free lectures presented by professors from universities around the world.

What You'll Be Using

To find free recordings of college lectures, you'll need to use the following:

▶ An Internet connection

▶ The iTunes program

Choosing a College in iTunes U

The iTunes U category lists all the universities that offer free lectures on various topics. Not every university offers lectures through iTunes U, but more universities are joining all the time, and the participating universities continue to add new lectures on different topics. With so many universities offering lectures through iTunes U, you're sure to find an interesting lecture if you look hard enough.

To find a college in the iTunes U category, follow these steps:

1. Click the iTunes icon on the Dock. (If the iTunes icon is not visible, double-click the **iTunes** icon in the Applications folder.) The iTunes window appears.
2. Click **iTunes Store** under the Store category in the left pane of the iTunes window.
3. Click **iTunes U** under the iTunes Store pane, as shown in Figure 41-1.

FIGURE 41-1: The iTunes U category displays a list of universities that offer free lectures.

4. Click a category, such as Find Education Provider or Featured Providers. A list of classes or schools appears, as shown in Figure 41-2.

FIGURE 41-2: *Every university offers multiple topics of study, which are divided into multiple lectures.*

5.   Click a course. (You may have to click several links until you find a list of audio files you can download, as shown in Figure 41-3.)

FIGURE 41-3: *Lectures appear as audio tracks.*

6.   Find a lecture you want to hear and click the **Get** button. After a few moments (depending on how fast your Internet connection may be), your chosen lecture appears in the Playlists category in the left pane of the iTunes window.

Listening to Downloaded Lectures

Each time you download a lecture, iTunes stores it in a playlist named after the university where you downloaded the file. Some lectures are audio files while others include video as well. To listen to or watch a lecture, follow these steps:

1. Click the iTunes icon on the Dock. (If the iTunes icon is not visible, double-click the **iTunes** icon in the Applications folder.) The iTunes window appears.
2. Click the university playlist to view all the audio lectures you've downloaded. A list of audio tracks appears.
3. Select (or clear) the checkboxes of the lectures you want to hear, as shown in Figure 41-4.
4. Click the play button.

FIGURE 41-4: To hear a lecture, check its checkbox.

Additional Ideas for Listening to Lectures

Listening to free college lectures can help you learn the latest developments in a particular field, refresh your memory on a topic you studied previously, expose you to new ideas taught from someone else's perspective, and give you an alternative to listening to the same collection of digital music files over and over again.

If you're currently in college, listening to lectures from other professors in other universities can help you learn even more about a specific subject by reinforcing different concepts. If you're not currently attending college, listening to college lectures can be a pleasant diversion to help you keep your mind active while you explore a new field from the convenience of your Macintosh computer.

With free access to some of the best minds in the country, you should take advantage of this unique learning opportunity made available by iTunes.

42

Listening to News, Music, and Talk Shows over the Internet

No matter how much you love the songs in your music collection, you'll probably get tired of listening to the same tunes all the time. You could keep expanding your collection, but that can get expensive. If you're like me, no matter how much music you have, sooner or later you'll crave something new and different. Fortunately, this problem is easy to solve. To hear something new, you can tune into an Internet radio station.

Internet radio stations are similar to ordinary radio stations, except they play streaming audio that can be heard only through the Internet. Ordinary radio stations are limited in number because they share limited radio air waves, but Internet radio stations have no such limitations. As a result, you'll find an almost unlimited number of Internet stations, catering to all sorts of tastes—whether it be Beatles music, foreign language instruction, or investing—24 hours a day. With such a wide variety of Internet radio stations available, you're sure to hear something you like.

Many Internet and traditional radio stations feature talk shows with interviews of interesting guests or discussions of specific topics such as real estate investing or New Age thinking. Since many people aren't able to hear these shows when they're originally broadcast (either due to time constraints or because they're out of range), radio stations often record their shows and store them as audio files known as *podcasts*. You can download podcasts and play them on your iPod or your Macintosh at your convenience.

Project goal: Explore and listen to free Internet radio stations and podcasts offering everything from music and talk show interviews to inspirational speeches and educational seminars.

What You'll Be Using

To listen to Internet radio stations and podcasts, you'll need the following:

▶ An Internet connection

▶ The iTunes program

Finding and Listening to an Internet Radio Station

The iTunes program, included with every Macintosh, can play audio CDs and files of your favorite music. However, iTunes is more than just an audio player. When you connect to the Internet, you can also use iTunes to find and connect to Internet radio stations worldwide.

Many Internet radio stations offer commercial-free alternatives to traditional radio stations, so you can listen to your favorite music, from hip hop to classical, 24 hours a day. You can also explore other music genres such as country, jazz, folk, dance, Latino, blues, or electronic.

Internet radio stations also offer tons of talk shows. Whether you're conservative or liberal, you can listen to talk shows geared to your particular point of view. You can tune into an Internet radio station located outside the United States and listen to music and talk shows in nearly any language. If you need a laugh or two, tune into an all-comedy Internet radio station and listen to humorous songs, interviews with your favorite comic, and audio clips of your favorite stand-up comedian's performances.

If you like classic rock, look for an Internet radio station that plays music from the '50s or '60s (or older if you like) so you can transport yourself to that time period. Some Internet radio stations even play nothing but old radio shows such as *Buck Rogers*, *Hopalong Cassidy*, or *Amos & Andy*. Some intersperse recordings of old radio shows with historical news broadcasts so you can hear news stories from the past. Relive the horror of the *Hindenburg* explosion or listen to the first news broadcast announcing the sinking of the *Titanic*. By listening to old radio broadcasts, you can make history come alive in ways that reading a history textbook can never do.

Check out these Internet radio stations for a trip back in time: ACB Radio Treasure Trove (*http://www.acbradio.org/treasure-trove.html*), AM 1710 Antioch (*http://radio.macinmind.com/*), Mystery Play I-Radio (*http://www.mystery-otr .com/*), and Ripley Retro Radio (*http://www.ripleys.com/retro-radio.php*), all under the Talk/Spoken Word category.

To tune into an Internet radio station, follow these steps:

1. Click the iTunes icon on the Dock. (If you can't find the iTunes icon on the Dock, double-click the **iTunes** icon in the Applications folder.) The iTunes window appears.

2. Click **Radio** under the Library category in the left pane. The right pane displays a list of radio station categories.

3. Click the triangle that appears to the left of your chosen category. The category expands and displays specific stations, as shown in Figure 42-1.
4. Click a radio station name.
5. Click the play button or press the spacebar to listen to the Internet radio station you chose.

FIGURE 42-1: *The iTunes Radio category displays a list of free Internet radio stations.*

✳ *NOTE:* **Some Internet radio stations offer two identical stations, each broadcasting at a different bit rate. For example, for high-speed Internet connections such as cable or DSL, a radio station may broadcast at 96 Kilobits per second (kbps), while for dial-up Internet connections, that same radio station may offer a slower 32 kbps broadcast. Choose the higher bit rate if you have a fast Internet connection and want to hear higher quality audio. Choose the lower bit rate if you have a slower Internet connection.**

Saving Internet Radio Stations in a Playlist

By exploring the many Internet radio stations available, you're sure to find a handful that you'll want to hear regularly. Rather than dig through the Radio category in the iTunes window each time you want to listen to a favorite station, you can save your favorites in a playlist. Then you can open your playlist and click the station you want to hear.

Here's how to create a playlist of your favorite Internet radio stations:

1. Click the iTunes icon on the Dock or double-click the **iTunes** icon in the Applications folder. The iTunes window appears.
2. Select **File ▸ New Playlist**. An untitled playlist appears under the Playlists category in the left pane of the iTunes window.
3. Type a descriptive name for your playlist, such as Radio Stations.

4. Click **Radio** under the Library category in the left pane. The right pane displays a list of radio station categories.
5. Click the triangle that appears to the left of your chosen category. The category expands and displays specific stations.
6. Move the mouse over an Internet radio station, hold down the mouse button, and then drag (move) the mouse over your playlist in the left pane of the iTunes window. When your playlist is highlighted, release the mouse button to store the Internet radio station in your playlist.

✱ *NOTE:* **You can create multiple playlists to store your favorite Internet radio stations. For example, you might create one playlist to store music radio stations and a second playlist for your favorite talk shows.**

Listening to Internet Radio Stations in a Playlist

Once you've stored radio stations in a playlist, selecting a station is easy:

1. Click the iTunes icon on the Dock, or double-click the icon in the Applications folder. The iTunes window appears.
2. Click your radio station playlist under the Playlists category in the left pane of the iTunes window. A list of your saved radio stations appears.
3. Click the radio station you want to hear, and then click the play button or press the spacebar.

Deleting an Internet Radio Station from a Playlist

If you want to remove a radio station in your playlist, you can delete it. (You can always add it back to that playlist later.) Follow these steps:

1. Click the iTunes icon on the Dock, or double-click the icon in the Applications folder. The iTunes window appears.
2. Click your radio station playlist under the Playlists category in the left pane of the iTunes window. A list of your saved radio stations appears.
3. Click the radio station you want to delete.
4. Choose **Edit ▸ Delete**. The radio station disappears from your playlist.

✱ *NOTE:* **You can also right-click a radio station and choose Delete from the shortcut menu.**

Finding Podcasts

You can access two basic types of podcasts: audio and video. Audio podcasts are usually recorded shows—typically popular radio talk shows such as National Public Radio's *Car Talk* or *Fresh Air* programs. However, many podcasts offer interviews or discussions that have never been broadcast. Others offer tutorials on topics such as meditation or foreign languages.

Video podcasts are like miniature TV shows. Their length can range from a few minutes to an hour or more. Many video podcasts are excerpts from television shows originally broadcast on networks such as the Discovery Channel or MSNBC. Others are self-contained shows such as sketch comedy shows (similar to *Saturday Night Live*), motivational speeches or sermons, and tutorials for improving your Photoshop skills or your golf swing.

Here's how to find an audio or video podcast:

1. Click the iTunes icon on the Dock, or double-click the icon in the Applications folder. The iTunes window appears.

2. Click **iTunes Store** under the Store category in the left pane of the iTunes window. The iTunes Store main page appears, as shown in Figure 42-2.

FIGURE 42-2: *The iTunes Store page displays the Podcasts category.*

3. Click **Podcasts** in the iTunes Store category. The iTunes Store displays several podcast categories, as shown in Figure 42-3:

    ▶ **Categories**   Lists groups of podcasts available, such as Arts, Health, Kids & Family, Music, or Technology. Search this group to find every available podcast.

    ▶ **Highlights**   Displays three tabs: What's Hot, New Audio, and New Video. This group can show you the newest podcasts available.

    ▶ **Featured Providers**   Lists popular and well-known producers of podcasts such as ABC News, Business Week, Comedy Central, and HBO.

    ▶ **Featured Video Podcasts**   Displays tabs organizing different video podcasts into groups such as Sports, Comedy, or Music. Search this group first to find a video podcast.

FIGURE 42-3: *The iTunes Store offers podcasts in several categories.*

4.   Click a selection in one of the podcast categories, such as a selection in Categories or Featured Providers. The iTunes window displays a list of various podcasts in your chosen category, as shown in Figure 42-4.

FIGURE 42-4: *The News & Politics podcast category provides a variety of specific podcasts from which to choose.*

5.   Click a podcast. The iTunes window displays a list of files for your chosen podcast, as shown in Figure 42-5.

6.   Click an audio file, and click the play button or press the spacebar to hear or see the podcast.

7.   (Optional) Click the **Get Episode** button for each podcast file you want to download and save to your Macintosh. By saving a podcast file to your computer, you can listen to or watch it at your convenience, or you can transfer it to your iPod.

FIGURE 42-5: *Podcasts often provide multiple files from which to choose.*

∗ **NOTE:** **If you click the Subscribe button for a podcast, iTunes will download all future episodes of the chosen podcast. That way, the latest episode of your favorite podcast will be available every time you connect to the Internet.**

Listening to Saved Podcasts

If you've saved podcasts by clicking the Get Episode button on one or more podcasts, your podcasts appear in the Podcasts category in the left pane of the iTunes window. To hear a podcast:

1.   Click the iTunes icon on the Dock, or double-click the icon in the Applications folder. The iTunes window appears.

2.   Click **Podcasts** under the Library category in the left pane of the iTunes window. A list of all saved podcasts appears in the right pane, as shown in Figure 42-6.

FIGURE 42-6: Podcasts appear organized as thumbnail images.

3. Double-click a podcast. A list of available podcast episodes appears, as shown in Figure 42-7.
4. Click the podcast file you want to hear, and then click the play button or press the spacebar. The iTunes program plays your podcast.

FIGURE 42-7: You can view all of the podcast episodes that you have downloaded.

Additional Ideas for Listening to Radio Stations and Podcasts

You can listen to your favorite talk radio show podcasts at your convenience. But you can do much more: how about using podcasts to learn a foreign language? You can visit the Education category in the iTunes Store Categories directory to download audio podcasts of foreign language lessons. Now you can hear and learn from native speakers in Spanish, Chinese, Arabic, French, and Japanese, as shown in Figure 42-8.

FIGURE 42-8: *The Education category offers a variety of foreign language lessons for free.*

Browse the Government & Organizations category in the iTunes Store Categories directory to find audio and video podcasts from the White House, the Pentagon, or the United Nations, as shown in Figure 42-9.

The News & Politics category of the iTunes Store Categories directory offers video podcasts from major news outlets such as ABC World News or BBC Radio News, as shown in Figure 42-10. You can listen only to those news stories that interest you and skip over the rest.

Browse through the Music category of the iTunes Store Categories directory to download music (for a small fee) and watch music videos of your favorite artists.

FIGURE 42-9: *Listen to government news and propaganda direct from the government's media outlets.*

FIGURE 42-10: *Major news media sources such as NBC News offer segments of their broadcasts as video podcasts.*

With so many different Internet radio stations and types of podcasts from which to choose, you'll never run out of great listening, no matter what type of music or topic interests you. With free access to Internet radio stations and podcasts from around the world, iTunes can turn your Macintosh into a full-fledged stereo, television, and education center.

43 Setting Up an Email Account

One of the most popular uses for the Internet is email, with which you can send and receive messages from people all over the world, absolutely free. When you pay for Internet access through an Internet service provider (ISP), you'll get an email account, which lets you send and receive email.

Many email accounts let you read and write messages through any web browser, such as Safari. However, you can also use a special email program to retrieve, read, and compose your email messages. To help you use email, every Macintosh comes with a free email program called Mail.

Project goal: Set up the Mail program to work with your email account.

What You'll Be Using

To set up an account to read and write email on your Macintosh, you'll need the following:

▶   The Mail program

▶   Email information from the company running your email account (such as an ISP)

Getting Your Email Account Information

When you sign up for Internet access through an ISP, you may receive a starter pack that lists the information needed to create and set up an email account on your computer. If not, get a piece of paper, contact the company responsible for running your email account (such as your ISP), and write down the following information:

▶ **Your email address** You can choose the first part of your email address, but the last part always contains the name of the company running your email account, such as *Bill@aol.com* or *JuneAllison@earthlink.net*. When you sign up with an ISP, you may need to specify a username, which your ISP will use to create your email account. You may have the option of creating additional email accounts as well.

▶ **Your password** You can choose your own password, but your email provider may have created an initial password for your account to help you get started.

▶ **The name of the computer that retrieves your email (often called a POP, IMAP, or Exchange server)** You must get this information from the company running your email account, such as your ISP. The server name is often as simple as the word *pop* or *mail* followed by the email company's name, such as *pop.ISP.net* or *mail.ISP.net*.

▶ **The name of the computer that sends out your email (often called an SMTP server)** You must get this information from the company running your email account. The server name is often as simple as the phrase *smtp* or *mail* followed by the ISP name, such as *smtp.ISP.net* or *mail.ISP.net*.

✳ *NOTE:* **If you don't know your email address, password, POP, IMAP, Exchange server name, or SMTP server name, you won't be able to retrieve your email using the Mail program. If you have a free email account (such as through Yahoo!), you may not be able to retrieve messages using a separate email program unless you pay an additional fee.**

Configuring the Mail Program for Your Email Account

After you have your email account information, you need to configure Mail to work with your email account. The first time you start the Mail program, it guides you through the process of typing in your email account information. If you have already set up an email account in Mail and want to configure a second account, Mail guides you through the same steps as if you were starting the Mail program for the first time.

Here's how to configure Mail to work with an email account:

1. Click the Mail icon on the Dock, or double-click the **Mail** icon in the Applications folder to start Mail.

2. Select **File ▸ Add Account**. (If you're starting Mail for the very first time, you won't have to select **File ▸ Add Account**.) A dialog appears, asking for your full name, email address, and password, as shown in Figure 43-1.

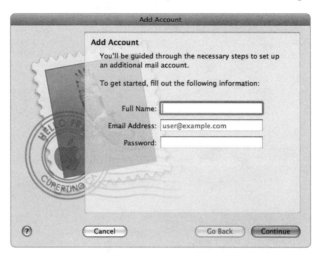

FIGURE 43-1: *A dialog appears asking for your initial email account information.*

3. Click in the **Full Name** text box and type your name. Whatever name (or nickname) you type here will appear in the From field when people receive your email messages.
4. Click in the **Email Address** text box and type your full email address, such as *JSmith@apple.com*. This email address is usually the account name provided by your ISP or the company that runs your email account.
5. Click in the **Password** text box and type your password. To prevent people from seeing your password, the Password text box masks your actual characters with dots. After you type your full name, email address, and password, an Automatically set up account checkbox appears already selected.
6. Click the **Create** button and Mail will try to finish configuring itself with your email account automatically. If this step fails, you'll need to follow the steps in the next section, "Configuring Mail Manually."

Configuring Mail Manually

If Mail cannot automatically configure itself to work with your email account, you may need to configure the remaining steps manually with the following steps:

1. Follow the steps in the preceding section, "Configuring the Mail Program for Your Email Account," until you reach the point at which Mail cannot automatically configure itself to work with your email account.

2. Click **Continue**. A dialog appears, asking for your incoming mail server, as shown in Figure 43-2.

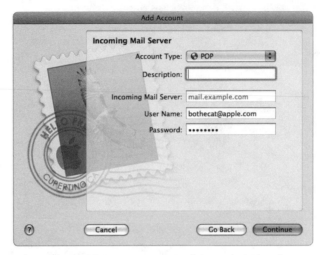

FIGURE 43-2: *The Incoming Mail Server dialog lets you define the name of the server that stores your email.*

3. Click the **Account Type** pop-up menu and choose **POP, IMAP,** or **Exchange.** In general, a POP account is used for individual accounts, while IMAP and Exchange accounts are more often used by corporations to set up email accounts for employees.
4. Click in the **Description** text box and type any text that identifies your email account, such as *Personal Mail.* Whatever you type here is for your benefit only, so you can make up any descriptive name.
5. Click in the **Incoming Mail Server** text box and type the server name, such as *popisp.net* or *mail.isp.net.* Mail tries to contact your email server to verify that you can access it.
6. Click **Continue.** An Incoming Mail Security dialog appears, as shown in Figure 43-3.
7. Click the **Authentication** pop-up menu and choose a method, such as Password. (Choose the other options only if your email account requires these other options, such as MD5 Challenge-Response or NTLM. The company running your email account can tell you which settings to choose.)
8. Click **Continue.** An Outgoing Mail Server dialog appears, as shown in Figure 43-4.
9. Click in the **Description** text box and type any text that helps you identify the mail server name, such as *Acme Mail Server.*
10. Click in the **Outgoing Mail Server** text box and type the mail server name (also called the outgoing mail server or the smtp server), such as *smtp.isp.net.*

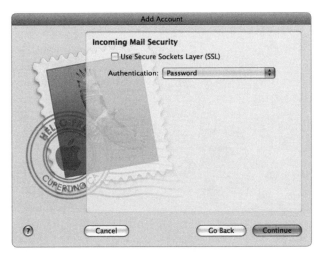

FIGURE 43-3: The Incoming Mail Security dialog lets you choose how to restrict access to your email account.

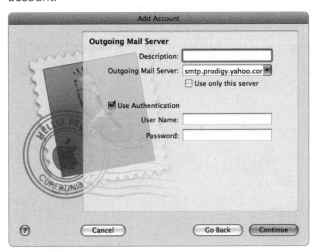

FIGURE 43-4: The Outgoing Mail Server dialog lets you define the name of the server that will send your messages out over the Internet.

11. Click in the **User Name** text box and type your username.
12. Click in the **Password** text box and type your password.
13. Click **Continue**. Mail tries to verify that your chosen mail server is working. If it succeeds, an Account Summary dialog appears, as shown in Figure 43-5.

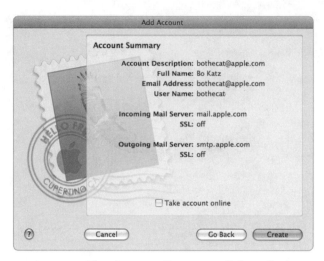

FIGURE 43-5: *The Account Summary dialog displays your email account information.*

14. (Optional) Select or clear the **Take account online** checkbox. If selected, this option tries to retrieve new messages from your email account as soon as you click the Create button.
15. Click **Create**. The Mail window appears and displays your account as an Inbox folder in the left pane.

Additional Ideas for Creating Accounts in Mail

Many people may need only a single email account, but Mail lets you retrieve email from multiple accounts if you want. For example, you might have a work email address and a personal email address. By configuring both accounts to work with Mail, you can read all your email from within a single program.

If you use another email program, you can transfer your saved messages into Mail by selecting **File ▶ Import Mailboxes**. Doing this makes it easy to switch from another email program to Mail.

Although configuring accounts can be a nuisance, take heart that you'll have to do this only on rare occasions, such as the first time you use Mail. After that, you can forget all about the technical details in configuring the email account and just enjoy reading and writing messages using Mail.

44

Reading and Writing Email

After you've set up the Mail program to work with your email account (see Project 43), you can start retrieving and sending messages. To read email messages, you can download and store them in the Mail program. To write a message, you can reply to a previous message or create a new message from scratch.

Project goal: Learn different ways to read and write email messages using the Mail program.

What You'll Be Using

To read and write email messages, you'll need the following:

▶ The Mail program configured to work with your email account

▶ An Internet connection

▶ The Address Book

Retrieving Email Messages

To read your messages, you have to retrieve them from the computer (called the *incoming mail server*) that runs your email account. You can retrieve messages manually or automatically.

Manually retrieving messages tells Mail, "Check for new messages right now." Automatically retrieving messages tells Mail, "Every few minutes, check for new messages and let me know how many new messages you find."

Manually Retrieving Messages

Generally, you'll want Mail to check for new messages periodically, such as every 15 minutes. However, if you're expecting a message and don't feel like waiting for Mail to retrieve it automatically, you can check for new messages immediately.

To retrieve messages manually, you have several choices:

▶ Click the **Get Mail** button.

▶ Select **Mailbox ▸ Get All New Mail**.

▶ Select **Mailbox ▸ Get New Mail** and then click the name of the email account you want to use.

If you have configured Mail to work with two or more email accounts, you can use the top two methods to retrieve messages for all your email accounts. If you choose the third method, you can selectively retrieve messages for a single email account.

Automatically Retrieving Messages

To make Mail retrieve messages automatically, you need to define how often Mail should check for new messages, such as every 5 minutes. To tell Mail how often to check for new messages, do the following:

1. Start Mail. (Click the Mail icon on the Dock or double-click the **Mail** icon in the Applications folder.)
2. Select **Mail ▸ Preferences**. A Preferences dialog appears.
3. Click the **General** icon. The General dialog appears, as shown in Figure 44-1.

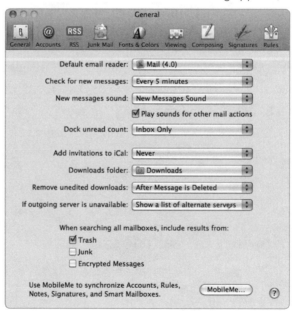

FIGURE 44-1: *The General dialog lets you define how often Mail should check for new messages.*

4. Click the **Check for new messages** pop-up menu and choose an option such as Every 5 minutes or Every 30 minutes.
5. (Optional) Click the **New messages sound** pop-up menu and choose a sound to play when you receive new email messages.
6. Click the close button of the General dialog.

Reading Your Messages

When the Mail program runs, it displays the number of new messages as a white number in a red circle in the upper-right corner of the Mail icon on the Dock, as shown in Figure 44-2. (If you don't leave the Mail program running, it can't retrieve your messages automatically.)

FIGURE 44-2: *When Mail is running, it shows you the number of new messages above the Mail icon.*

To read your messages, do the following:

1. Click the Mail icon on the Dock. The Mail window appears.
2. Click the **Inbox** folder under the Mailboxes category in the left pane of the Mail window. The right pane displays all your messages, where new messages appear with a blue dot in front of them.
3. Click a message that you want to read. The contents of the chosen message appear in the preview pane of the Mail window, as shown in Figure 44-3.
4. (Optional) Double-click a message to display that message in a separate window, as shown in Figure 44-4.

Retrieving a File Attachment

Many messages contain only text, but some messages can include a file, which is called a *file attachment*. A file attachment can be a word processor document, a picture, a movie, a song, or any other type of file stored on your Macintosh.

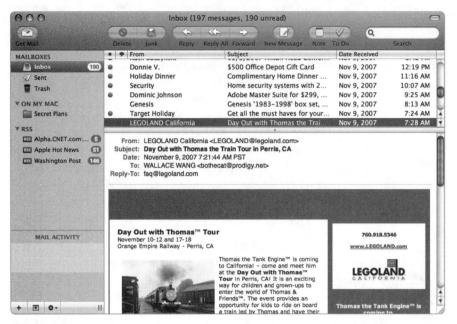

FIGURE 44-3: *You can read a message in the preview pane.*

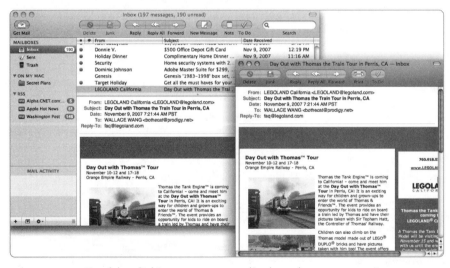

FIGURE 44-4: *Double-clicking a message displays that message in a separate window.*

When you receive a file attachment, you'll see two buttons labeled *Save* and *Quick Look*, as shown in Figure 44-5. You may also see an icon representing the file displayed in the Message window or preview pane.

To peek at the contents of the file attachment, click **Quick Look**. To save the file attachment into your Downloads folder, click **Save**.

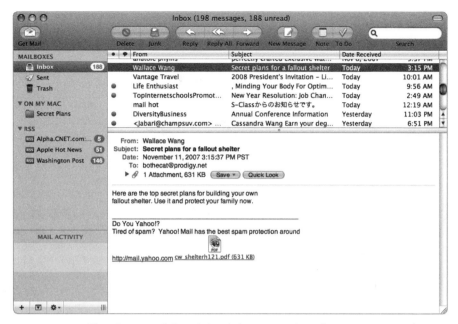

FIGURE 44-5: *The Save and Quick Look buttons identify a message with a file attachment.*

Defining Where to Store a File Attachment

Normally, Mail saves all file attachments in your Downloads folder, but you can specify a different folder to store file attachments. Here's how:

1. Select **Mail ▸ Preferences**. A Preferences dialog appears.
2. Click the **General** icon. The General dialog appears (see Figure 44-1).
3. Click the **Downloads folder** pop-up menu and choose **Other**. A dialog appears, displaying all the drives and folders on your hard disk.
4. Click a folder in which you want to store saved file attachments and click **Select**.
5. Click the close button of the General dialog.

Deleting a Message

After you read a message, you can delete it if you don't need it any more. Here's how to delete a message:

1. Start the Mail program. The Mail window appears.
2. Click the **Inbox** folder under the Mailboxes category in the left pane.
3. Click a message you want to delete. (To select multiple messages, hold down the ⌘ key as you click each message that you want to delete.)
4. Click the **Delete** button (or select **Edit ▸ Delete**).

Saving Email Addresses

You can't send a message without having the email address of the recipient. To avoid having to type email addresses and losing email addresses, you can save them in the Address Book program. You can save addresses from emails you receive in the Address Book program or just type email addresses from scratch by opening the Address Book program.

To save an email address from a message you've received, do the following:

1. Click the **Inbox** folder under the Mailboxes category in the left pane.
2. Click a message sent by someone whose email address you want to save. Select **Message ▸ Add Sender to Address Book**. The email address of the sender is now stored in your Address Book.

Writing a Message

Before you can send a message, you need to type the email address of the recipient. Then you can type a message and add an optional file attachment. To create an email message, you can create a new message or reply to an email message you received.

✳ *NOTE:* **Before sending a message, select Edit ▸ Spelling and Grammar ▸ Check Document Now to spell check your message.**

Creating a New Message

Creating a new message is useful if you're writing email to someone for the first time, or if you want to contact someone without replying to a previous message. Here's how to create a new message:

1. Select **File ▸ New Message**. A New Message window appears.
2. Click in the **To** text box and type an email address. (Or click the **Address** icon, and when the Address Book window appears, double-click a name to paste that person's email address into the To text box. Then click the close button of the Address Book window.)

✳ *NOTE:* **You can send a message to multiple email addresses by typing multiple addresses in the To text box, separating each email address with a comma.**

3. Click in the **Subject** text box and type a word or phrase that describes the topic of your message.
4. Click in the Message window and type your message.
5. Click the **Send** button.

Replying to a Message

When you reply to an existing message, Mail automatically adds the sender's email address and includes the sender's message to help the recipient better understand your reply. Here's how to reply to a message:

1. Click the **Inbox** folder that appears under the Mailboxes category in the left pane of the Mail window.
2. Click a message to which you want to respond.
3. Click the **Reply** button. (If you're responding to a message that several people received, clicking the Reply All button lets you send a message to everyone who received the same message from the sender.) A message window appears that includes the sender's email address and the text that the sender had written to you.
4. Type your own message.
5. Click the **Send** button.

Forwarding a Message

Rather than reply to an existing message, you might want to pass a message along to someone else; this is known as *forwarding* a message. Here's how to forward a message:

1. Click the **Inbox** folder that appears under the Mailboxes category in the left pane of the Mail window.
2. Click a message that you want to forward to someone else.
3. Click the **Forward** button. A message window appears that includes the text of the message.
4. Click in the **To** text box and type an email address. (Or click the **Address** icon, and when the Address Book window appears, double-click a name to paste that person's email address into the To text box. Then click the close button of the Address Book window.)
5. Type your own message.
6. Click the **Send** button.

Attaching a File to a Message

If you want to send an attached file with a message, first create a new message or reply to an existing message. Then, before clicking the Send button, do the following:

1. Click the **Attach** button. A dialog appears, listing all the drives and folders on your Macintosh, as shown in Figure 44-6.
2. Click the file you want to attach to your message. (You may need to navigate through several folders to find the file you want.)
3. Click **Choose File**.

FIGURE 44-6: *A dialog appears so you can choose a file to attach to a message.*

❋ **NOTE:** Many email accounts limit the size of file you can attach to a message, such as a 10MB maximum. If you try to send a file attachment that's larger than your email account's maximum limit, you'll likely see an error message that displays the maximum file size limit allowed. If you need to send an extremely large file, consider using a free digital delivery service such as YouSendIt (*http://www.yousendit.com/*), Megaupload (*http://www .megaupload.com/*), or SendThisFile (*http://www.sendthisfile.com/*).

Saving Messages as Drafts

If you need to write a lengthy message, you may not have time to write the entire message in one sitting. In this case, you can save your message in the Drafts folder. Here's how:

1. Create a new email message or respond to an existing one to display a message window on the screen.
2. Type your message.
3. Click the **Save As Draft** button.

4. Click the close button of the message window. The left pane of the Mail window displays your Drafts folder along with a number to identify how many messages are currently stored in the Drafts folder, as shown in Figure 44-7.

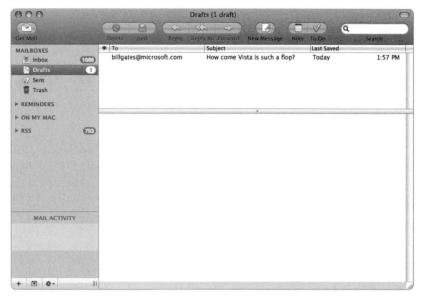

FIGURE 44-7: *The Drafts folder displays the number of messages stored but not sent yet.*

After you've saved an email message in the Drafts folder, you can open that message to edit and send it by doing this:

1. Click the **Drafts** folder that appears in the left pane of the Mail window. The right pane lists all your saved messages.
2. Double-click a message. Your chosen message appears in a separate window.
3. Type or edit your message.
4. Click the **Send** button (or click the **Save As Draft** button to save your message in the Drafts folder again). When Mail sends your message, that message disappears from the Drafts folder.

Additional Ideas for Reading and Writing Messages

Using email can be fun. You can make it even more fun by making some changes to your email messages. For example, if the text of an email message appears too small (or too large), you can modify the text size by opening a message and selecting Format ▸ Style ▸ Bigger (or Smaller), or you can press ⌘-+ (plus sign) to make text appear bigger or ⌘-− (minus sign) to make text appear smaller.

As an alternative to changing the size of text in a message, you can make your Macintosh read your messages to you by selecting Edit ▸ Speech ▸ Start Speaking. This makes your Macintosh read your message to you in a computer-synthesized voice.

The Mail program makes it easy to read and write messages, so you can immediately start sending email to friends, relatives, and co-workers all over the planet. The more people you contact, the more likely you'll get interesting email from people you want to hear from in return, and that can make everyone happy.

45 Making Email Look Pretty

Typing plain ol' text in an email message may be functional, but it's also a bit boring. To make your email look prettier, the Mail program includes stationery and signatures. Stationery provides pretty graphics for holding text and pictures. Signatures let you include text at the end of every message you send, such as your name and phone number or a funny saying that you want to share with others.

Project goal: Learn to use stationery and signatures to create visually interesting email messages.

What You'll Be Using

To read and write pretty email messages, you'll need the following:

▶ The Mail program configured to work with an email account

▶ An Internet connection

▶ Photos stored in iPhoto

Using Stationery

You can use stationery when creating a new message. Stationery provides a pre-designed background and graphics to which you can add text and pictures.

NOTE: **Stationery uses HTML (HyperText Markup Language) to create its fancy designs, which is the same computer language used to create web pages. If someone's email program cannot display HTML messages (or if that person has turned off this feature), your recipient won't see your fancy stationery designs.**

Here's how to use stationery:

1. Start Mail. (Click the Mail icon on the Dock or double-click the **Mail** icon in the Applications folder.)

2. Select **File ▶ New Message**. A New Message window appears.

3. Click the **Show/Hide Stationery** button in the upper-right corner of the New Message window. A list of stationery categories appears on the left.

4. Click a stationery category, such as Birthday or Announcements.

5. Click a specific stationery design. Your chosen design appears in the message window, as shown in Figure 45-1. Stationery displays dummy text and pictures as placeholders for you to replace with your text and pictures.

FIGURE 45-1: *When you choose a stationery template, the chosen design appears, ready for you to modify.*

6. Click the text you want to replace and type your own text.

7. (Optional) Click the **Photo Browser** button in the upper-right corner of the New Message window. The Photo Browser window appears, displaying all the pictures you've stored in iPhoto, as shown in Figure 45-2. (If you haven't stored any pictures in iPhoto yet, the Photo Browser window appears empty.)

FIGURE 45-2: *The Photo Browser window lets you retrieve pictures stored in iPhoto and add them to your stationery.*

8. (Optional) Drag a picture out of the Photo Browser window and drop it over the placeholder picture in your stationery. Your chosen picture appears in your stationery.

* **NOTE: You can also drag and drop pictures from your Pictures folder, or even from another program window, into stationery placeholders. For example, you could drag a picture from a web page displayed in Safari and drop it into a stationery placeholder.**

9. Click in the **To** text box and type an email address. (Or click the **Address** icon and when the Address Book window appears, double-click a name to paste that person's email address into the To text box. Then click the close button of the Address Book window.)

10. Click the **Send** button.

Using Signatures

A signature automatically adds text at the bottom of every message you send. A signature can display a funny saying or your company's name, your title, and your phone number so that anyone receiving your message can contact you. To use a signature, you must first create the text you want to appear. Next, you must tell Mail to add your signature to your messages.

Creating a Signature

Here's how to create a signature:

1. Start the Mail program.
2. Select **Mail ▸ Preferences**. A Preferences window appears.
3. Click the **Signatures** button. The Signatures window appears.
4. In the left pane, click the email account for which you want to use a signature.
5. Click the plus button. The middle pane displays a name for your signature (such as Signature #1).
6. Double-click the signature name in the middle pane and type a descriptive name for your signature.
7. Double-click the text in the right pane and type the signature text you want to appear at the end of all your messages, as shown in Figure 45-3.

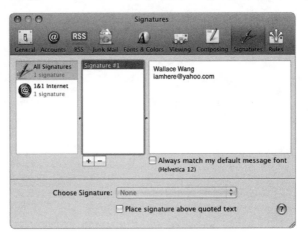

FIGURE 45-3: *The Signatures window lets you create signatures.*

8. (Optional) Click the **Choose Signature** pop-up menu and choose **None**, **At Random**, or **In Sequential Order**. The last two options automatically choose a different signature for every message. If you have only one signature, either of these two options automatically includes that one signature in every message.
9. Click the close button of the Signatures window.

Using a Signature

Each time you create a new email message or reply to a message, you can attach a signature to the bottom of the message. To choose a signature for a message, do the following:

1. Create a new message or reply to an existing message.
2. In the message window, click the **Signature** pop-up menu that appears under the Subject text box, as shown in Figure 45-4.

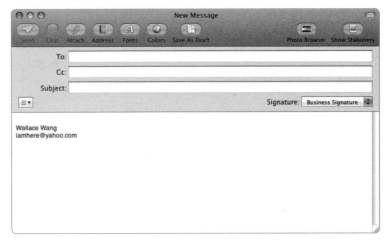

FIGURE 45-4: *The Signature pop-up menu lets you choose a specific signature file.*

3. Choose a signature file to use.
4. (Optional) Type or edit the text in the To and Subject text boxes.
5. Type your message in the message window.
6. Click the **Send** button.

Deleting a Signature

Eventually you may want to delete a signature. Here's how:

1. Start the Mail program.
2. Select **Mail ▸ Preferences**. A Preferences window appears.
3. Click the **Signatures** button. The Signatures window appears.
4. In the left pane, click the email account that contains your signature.
5. Click the signature filename you want to delete.
6. Click the minus button. A dialog appears, asking if you want to delete your signature file.
7. Click **OK**.
8. Click the close button of the Signatures window.

Additional Ideas for Making Email Look Pretty

The Mail program organizes stationery into categories, but it also includes a Favorites category where you can drag your favorite stationery so you won't have to hunt through the stationery categories every time. If you find the stationery selections provided by Mail too limiting, you can buy additional stationery from Equinux (*http://www.equinux.com/*). If you have technical expertise, you can even create your own stationery by reading Apple's stationery creation guide, "Creating Mail Stationery Bundles" (*http://developer.apple.com/documentation/AppleApplications/Conceptual/MailArticles*).

If you want to spice up your email messages with signatures, create several signatures that display a saying or phrase to share with others. By creating several signature files and letting Mail choose them randomly or in sequential order, everyone receiving your messages can receive different signatures.

If you're adding a signature for business use, include your company name, motto, and website address to promote your business every time you send email. Since recipients may forward your email messages to others (including the text of your signature file), this can be a free form of advertising.

Whether you use stationery or signatures (or both), there's no reason why your email messages need to be plain and boring. Now all you have to do is make sure your messages are worth reading in the first place.

46 Organizing Your Email

All new email messages usually appear in your Inbox folder. However, the more messages you get, the more crowded your Inbox folder can get, so it can be difficult to find anything.

To solve this problem, the Mail program can help you sort, search, and organize your email. By sorting and searching your email, you can stay as disorganized as you want and still find what you need. By organizing your messages into folders, you'll always be able to find what you want without wasting time searching for it.

Project goal: Learn to sort and search your email messages and organize them in separate folders.

What You'll Be Using

To sort, search, and organize email messages, you'll need the following:

▶ The Mail program configured to work with an email account

▶ An Internet connection

Sorting Messages

To help you find a particular message, you can sort all messages by clicking a heading, such as the following:

▶ **From** Sorts alphabetically by the sender's name or email address

▶ **Subject** Sorts alphabetically by the email's subject text

▶ **Date Received** Sorts chronologically by the date you received the message

Each time you click a heading, Mail switches between sorting your messages in ascending order (such as putting the newest messages at the top) and descending order (such as putting the oldest messages at the top). The currently sorted heading (Date Received) appears highlighted, as shown in Figure 46-1.

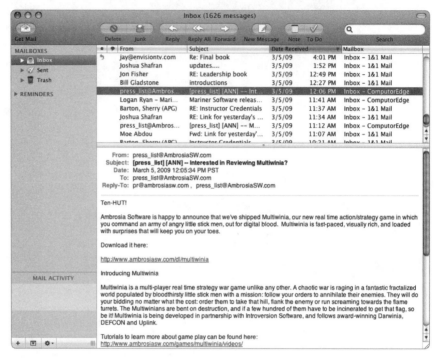

FIGURE 46-1: *Clicking a column heading sorts all messages stored in Mail according to that heading.*

＊ **NOTE:** You can sort your messages using only one column at a time.

Searching for Messages

Searching allows you to find all messages that contain text stored in the following parts:

▶ **From**   Finds all messages sent by certain people

▶ **Subject**   Finds all messages related to a specific topic

▶ **Message**   Finds all messages that contain certain text

Here's how to search for a message:

1. Start Mail. (Click the Mail icon on the Dock or double-click the **Mail** icon in the Applications folder.)
2. Click in the **Search** text box that appears in the upper-right corner of the Mail window.

3. Type the text you want to find. As you type, Mail displays all messages that match your typed text, as shown in Figure 46-2. The messages that most closely match your text (found in the sender's name, the email subject, or the message itself) appear at the top of the Mail window.

FIGURE 46-2: *The Search text box lets you define the text to find in your stored messages.*

❋ **NOTE:** Now that you've filtered your inbox to a smaller set of your messages, you can sort these results by different fields, such as **Subject** or **From**, just as you did with your entire mailbox.

4. Click a message to read it.
5. Click the close button of the Search text box to clear the box. All your messages appear in the order they were in before you started your search.

Using Smart Mailboxes

Typing text into the Search text box to find certain messages can get tedious. To simplify this process, you can create a *Smart Mailbox*, which lets you define the type of messages you want to find. Every time a new message matches the criteria you have selected, that message appears inside your Smart Mailbox in the left pane of the Mail window, which updates its list of messages automatically as you add or delete messages.

❋ **NOTE:** A Smart Mailbox doesn't physically move messages out of your Inbox folder. Instead, the Smart Mailbox simply provides a link to messages stored in your Inbox folder.

Creating a New Smart Mailbox

Here's how to create a new Smart Mailbox:

1.   Select **Mailbox ▸ New Smart Mailbox**. A New Smart Mailbox dialog appears, as shown in Figure 46-3.

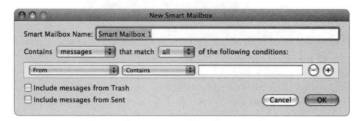

FIGURE 46-3: *The New Smart Mailbox dialog lets you define what type of messages you want Mail to find and store.*

2.   Click in the **Smart Mailbox Name** text box and type a descriptive name for your Smart Mailbox.
3.   Click the **Contains** pop-up menu and choose **messages**. (If *messages* already appears, you can skip this step.)
4.   Click the **that match** pop-up menu and choose **all** or **any**.
5.   Click the first conditions pop-up menu that appears directly under the Contains pop-up menu. A list of condition options appears, as shown in Figure 46-4.

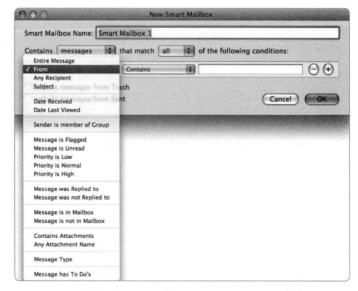

FIGURE 46-4: *The first condition pop-up menu defines what to search for.*

6. Click the next pop-up menu and choose an option, such as **Contains**, **Does not contain**, **Begins with**, **Ends with**, or **Is equal to**.
7. Click in the next text box and type the text you want to search for.
8. (Optional) Click the plus button to define another condition and repeat the above five steps.
9. Click **OK**. Your Smart Mailbox appears under the Smart Mailboxes category in the left pane of the Mail window.

Editing a Smart Mailbox

After you create a Smart Mailbox, you may want to modify its criteria. Here's how to do this:

1. Click a Smart Mailbox under the Smart Mailboxes category in the left pane of the Mail window.
2. Select **Mailbox ▸ Edit Smart Mailbox**. A Smart Mailbox dialog appears (similar to Figure 46-3).
3. Change the conditions used by the Smart Mailbox to store your messages.
4. Click **OK**.

Deleting a Smart Mailbox

Eventually you may want to delete a Smart Mailbox, which you can do as follows:

1. Start the Mail program.
2. Click a Smart Mailbox under the Smart Mailboxes category in the left pane of the Mail window.
3. Select **Mailbox ▸ Delete Mailbox**. A dialog appears, asking if you really want to delete the selected Smart Mailbox.
4. Click **Delete**. The chosen Smart Mailbox disappears.

✳ *NOTE:* Deleting a Smart Mailbox doesn't physically delete any messages, since those same messages still appear in your Inbox.

Using Rules to Sort Messages

Another way to organize messages is to use rules. A *rule* defines what type of message you want to look for, such as messages from certain email addresses, and then routes those messages to a separate folder instead of the Inbox folder.

✳ *NOTE:* Smart Mailboxes contain links to messages physically stored in the Inbox folder. Rules physically move messages into a specific folder.

Creating a Folder for Sorted Messages

Here's how to create a folder to hold messages sorted by rules:

1. Start the Mail program.
2. Select **Mailbox ▸ New Mailbox**. A New Mailbox dialog appears, as shown in Figure 46-5.

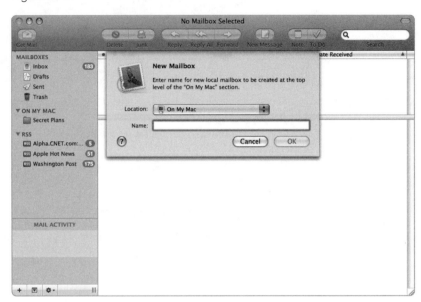

FIGURE 46-5: *The New Mailbox dialog lets you create a descriptive name for your new mailbox folder.*

3. (Optional) Click the **Location** pop-up menu and choose a location in which to store your mailbox folder. (The default is On My Mac.)
4. Click in the **Name** text box and type a descriptive name for your mailbox folder.
5. Click **OK**.

Creating a Rule

Rules tell the Mail program how to route certain messages into different folders. For example, you might create one rule for routing messages from co-workers into one folder and a second rule for routing messages from your friends into another folder.

Here's how to create a rule:

1. Start the Mail program.
2. Select **Mail ▸ Preferences**. A Preferences window appears.
3. Click the **Rules** button. The Rules window appears, as shown in Figure 46-6.

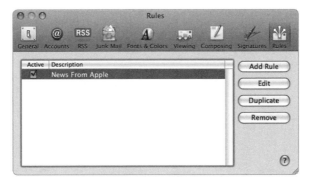

FIGURE 46-6: *The Rules window lets you create and manage rules for routing messages.*

4. Click **Add Rule**. A Rules dialog appears, as shown in Figure 46-7.

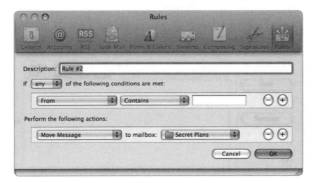

FIGURE 46-7: *The Rules dialog displays pop-up menus and text boxes for describing the type of messages you want to route into another folder.*

5. Click in the **Description** text box and type a descriptive name for your rule.
6. Click the **If** pop-up menu and choose **any** or **all**. If you create two or more rules, the all option routes only messages that match all your defined conditions. The any option routes messages if they match one or more defined conditions.
7. Click the first pop-up menu (which usually displays the word *From*) and choose an option for how to identify and route a message, such as **From**, **Subject**, or **Date Received**, as shown in Figure 46-8.
8. Click the second pop-up menu (which usually displays the word *Contains*) and choose how to apply the rule, such as **Contains**, **Begins with**, or **Ends with**.

FIGURE 46-8: *The first pop-up menu defines what criteria your rule uses to sort your messages.*

9.   Click in the text box that appears next and type the text for your condition. An example of a condition using the previous two pop-up menus might look like this: *From Contains Fred*, which would identify all messages whose From field contained *Fred*.

10.   (Optional) Click the plus button to create another rule and repeat the preceding steps.

11.   Make sure the first pop-up menu under the Perform the following actions displays the words *Move Message*.

12.   Click the **to mailbox** pop-up menu and choose the folder where you want to route your messages.

13.   Click **OK**. Now all messages that match your rules will be moved to your chosen folder automatically.

Editing and Deleting a Rule

In case you want to change or delete a rule, you can do the following:

1.   Start the Mail program.

2.   Select **Mail ▸ Preferences**. A Preferences window appears.

3.   Click the **Rules** button. The Rules window appears (see Figure 46-6).

4. Click **Edit Rule** and modify your rules in the Rules dialog (see Figure 46-7), and then click the close button of the Preferences window. (Or click **Remove**, and when another dialog appears, click **Remove** again.)

✻ *NOTE:* **If you delete a Smart Mailbox, you will not delete any messages. If you delete a folder that contains messages routed there by a rule, however, you will physically delete any messages stored in that folder.**

Additional Ideas for Organizing Email

If you don't want to take time to organize your email, you can stick to sorting (by clicking column headings such as From, Subject, and Date Received) and searching (by typing text in the Search text box in the upper-right corner of the Mail window).

If you're willing to take time to organize your email, use Smart Mailboxes and rules. Since Smart Mailboxes create links to messages physically stored in the Inbox folder, you can look for messages in both the Smart Mailbox and the Inbox folder. If you prefer reducing clutter, use rules to move messages physically into specific folders.

Both Smart Mailboxes and rules help you organize your email into categories. If you shop online, you can create a Smart Mailbox or folder to hold any email verifications you receive from merchants such as Amazon.com. That way, browsing the messages in that Smart Mailbox or folder can show you when you placed your order and when your order delivery was promised.

If you're looking for a job and waiting to hear from certain companies, route their emails into their own folder so you won't miss them when they arrive. If you're involved in a long-distance romance, route your lover's email messages to a folder so you'll always know where to find them so you can read and re-read them all easily.

Staying organized may not be easy, but the consequences of not doing so can mean missed messages, which could lead to lost opportunities or missed deadlines just because you couldn't find an important email message when you needed it. So take time now to make Mail organize your messages automatically and you'll be glad you did.

47 Dealing with Junk Email

If you have an email account, you'll eventually start receiving junk email. To avoid wasting time deleting junk email manually, you can make the Mail program identify or even delete most junk email automatically. That way, Mail can show you only the important messages without annoying you with the junk.

Project goal: Learn different ways to make the Mail program handle junk email automatically.

What You'll Be Using

To handle junk email messages, you'll need the following:

▶   The Mail program configured to work with an email account

▶   An Internet connection

Bouncing Messages

One trick for dealing with unwanted email messages is to *bounce* them. This acts like stamping a "Return to Sender, Addressee Unknown" notice on the front of your received message. When you bounce an email message, the sender receives the bounced message, which makes your email address appear invalid.

Bouncing a message back to the sender works only if the sender's return email address is correct. Since many people and companies send junk email (known as *spam*) using fake email addresses, bouncing a message back to a fake email address will just return the bounced message back to you again.

Because of this, you should bounce a message only when you know the sender's email address is valid. For example, you can bounce a message sent by someone you don't like anymore (such as an ex-boyfriend or girlfriend).

Here's how to bounce a message:

1. Start Mail. (Click the Mail icon on the Dock, or double-click the **Mail** icon in the Applications folder.)
2. Click the message you want to bounce.
3. Select **Message ▸ Bounce**. A dialog appears, asking if you want to bounce the message.
4. Click **Bounce**. Mail moves the message into your Trash folder and sends a bounce message back to the sender.

Using Junk Mail Filtering

To deal with the inevitable flood of junk email every email account receives, the Mail program includes built-in junk mail filtering. To use Mail's junk mail filtering, you need to turn it on, tell Mail what to do with junk mail, and tell Mail how to identify junk mail.

Configuring the Junk Mail Filter

By default, Mail's junk mail filter is turned on, but here's how you can turn it off or on and modify how the filter behaves:

1. Select **Mail ▸ Preferences**.
2. Click the **Junk Mail** button. A Junk Mail window appears, as shown in Figure 47-1.

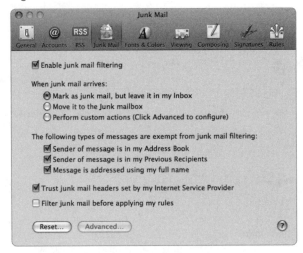

FIGURE 47-1: *The Junk Mail window lets you configure Mail's filter.*

3.   Select or clear the **Enable junk mail filtering** checkbox, which is initially checked by default. If you remove the checkmark, Mail won't filter out junk mail.

4.   Click a radio button under the When junk mail arrives group. You have three choices:

   ▶   **Mark as junk mail, but leave it in my Inbox**   Identifies junk mail but lets you decide to delete it manually

   ▶   **Move it to the Junk mailbox**   Automatically routes junk mail to a special Junk mailbox folder, which is created for you automatically, but Mail may also mistakenly route valid email into the Junk mailbox folder

   ▶   **Perform custom actions**   Lets you define additional rules for identifying and routing junk mail

5.   (Optional) Select or clear any checkboxes under *The following types of messages are exempt from junk mail filtering*. By default, all of these checkboxes are selected, since Mail assumes if the sender is in your Address Book or knows your full name, the message probably isn't junk.

6.   (Optional) Select or clear the **Trust junk mail headers set by my Internet Service Provider** checkbox. Most email accounts also use built-in junk mail filters that can identify likely junk mail to help Mail filter out junk more effectively.

7.   Click the close button of the Junk Mail window.

Identifying Junk Mail

After you've configured Mail's junk filter, Mail can identify most junk mail, but some junk mail will still slip past. When you find junk mail that Mail's filters have missed, you can manually label the message as junk, which helps "train" Mail to recognize similar junk email in the future.

When Mail recognizes a junk mail message, it displays that message in a different color. To identify junk mail manually (or remove an incorrect junk mail label from a valid message), do the following:

1.   Click a message that Mail's junk mail filter missed.

2.   Select **Message ▶ Mark ▶ As Junk Mail** (or click the **Junk** button at the top of the Mail window). The preview pane displays *You marked this message as Junk Mail*, as shown in Figure 47-2.

3.   (Optional) Click the **Not Junk** button if a message is labeled as junk mail by mistake.

Deleting Junk Mail

After you've identified junk mail, you can delete junk messages manually by doing the following:

1.   Click the junk email message you want to delete (or hold down the ⌘ key as you click multiple messages).

2.   Select **Edit ▶ Delete** (or click the **Delete** button at the top of the Mail window).

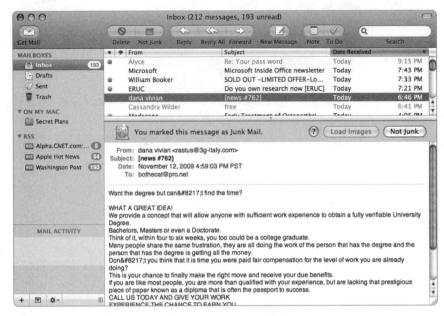

FIGURE 47-2: *Mail can identify junk mail by labeling it as junk.*

If you configured Mail to route suspected junk messages to a Junk mailbox folder automatically, you should browse through this Junk mailbox folder periodically to look for any valid messages mistakenly identified as junk by Mail's filters. When you're sure the Junk mailbox folder only contains useless messages, delete your Junk mailbox folder by selecting **Mailbox ▸ Erase Junk Mail**.

Additional Ideas for Dealing with Junk Email

Junk email is inevitable. The simplest way to avoid junk mail is to give out your email address only to trusted friends.

Since many online merchants ask for your email address, you could create and use a free email account (through Yahoo! or another free email account company) and use these "dummy" email addresses whenever you need to give out an email address. If junk mail overwhelms your free email account, you can simply shut it down and create a new one.

Junk email will always be a nuisance, like death and taxes, but with Mail's built-in junk mail filtering, you can reduce a potential flood of junk email into a manageable trickle.

48

Instant Messaging with iChat

Sending and receiving email is a fun way to communicate with your friends and family members, but sometimes you may want instant communication. To satisfy your need for real-time communication, every Macintosh comes with a program called *iChat*. With iChat, you have a choice of sending text messages, audio messages, or video messages.

Text messaging lets you type messages, audio messaging lets you use your Macintosh like a telephone, and video messaging lets you see who you're talking to. If you want to stay in touch, iChat can help you do it with nothing more than a high-speed Internet connection.

Project goal: Learn how to use iChat to talk to your friends and family members (who you probably would never have picked to be your friends).

What You'll Be Using

To learn how to communicate in real time with your Macintosh, you'll be using:

▶ The iChat program

▶ An Internet connection

Setting Up an iChat Account

Before you can use iChat, you need to set up an iChat account, which you can do in one of three ways:

▶   Create or use an existing MobileMe email account

▶   Create or use an existing America Online Instant Messenger (AIM) account

▶   Create or use an existing Google Talk or Gmail account (which includes an instant messaging function)

An AIM (*http://www.aim.com/*) or Gmail (*http://mail.google.com/*) account is completely free to create, but you'll need to pay a $99 annual fee to create a MobileMe account. You only need to create an AIM, Gmail or Google Talk, or MobileMe account once. If you don't already have one of these accounts, or if you're unsure of which kind of account to create first, you should ask your friends what they use—as you'll probably want to chat with them anyway.

And you don't have to choose one or the other. You can sign onto iChat using multiple accounts, all at the same time. This way you can chat with your friends who use AIM and those who use Google Talk.

✳ *NOTE:* **You can also use a Jabber or an older .Mac account. If you don't know what Jabber or .Mac are, then just stick with creating an AIM, Gmail, or MobileMe account.**

To set up your iChat account, do this:

1.   Click the iChat icon on the Dock. (If you don't see the iChat icon on the Dock, click the Finder icon on the Dock, click **Applications** in the left pane of the Finder window, and then double-click the **iChat** icon.) A Welcome dialog appears.

2.   Click the **Continue** button. An Account Setup dialog appears, as shown in Figure 48-1.

FIGURE 48-1: The iChat Account Setup dialog

∗ *NOTE:* If you use a MobileMe account to set up iChat, you'll have the option of using encryption to protect your text, audio, and video chats with other MobileMe users.

3. Click the **Account Type** pop-up menu and choose **AIM**, **Google Talk**, or **MobileMe**.
4. Click in the **Screen Name** text box and type your screen name or email address. (If you selected MobileMe in the previous step, then click in the **MobileMe Name** text box and type your MobileMe account name.)
5. Click in the **Password** text box and type the password to your account.
6. Click the **Continue** button. A dialog appears, letting you know that you have finished setting up your iChat account.
7. Click the **Done** button.

∗ *NOTE:* You can repeat this process for any other chatting accounts you'd like to add. Just select iChat ▸ Preferences, then click the Accounts button. To add another account, click the plus (+) button in the lower-left corner. You can delete accounts using the minus (–) button.

Starting iChat

After you've set up an iChat account, you'll be ready to start chatting with your friends. First, make sure you're connected to the Internet. Then choose one of the following two ways to start up iChat:

▶ Click the iChat icon on the Dock

▶ Click the Finder icon on the Dock, click **Applications** in the left pane of the Finder window, and then double-click the **iChat** icon

Each time you start iChat, a dialog pops up, asking for your Login ID and Password, as shown in Figure 48-2. Your Login ID is your AIM, Gmail, or MobileMe screen or account name and your password is your AIM, Gmail, or MobileMe account password.

After you type this information, click the **Log In** button.

FIGURE 48-2: You must type an ID and Password to log in to your iChat account.

Adding a Name to Your Buddy List

The friends list or *Buddy List* is meant to store the names of your friends so you can contact them easily without remembering and typing their account name. To add a name to the Buddy List, do this:

1. Start iChat. The Buddy List window appears.
2. Click the plus icon in the bottom-left corner of the Buddy List window. A pop-up menu appears, as shown in Figure 48-3.
3. Click **Add Buddy**. A dialog appears, asking for the account name, as shown in Figure 48-4.

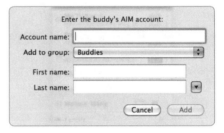

FIGURE 48-3: *The Buddy List window stores the names of all your friends.*

FIGURE 48-4: *You can type someone's account name and real name into your Buddy List.*

4. Click in the **Account name** text box and type the account name of the person you want to contact. (Account names can be a person's MobileMe or Gmail email address or AIM screen name. You may need to ask other people what their account names are.)
5. (Optional) Click the **Add to group** pop-up menu and choose a category to store your friend's name in the Buddy List window.
6. Click in the **First name** and **Last name** text boxes and type your friend's real first and last name.
7. Click the **Add** button to add the name to your Buddy List.

At this point, you can start chatting. All you need to do is decide who you want to chat with and what type of chat you want, such as a text, audio, or video chat.

Starting a Text Chat

A text chat lets you type messages back and forth. Text messaging is best when using a slow Internet connection or when you're chatting with someone who doesn't have a microphone or webcam that would allow them to participate in an audio or video chat.

To start a text chat, do this:

1. Start iChat. The Buddy List window appears, as shown in Figure 48-5.
2. Click the name of a Buddy in your Buddy List who is currently online.

✱ **NOTE:** If you want to chat with someone who isn't stored in your Buddy List, choose File ▸ New Chat to open a New Chat dialog. Then type that person's screen name in the To: text box.

3. Click the Start a text chat icon at the bottom of the Buddy List window. A Chat window appears, as shown in Figure 48-6.

Start a video chat
Start an audio chat
Start a text chat

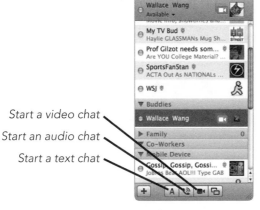

FIGURE 48-5: *The Start a text chat, Start an audio chat, and Start a video chat buttons*

FIGURE 48-6: *The Chat window lets you send and receive text messages.*

4. Click in the text box at the bottom of the Chat window, type a message, and then press the RETURN key. Your messages and your friend's messages will appear in the scrolling Chat window.
5. Click the close button in the Chat window when you want to quit chatting.

Starting an Audio Chat

An audio chat lets you turn your Macintosh into a telephone, as long as the other person has a microphone and speakers. To start an audio chat, do this:

1. Start iChat. The Buddy List window appears (see Figure 48-5).
2. Click the name of a Buddy in your Buddy List who is currently online.

* **NOTE: If you want to chat with someone who isn't stored in your Buddy List, choose File ▸ New Chat to open a New Chat dialog. Click the Type pop-up menu and choose Audio Chat. Then type that person's screen name in the To: text box.**

3. Click the Start an audio chat icon at the bottom of the Buddy List window. An Audio Chat window appears, as shown in Figure 48-7.
4. Start speaking. (You can also adjust the volume or mute your microphone.)
5. Click the close button in the Audio Chat window when you want to quit chatting.

FIGURE 48-7: *The Audio Chat window for talking to a friend*

Starting a Video Chat

A video chat lets you talk and see the other person, just as long as that other person has a webcam, a microphone, and speakers. Video chats work best with high-speed Internet connections, while text chats are ideal for slower Internet connections. To start a video chat, do this:

1. Start iChat. The Buddy List window appears (see Figure 48-5).
2. Click the name of a Buddy in your Buddy List who is currently online.

* **NOTE: If you want to chat with someone who isn't stored in your Buddy List, choose File ▸ New Chat to open a New Chat dialog. Click the Type pop-up menu and choose Video Chat. Then type that person's screen name in the To: text box.**

3. Click the Start a video chat icon at the bottom of the Buddy List window. A Video Chat window appears, as shown in Figure 48-8.
4. Start speaking. (You can also adjust the volume or mute your microphone.)
5. Click the close button in the Video Chat window when you want to quit chatting.

FIGURE 48-8: *The Video Chat window for talking to and seeing a friend*

Additional Ideas for Using iChat

The text messaging feature of iChat is perfect when you're stuck in a boring lecture or meeting and want to act like you're typing notes, but are really just chatting with your friends and making plans.

Audio chats are great for times when you want to talk to others but don't want to waste the money on long-distance phone calls. If you have a high-speed Internet connection, you might want to choose a video chat so you can see the other person and chat at the same time. Of course, this means having to stare at the other person and having them stare back at you, so if this makes you uncomfortable, you might prefer an audio chat, which more closely mimics a telephone call.

Perhaps one of the most advanced features of iChat is the *Share a Screen* option, which literally lets you control someone else's Macintosh (or vice versa). This is great for when you need help and want someone to show you exactly which icons or menus to click, or if you want to show someone else how to use their Macintosh without having to drive over to that person's home or office.

This Share a Screen feature requires a high-speed Internet connection, but by talking to someone and moving their mouse pointer on the screen, you can remotely teach that person what to do, so they can quickly learn all the joys of using a Macintosh.

PART 5

Maintaining Your Macintosh

49

Learning About Your Macintosh

Look on the side of any software package and you'll see the words *System Requirements* atop a list that defines the minimum hardware (hard disk size, memory) and software (OS X version) requirements that your Macintosh must meet to run that particular software. System requirements are useful, but only if you know enough about your Macintosh in the first place. If you don't know which version of the Mac OS X operating system your computer is running or how much memory your computer has available, these system requirements won't mean a whole lot.

If you want to save files to a CD or DVD, you may encounter another challenge. All recent Macintosh computers can play and write data to CDs, and newer Macintosh computers can also play and write data to DVDs. However, with so many different CD/DVD disc types available for purchase, if you purchase the wrong type, you won't be able to use it in your Macintosh.

Project goal: Determine what OS X version your Macintosh uses and how much disk space it has available so you'll know whether your computer can run certain programs or use certain types of CDs and DVDs.

What You'll Be Using

To examine your Macintosh, you'll use the following:

▶ The Finder

▶ The System Profiler program

Identifying Your Operating System Version, Processor Type, and Memory

Every Macintosh uses the Mac OS X operating system. However, dozens of different versions of the Mac OS X system have been released to date, such as version 10.4.11, 10.5.7, and 10.6. Many programs won't work if your computer uses a version of the Mac OS X program that doesn't meet the software publisher's requirements, so you need to know which version your computer is running before you buy.

In addition, many programs won't run unless your Macintosh has a minimum amount of available memory. For example, if your program needs 2GB (gigabytes) of RAM but your Macintosh has only 1GB of RAM, you can't run that program, even if your computer uses the correct version of the operating system. (If all this talk about RAM and gigabytes confuses you, relax. You simply need to know how much memory your computer has and don't need to get bogged down in the technical details.)

✳ *NOTE:* **The amount of memory (RAM, which stands for *Random Access Memory*) that is considered the bare minimum is 1GB, which is perfectly fine for word processing, using email, or browsing the Internet. If you plan to do more heavy-duty computing, such as spreadsheet number crunching, computer-aided design, or desktop publishing, you could get by with 1GB, but most high-end programs need at least 2GB. Of course, the more memory you add, the faster your Macintosh will run, since it can automatically detect and use all the memory available.**

Some programs are also picky about the speed of the processor used in your computer. Since the processor acts like the brain of the computer, some programs won't run unless your computer has a certain type of processor that operates at a specific minimum speed (typically measured in gigahertz, or GHz). If your computer processor speed is too slow, it may not be capable of running certain programs.

✳ *NOTE:* **The two types of processors used in the Macintosh are PowerPC and Intel processors. PowerPC processors were used in older Macintosh models, while Intel processors are used in all newer Macintosh models. Mac OS X 10.6 Snow Leopard can only run on Macintosh computers that use Intel processors.**

Fortunately, the Macintosh makes it easy to determine which version of the Mac OS X operating system is running on your computer, the total amount of RAM available, the processor type, and processor speed. Simply do the following:

1. Click the Apple menu and choose **About This Mac**. An About This Mac window appears, as shown in Figure 49-1.
2. Click the close button of the About This Mac window.

FIGURE 49-1: *The About This Mac window displays basic information about your Macintosh.*

Identifying the Types of CD and DVD Discs Your Mac Can Use

Look in any computer or office supply store and you'll find a bewildering array of CD and DVD discs. Some cost more than others, but all have some designation on the package, such as CD-R or DVD+RW. Before you buy a stack of CD or DVD discs, you need to make sure your Macintosh can use them. Table 49-1 lists the different types of CD and DVD discs you'll likely find.

* **NOTE:** If you want to create an audio CD or video DVD on your Macintosh, make sure the discs you use can also be played in other types of disc players, such as your car stereo's CD player. In general, most audio CD players can recognize CD-R discs, and most DVD players can recognize DVD-R and DVD+R discs.

Table 49-1: Types of CD/DVD Discs Available

Disc Name	What It Means	Storage Capacity	Purpose
CD-R	Compact Disc-Recordable	650–700MB	Can save data only once
CD-RW	Compact Disc-ReWritable	650–700MB	Can be reused to store, modify, and erase data
DVD-R	Digital Video Disc, Recordable	4.7GB	Can save data only once
DVD+R	Digital Video Disc, Recordable	4.7GB	Can save data only once
DVD-RW	Digital Video Disc, ReWritable	4.7GB	Can be reused to store, modify, and erase data
DVD+RW	Digital Video Disc, ReWritable	4.7GB	Can be reused to store, modify, and erase data
DVD-R DL	Digital Video Disc, Recordable, Double Layer	8.5GB	Can save data only once
DVD+R DL	Digital Video Disc, Recordable, Double Layer	8.5GB	Can save data only once

✳ *NOTE:* **With DVD discs, the two competing standards are the minus (–) and plus (+) standards, such as DVD-R and DVD+R. Technically, a DVD-R is different from a DVD+R disc. However, most newer Macintosh computers can read and recognize both the plus and minus types of discs. Older Macintosh computers (and DVD players) may not be able to read and write to different types of discs.**

Older Macintosh computers include a drive that can read and write to CDs but cannot use DVDs. Later Macintosh computers include a drive called a *combo drive*, which can read and write to CDs but only read DVDs. The very latest Macintosh computers include a drive called a *SuperDrive*, which can read and write to DVDs and CDs. It's super!

To determine your computer's drive capabilities, do the following:

1. Click the Apple menu and choose **About This Mac**. The About this Mac window appears (see Figure 49-1).
2. Click the **More Info** button. The System Profiler window appears, as shown in Figure 49-2.
3. Click the triangle to the left of the word *Hardware* under the Contents category. A list of hardware components appears.

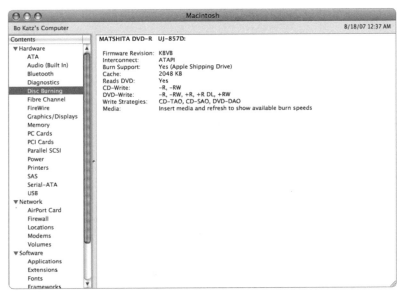

FIGURE 49-2: *The System Profiler window can identify the capabilities of your computer's CD/DVD drive.*

4. Click **Disc Burning**. The right pane of the System Profiler window lists all the types of CD/DVD discs your Macintosh can use.
5. Select **System Profiler ▸ Quit System Profiler**.

Additional Ideas for Identifying the Parts of Your Macintosh

Since the System Profiler program can show you what equipment is connected to your Macintosh, you can use it for simple troubleshooting.

Open the System Profiler window and click **Printers** under the Hardware category. The System Profiler will show information about the printer your Macintosh thinks is connected to your computer (as shown in Figure 49-3). If a different printer is hooked up to your Macintosh or you don't see any information about printers, you may need to install a print driver to make sure your printer works with your Macintosh.

A *print driver* is a small program designed to make your Macintosh work with a specific printer. If you visit the website of the company that manufactures your printer, you should be able to download the appropriate print driver for your printer.

If you click Applications under the Software category, you can see all the programs installed on your Macintosh and their version numbers, as shown in Figure 49-4. Because software companies keep producing newer, more advanced

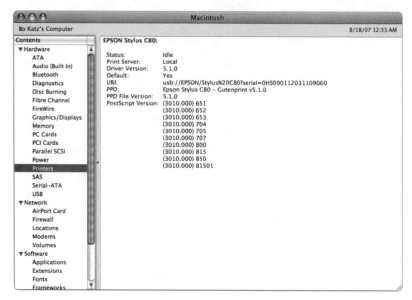

FIGURE 49-3: *The System Profiler window can identify your current printer.*

versions of their programs, glancing at the version number and then looking up the latest version available online can show whether you're running an old program or the latest one.

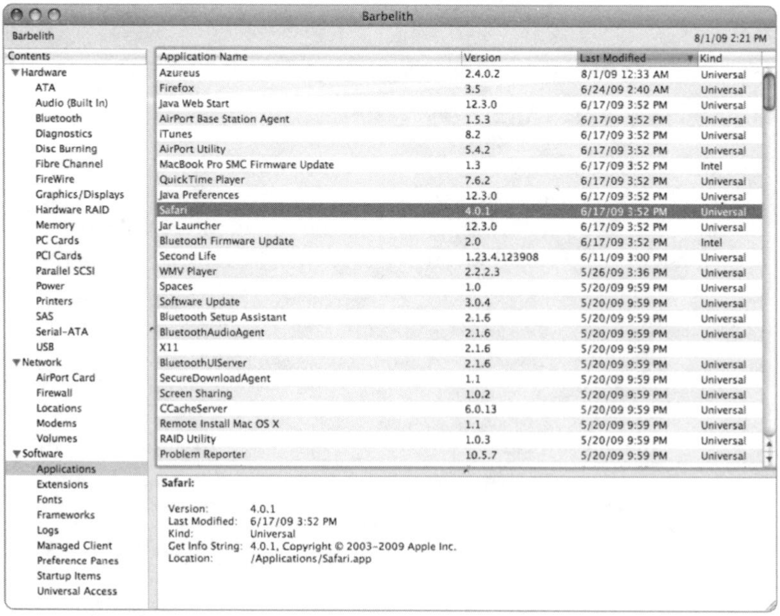

FIGURE 49-4: *The System Profiler window can identify versions of programs installed on your Macintosh.*

To find the latest version of a program, visit the website of the software publisher (such as Microsoft or Adobe), browse through the list of the latest versions of programs on VersionTracker (*http://www.versiontracker.com/*), or click the Help or Application Name menu (that contains the program's name) of a program and look for a Check for Updates option, as shown in Figure 49-5.

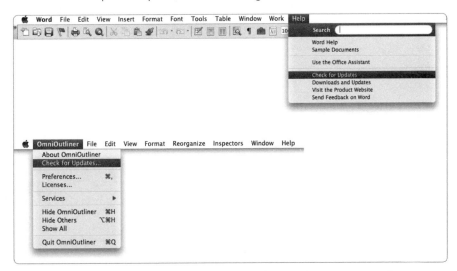

FIGURE 49-5: *Many programs offer a Check for Updates command to make it easy for you to verify whether you have the latest program version installed.*

If you look at the Kind column of the System Profiler window when viewing your software, you'll see one of three designations: PowerPC, Universal, or Intel. PowerPC programs were designed to run on older Macintosh computers that use PowerPC processors. PowerPC programs can run on the newer Macintosh computers, but you should probably look for a newer version of the program. Universal programs are designed to run equally well on both PowerPC and Intel processors. Intel programs are designed to run only on the newest Macintosh models. If you have an Intel program, you won't be able to run it on an older Macintosh that has a PowerPC processor.

By using the System Profiler program, you can see exactly what's inside every Macintosh. Even if you don't understand all the technical gibberish the System Profiler program displays, you can use much of it to learn a little bit more about your Macintosh so that you can make decisions about what programs you can run and whether your software is up to date.

50

Installing, Updating, and Uninstalling Software on Your Macintosh

Apple crams every new Macintosh with loads of software so you can start being productive with your computer right away. However, you'll likely need to install other programs on your Mac to accomplish some tasks, such as balancing your checkbook, creating astrological charts, predicting lottery numbers, or playing video games. Whatever task you need to accomplish, you can find a program to help you do it on your Macintosh.

Since your Macintosh is only as useful as the software it can run, you need to know how to install programs, update them, and uninstall and get rid of them if necessary, which you'll learn about in this chapter.

Before you can use any program, you must install it on your computer. Installing simply stores a program on your Macintosh so you can start using it.

After you have installed some programs, you may find that you no longer use one or more programs. Rather than let them clutter up your hard disk and take up space on your Macintosh, you can uninstall them.

In addition, software publishers often release improvements (updates or patches) that are designed to add new features or make their software run more reliably. You can usually get these modifications by downloading and installing them from the Internet.

Project goal: Learn how to install, update, and uninstall software on your Macintosh.

What You'll Be Using

To install and uninstall software on your Macintosh, you'll need the following:

▶ The Finder

▶ A software program

▶ An Internet connection

Installing Software from a CD or DVD

You can install software on your Macintosh in two different ways: by copying a program into the Applications folder on your hard disk or by using a separate installer application that copies a program to your Applications folder automatically. The method that you'll use will depend on the program you're installing.

＊ *NOTE:* **You can store programs anywhere on your Macintosh. However, it's a good idea to store all programs in the Applications folder so you'll always know where to find them.**

If you purchased a program on a CD or DVD, when you insert that disc into your computer, a program icon may appear on your Desktop. If so, you should be able to install the program simply by dragging the program icon into the Applications folder (as shown in Figure 50-1).

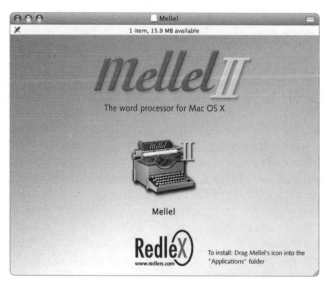

FIGURE 50-1: *To install a program, you may be prompted to drag a program icon into the Applications folder.*

Other times, you may see an installer application icon that looks like a box with its top opened up, as shown in Figure 50-2. When you see an installer application icon, you must double-click it to run it and store the program in your Applications folder.

Here's how to install a program by dragging a program icon into the Applications folder:

1. Insert the CD/DVD into your Macintosh. A Finder window appears, displaying the program's icon. (If a Finder window does not appear, click the Finder icon on the Dock and then double-click the **CD/DVD** icon in the left pane of the Finder window to display the program's icon.)

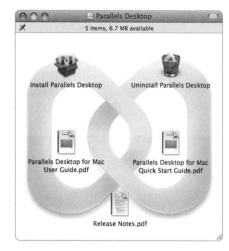

FIGURE 50-2: *Many programs use an installer application icon that you must double-click to install the program in the Applications folder.*

2. Click the Finder icon on the Dock, and then select **File ▸ New ▸ New Finder Window**.
3. Move the Finder window so that it appears next to the window that displays the program icon from the CD/DVD.
4. Move the mouse over the program icon in the CD/DVD window, hold down the mouse button, and drag the icon over the Applications folder in the other Finder window, as shown in Figure 50-3.
5. Release the mouse button. Your program should now be installed on your Macintosh.

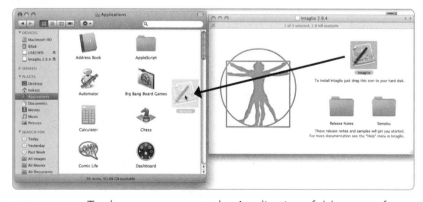

FIGURE 50-3: *To drag a program to the Applications folder, you often need to display two Finder windows side by side.*

Here's how to run an installer application to install a program into the Applications folder:

1. Insert the program CD/DVD into your Macintosh. A Finder window appears, displaying an installer icon that resembles an open box. (You may see other files displayed here as well.)
2. Double-click this installer icon (or click the installer icon and select **File ▸ Open**). The installer application will run and display instructions telling you what to do next (as shown in Figure 50-4). When following these onscreen instructions, you can often tell the installer application where to install the program or choose which parts of a program you want to install. For example, you might install a spell checker for English but not for Spanish if you don't plan to use Spanish.

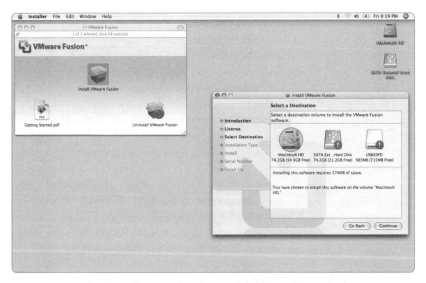

FIGURE 50-4: *An installer application guides you through the steps needed to install a program on your Macintosh.*

Installing Software over the Internet

Although many stores sell packaged Macintosh software, you'll find a much greater variety of software by searching the Internet.

* *NOTE:* Selling software in stores is expensive. The software publisher needs to pay for a CD or DVD and a pretty box, and then it sells the product to a distributor who then sells and ships it to a store. By selling software directly over the Internet, software publishers save money, so they may pass the savings on to you by offering a discount if you buy and download their programs over the Internet.

When you buy software over the Internet, the software publisher can send you a CD/DVD containing the program, but more than likely you'll download the program online, typically as a compressed (shrunken) file.

The most common way for people to compress Macintosh software is as a *disc image file*, often abbreviated as a *.dmg file* since that's the extension that appears on the file (as shown in Figure 50-5).

FIGURE 50-5: *Compressed files of software often appear as .dmg files.*

To install a program stored as a *.dmg* file, do the following:

1. Double-click the *.dmg* file (or click the *.dmg* file and select **File ▸ Open**). A device icon appears on the Desktop, along with a window displaying the contents of the *.dmg* file (as shown in Figure 50-6). This device icon appears as a separate storage device and contains the contents of the disc image file.

* **NOTE:** Sometimes when you download a *.dmg* file, it will automatically uncompress itself and create a device icon on your Desktop; then it will start running an installation program.

2. At this point, you can install the program either by dragging its program icon into the Applications folder or by double-clicking the installation application icon, if one exists.
3. After you install the program, drag the device icon to the Trash or click it and select **File ▸ Eject** to remove the device icon.

Device icon

FIGURE 50-6: *Opening a .dmg file creates a device icon on the Desktop and opens a window that displays the contents of the disc image file.*

✳ **NOTE:** After you install a program, keep the *.dmg* file in a safe place. That way you'll have it if you need to reinstall the program later.

Updating Software

Most software publishers release improvements to their programs frequently, and each may have its own way of providing these updates. To make updating easy, Apple provides a simple way to update not only the entire Mac OS X operating system, but also all Apple programs.

✳ **NOTE:** Minor updates to a program are usually free. Major updates to a program usually cost money.

Here's how to update Apple's software:

1. Make sure that you're connected to the Internet.
2. Click the Apple menu and choose **Software Update**. A Software Update window appears, listing all the available updates for your Apple programs, as shown in Figure 50-7.
3. Select the checkboxes of the software updates you want to install, and uncheck those that you don't want.

✳ **NOTE:** You don't necessarily need every software update, especially those intended for programs you never use.

4. Click **Install x Items**. After installing certain updates, you may be asked to restart your Macintosh.

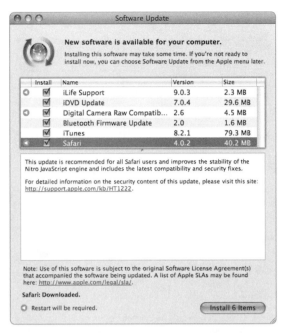

FIGURE 50-7: *The Software Update window lists all available updates to your Apple programs.*

Checking and downloading software updates periodically can get tedious. To automate this process, you can tell your Macintosh to check for updates, which it can do if you have an Internet connection (via a DSL, cable, or other fast connection; this will not work if you use a dial-up Internet connection). Here's how to tell your Macintosh to check for updates automatically:

1. Click the Apple menu and choose **System Preferences**. A System Preferences window appears.
2. Click the **Software Update** icon under the System category. A Software Update window appears, as shown in Figure 50-8.
3. Select (or clear) the **Check for updates** checkbox. After you select this checkbox, click the **Check for updates** pop-up menu and choose **Daily**, **Weekly**, or **Monthly**.
4. Select (or clear) the **Download important updates automatically** checkbox.
5. Click the close button of the Software Update window.

✳ *NOTE:* **To update non-Apple software, you may need to visit the software publisher's website periodically or look for a Check for Updates command buried in a program menu, as shown in Figure 50-9.**

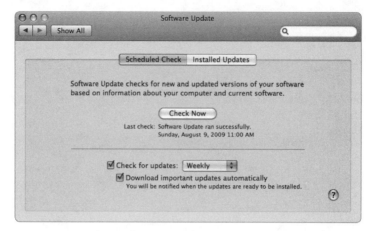

FIGURE 50-8: *The Software Update window lets you define how often your Macintosh should check for the latest software updates.*

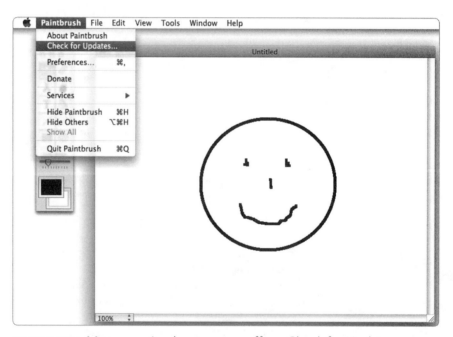

FIGURE 50-9: *Many non-Apple programs offer a Check for Updates command hidden somewhere in a menu.*

Uninstalling Software

The Macintosh makes uninstalling software as simple as dragging a file or folder icon into the Trash. Here's how to uninstall a program:

1. Click the Finder icon on the Dock. A Finder window appears.
2. Click the **Applications** folder in the left pane of the Finder window. The contents of the Applications folder appear in the right pane.
3. Move the mouse over the program file or folder and drag it over the Trash icon on the Dock. (You can also click a program file or folder and then select **File ▸ Move to Trash**.)

✳ *NOTE:* **Make sure you really want to uninstall a program before you trash it! Once you dump the Trash, it's not coming back.**

Additional Ideas for Installing Software on Your Macintosh

After you install software on your Macintosh, always store the original CD or DVD that contains the program in a safe place. That way, if your hard disk crashes or your Macintosh fails, you can always reinstall the program.

When you download programs from the Internet, keep a copy of those programs (the *.dmg* disc image files) in a safe place, such as a special folder on your hard disk as well as on a CD or DVD (in case your hard drive fails).

You may never have to reinstall a program after you've installed it, but when you get a new Macintosh or accidentally uninstall a program, a spare copy of your programs and registration keys can make sure you can reinstall your programs and get up and running as quickly as possible.

51 Ejecting Stuck CDs or DVDs

On older computers, you loaded a CD or DVD by opening a CD/DVD tray, dropping your disc in that tray, and sliding the tray back into your computer. The latest Macintosh computers have eliminated the tray and now let you load a CD or DVD just by sliding the disc into a slot. While this requires fewer moving parts (and fewer parts that could break), the biggest disadvantage of the CD/DVD slot is that sometimes the disc can get stuck inside your computer with no physical way of yanking it back out again. (The old CD/DVD trays could sometimes be forced open to retrieve a stuck disc.)

If a disc gets stuck in your computer, your Macintosh offers a variety of ways to eject it. By trying each method, you can eventually eject a stuck disc without having to call for help or physically harming your Macintosh.

Project goal: Learn how to eject a CD or DVD that's stuck inside your Macintosh and refuses to eject.

What You'll Be Using

To learn how to eject a stuck CD or DVD, you'll be using the following:

▶ The keyboard

▶ The Finder

▶ The Disk Utility program

▶ The Terminal program

How to Eject a CD or DVD Normally

Your Macintosh offers several ways to eject a CD or DVD normally:

▶ Press the eject key on the keyboard.

▶ Drag the CD/DVD icon from the Desktop to the Trash icon on the Dock.

▶ Click the eject button that appears to the right of a CD or DVD in the iTunes window or in the sidebar of the Finder window, as shown in Figure 51-1.

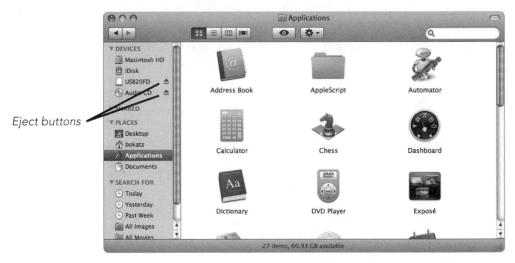

FIGURE 51-1: *An eject button appears next to every removable storage device connected to your Macintosh.*

Whenever you want to eject a CD or DVD, try one of the three methods. (Stick a CD or DVD in your Macintosh right now and try all three methods, one after the other, to see how they work.)

How to Eject a Stuck CD or DVD

One of the biggest problems with a stuck CD or DVD is that its icon may not appear on the Desktop or in the Finder or iTunes window. Even though you know the CD/DVD is stuck in your Macintosh, none of the other programs may recognize the CD/DVD, and thus you won't be able to eject the disc using the normal methods.

If this occurs, you may have to resort to one of the following alternative ways to eject a CD or DVD from your Macintosh.

Eject from the Disk Utility Program

In addition to fixing problems on disks, the Disk Utility program can also eject CDs and DVDs. Here's how to use Disk Utility to eject a stuck CD or DVD:

1. Click the Finder icon on the Dock. The Finder window appears.
2. Select **Go ▸ Utilities**.
3. Double-click the **Disk Utility** icon. The Disk Utility window appears, as shown in Figure 51-2.

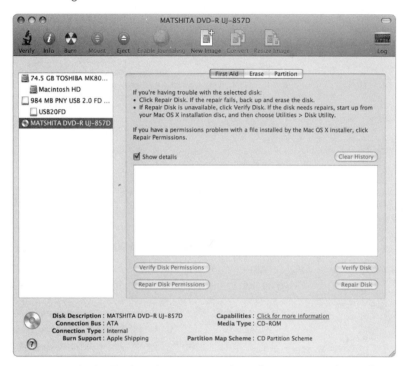

FIGURE 51-2: The Disk Utility program lists the CD/DVD drive of your Macintosh.

4. Click the CD/DVD drive in the left pane of the Disk Utility window.
5. Click the **Eject** icon near the top of the Disk Utility window, select **File ▸ Eject**, or press ⌘-E.

Eject from the Terminal Program

The Terminal program gives you access to the guts of your Macintosh without the fancy user interface of windows, menus, and buttons. Here's how to use the Terminal program to eject a CD or DVD:

1. Click the Finder icon on the Dock. The Finder window appears.
2. Select **Go ▸ Utilities**.

3. Double-click the **Terminal** icon. The Terminal window appears, as shown in Figure 51-3.

4. Type **drutil tray eject** and press RETURN.

5. Select **Terminal ▸ Quit Terminal**.

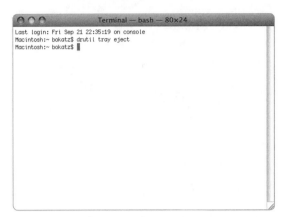

```
                  Terminal — bash — 80×24
Last login: Fri Sep 21 22:35:19 on console
Macintosh:~ bokatz$ drutil tray eject
Macintosh:~ bokatz$ ▐
```

FIGURE 51-3: *You can have the Terminal program eject a CD or DVD by typing the* drutil tray eject *command.*

Restart and Hold Down the Left Mouse Button

If you hold down the left mouse button while your Macintosh is starting up, it will often eject a CD or DVD stuck inside. Here's how to use this method:

1. Click the Apple menu and select **Restart**. (If your Macintosh won't let you access the Apple menu, press the Mac's power button or press CTRL-eject key to display the dialog shown in Figure 51-4. Then click **Restart**.)

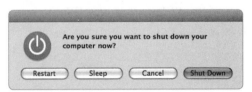

Are you sure you want to shut down your computer now?

Restart   Sleep   Cancel   Shut Down

FIGURE 51-4: *Press the Mac's power button or press CTRL-eject key to display a dialog so you can restart your Macintosh.*

2. Hold down the left mouse button as your Macintosh restarts. (Start holding down the left mouse button immediately after you choose the Restart command in the preceding step.)
3. Release the left mouse button as soon as the CD/DVD ejects from your Macintosh.

Restart and Hold Down the C Key

If you hold down the C key while your Macintosh is starting up, your Macintosh will try to boot off the CD/DVD. If your stuck CD/DVD is not a bootable CD/DVD (such as your original Mac OS X installation disc), your Macintosh will eject it. Here's how to use this method:

1. Click the Apple menu and select **Restart**. (If your Macintosh won't let you access the Apple menu, press the Mac's power button or press CTRL-eject key to display a dialog. Then click **Restart**.)
2. Hold down the C key as your Macintosh restarts.
3. Release the C key after your Macintosh ejects the CD/DVD.

Additional Ideas for Ejecting and Preventing Stuck CDs or DVDs

To prevent CDs and DVDs from getting stuck in your Macintosh, clean your discs periodically. Sometimes dirt on the discs can keep your Macintosh from reading them correctly. If a disc is scratched, you may need to get a replacement disc or else it might get jammed in your Macintosh again.

Although stuck CDs and DVDs may be an occasional minor inconvenience, you will generally be able to rely on your Macintosh. However, if you try all of the methods listed in this project and still can't eject your CD/DVD, your CD/DVD drive may have physical problems that will require repairs or a replacement, so take your Macintosh to a repair shop and let the technicians worry about it.

52

Password Protecting Your Macintosh

Nobody wants strangers peeking at their files, messing up their settings, or wiping out their data. To protect your Macintosh from prying eyes, you could lock it behind closed doors, and perhaps you do. However, if this isn't possible (or desirable), try the next best solution and password protect your Macintosh instead.

Password protection keeps people from accessing your Macintosh unless they know your password. (When you first unpacked your Macintosh and turned it on, you had to type your name and a password.) Password protection is like locking your front door: It won't guarantee that intruders will stay out, but it can slow them down.

Project goal: Lock out anyone who doesn't know your password.

What You'll Be Using

To password protect your Macintosh, you need to use the following:

► The System Preferences program

Password Protecting Screensaver and Sleep Mode

To protect your computer, you should password protect your screensaver and sleep mode. If you don't do this and you walk away from your computer, your screensaver can start up or your Macintosh may go to sleep. Anyone can wake your Macintosh out of screensaver or sleep mode and access your files.

By password protecting both your screensaver and sleep mode, you can safely walk away from your computer. The moment you return, tap a key to exit out of screensaver or sleep mode. Type your password and access your computer once more.

To password protect your screensaver and sleep mode, do the following:

1. Click the Apple menu and choose **System Preferences**. The System Preferences window appears.
2. Click the **Security** icon under the Personal category. The Security window appears.
3. Click the **General** tab to view the General options.
4. Click the lock icon in the bottom-left corner of the Security window. (Skip this step if the lock icon already appears opened.) When a dialog appears, type your password and click **OK**.
5. Select the **Require password after sleep or screen saver begins** checkbox, as shown in Figure 52-1.
6. Click the **Require password** pop-up menu and choose a time, such as immediately, 15 minutes, or 5 seconds.
7. Click the close button of the System Preferences window.

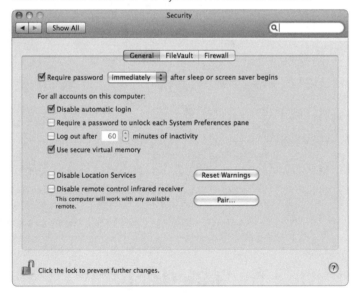

FIGURE 52-1: *You can password protect your screensaver and sleep mode in the Security window.*

Password Protecting System Preferences

The System Preferences window is another area of your computer that you can password protect, and it's an important one. It provides access to settings that determine how your Macintosh behaves. You don't want just any user (such as your 10-year-old son) to change the way your mouse or keyboard works or make your Macintosh start up using a different hard disk, for example. If someone accesses the System Preferences window without your knowledge, he or she can literally change your Macintosh. Think of the System Preferences window as the keys to your computer's "house"; you wouldn't give these keys to just anyone, nor would you give them tools for ripping out the carpet and knocking down the walls.

To control access to System Preferences, password protect it like so:

1. Click the Apple menu and choose **System Preferences**. The System Preferences window appears.
2. Click the **Security** icon under the Personal category. The Security window appears.
3. Click the **General** tab. The Security window appears (see Figure 52-1).
4. Click the lock icon in the bottom-left corner of the Security window. (Skip this step if the lock icon already appears opened.) When a dialog appears, type your password and click **OK**.
5. Select the **Require password to unlock each System Preferences pane** checkbox.
6. Click the close button of the Security window.

Disabling Automatic Login

Every Macintosh consists of at least one user account, which you set up when you first started using your new Macintosh. The user account acts like a door. If no passwords are used to protect your user account, anyone could use your Macintosh and open any door. With a password, which is like a key, the door to your Macintosh is locked until the key is used to open it.

When you create multiple accounts on your Macintosh, you essentially create multiple doors to your Macintosh, and each door (account) can be locked with a different key (password). Each time you turn on your computer, your Macintosh automatically accesses one account without requiring you to type a password. (Accessing an account is known as *logging in*. Exiting out of an account is known as *logging out*.)

The problem with this automatic login feature, however, is that anyone can turn your Macintosh on to access an account on your computer. Therefore, the first step in password protecting your Macintosh is to turn off the automatic login feature so that only people with a password can gain access. Here's how to turn off automatic login and define an automatic logout inactivity time:

1. Click the Apple menu and choose **System Preferences**. The System Preferences window appears.
2. Click the **Security** icon under the Personal category. The Security window appears.

3. Click the **General** tab. The Security window appears (see Figure 52-1).
4. Click the lock icon in the bottom-left corner of the Security window. (Skip this step if the lock icon already appears opened.) When a dialog appears, type your password and click **OK**.
5. Make sure a check mark appears in the **Disable automatic login** checkbox. (If the checkbox is empty, click the checkbox.)
6. Select the **Log out after** checkbox.
7. Type a number in the **Log out after** text box, such as 10 or 15, to define how long your Macintosh waits before automatically logging out.
8. Click the close button of the Security window.

Turning Automatic Login Back On

If you've disabled automatic login but you want to turn it on again, here's how:

1. Click the Apple menu and choose **System Preferences**. The System Preferences window appears.
2. Click the **Accounts** icon under the System category. The Accounts window appears.
3. Click the lock icon in the bottom-left corner of the Accounts window. A dialog appears, asking for your password.
4. Type your password in the Password text box and click **OK**.
5. Click **Login Options** in the lower-left corner of the Accounts window, as shown in Figure 52-2.
6. Click the **Automatic login** pop-up menu and choose an account name. You can define only one account for your Macintosh to log in to automatically.
7. Click the close button of the Accounts window.

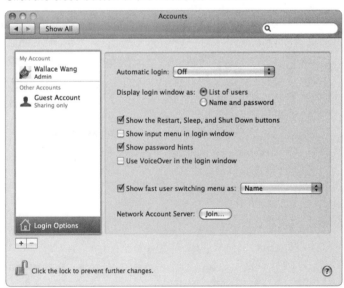

FIGURE 52-2: The Accounts window lets you define which account your Macintosh will automatically log in to.

Logging Out Automatically

If you step away from your computer, you may want your Macintosh to log out automatically after a certain amount of time in which no activity (that is, no mouse clicks or typing at the keyboard) has occurred.

Ideally, you should make the inactivity time period short—say, 10 or 15 minutes. But don't make it too short: If you define too short a time, you could be reading on screen and your Macintosh may suddenly log you out because you're not typing or clicking.

By the same token, don't set the inactivity time too long, because that may give someone time to access your account while you've stepped away. Here's how to make your Macintosh log out automatically:

1. Click the Apple menu and choose **System Preferences**. The System Preferences window appears.
2. Click the **Security** icon under the Personal category. The Security window appears.
3. Click the **General** tab to view the General options.
4. Click the lock icon in the bottom-left corner of the Security window. (Skip this step if the lock icon already appears opened.) When a dialog appears, type your password and click **OK**.
5. Select the **Log out after ___ minutes of inactivity** checkbox (see Figure 52-1).
6. Click in the **Log out after** text box and type a number such as 8 or 15 to define how many minutes to wait before logging out automatically.
7. Click the close button of the Security window.

Choosing and Changing Your Passwords

You should choose a password that's not easy for anyone to guess. For example, your first name, street address, *123*, or simply *PASSWORD* are all bad passwords.

To create a password that's difficult to guess, use a mix of uppercase and lowercase letters with symbols and numbers, such as *Dj8$eR2Lp*. If you need help creating a good password, use a random password generator such as the one available at *http://www.pctools.com/guides/password/*. When you create a password of random characters, the odds of someone guessing the password are very low (but the odds of you forgetting your own password are much higher).

Here's how to change your password:

1. Click the Apple menu and choose **System Preferences**. The System Preferences window appears.
2. Click the **Accounts** icon under the System category. The Accounts window appears.
3. Click the lock icon in the bottom-left corner of the Security window. (Skip this step if the lock icon already appears opened.) When a dialog appears, type your password and click **OK**.
4. Click **Change Password**. A dialog appears, as shown in Figure 52-3.

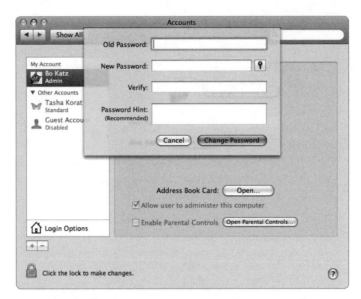

FIGURE 52-3: *To change your password, you must first type your old password and then type a new password.*

5. Click in the **Old Password** text box and type your old password.
6. Click in the **New Password** text box and type your new password.
7. Click in the **Verify** text box and type your new password a second time to verify that you typed it correctly.
8. Click in the **Password Hint** text box and type a descriptive phrase that will help you remember your new password.
9. Click **Change Password**.
10. Click the close button of the Accounts window.

Additional Ideas for Password Protecting Your Macintosh

Passwords won't keep out a determined intruder, but they will keep out the casual intruder or troublemaker.

Still, if you're among the truly paranoid, consider creating a separate, dummy account (see Project 16) and fill it with seemingly important files so that if someone breaks into that account he or she won't know to look elsewhere.

You can turn on the automatic login feature to load this dummy account any time someone restarts your Macintosh in an attempt to gain access. A dummy account (also called a *honeypot*), can mislead intruders. If you create several accounts and password protect them all, an intruder would need to know each account password, but he or she would also need to know which account contains your crucial files. This convoluted setup may make take some time to create and organize, but if you have important data that you need to keep away from prying eyes, it can keep potential intruders from invading your privacy.

53 Encrypting Your Data

The safest way to protect your data is to lock your computer behind closed doors. The second safest way to protect your data is to use encryption.

Encryption scrambles your data and password-protects it—to read the data, you must type the correct password. As long as you're the only one who knows your password, you'll be the only person who can read encrypted files.

NOTE: If you encrypt data with a password and forget that password, you'll never be able to read that data ever again. If you encrypt data with a simple password that's easy to guess (such as *123* or *PASSWORD*), an intruder could guess your password and access your data. Your data is only as safe as your password.

Project goal: Learn to encrypt the data on your Macintosh.

What You'll Be Using

To encrypt data, you'll need the following:

▶ The System Preferences program

▶ The FileVault program

Encrypting Your Home Folder

Turning on the FileVault program encrypts the information in your home folder using the password you use for your account. For safety, you can also set a *master* password. That way, if you forget your account password, you can still read your files using the master password. If you forget both your account password and master password, you can never read your data again.

* *NOTE: FileVault uses an encryption algorithm called Advanced Encryption Standard (AES), which even government agencies can't crack (theoretically).*

Setting a Master Password

Before turning on encryption, you should create a master password that will allow you to read all encrypted data stored on your Macintosh. Here's how to create a master password:

1. Click the Apple menu and select **System Preferences**. A System Preferences window appears.
2. Click the **Security** icon under the Personal category. The Security window appears.
3. Click the **FileVault** tab, as shown in Figure 53-1.

FIGURE 53-1: *The Security window lets you set a master password.*

4. Click **Set Master Password**. A dialog appears, as shown in Figure 53-2.
5. Click in the **Master Password** text box and type a master password.
6. Click in the **Verify** text box and retype your master password.

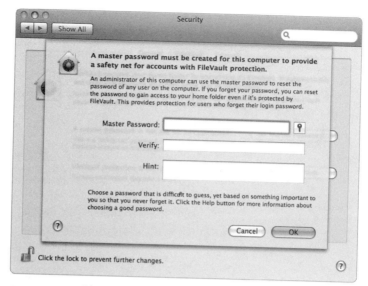

FIGURE 53-2: *You must type a master password twice to make sure you typed it correctly.*

7. Click in the **Hint** text box and type a word or phrase that can help you remember your master password.
8. Click **OK**.
9. Click the close button of the Security window.

Securely Erasing Files and Virtual Memory

After you define a master password, you can turn on FileVault to encrypt all files stored in your home folder. When you turn on FileVault, you also have the option of turning on two additional features called *Secure Erase* and *Secure Virtual Memory*.

Normally, when you delete a file by emptying the Trash, that file still remains physically on your hard disk, which makes it possible for others to retrieve that file later. When you empty the Trash with the Secure Erase feature turned on, your Macintosh writes over the deleted file with random data, making that file nearly impossible to read—just as scribbling over a printed word can make that word more difficult to read.

In addition to protecting your deleted files, FileVault can also encrypt your virtual memory. When programs run, they often store data on the hard disk, which mimics your computer's actual memory. Thus it's possible to type a secret document and your word processor will store that data in virtual memory on your hard disk. When you quit the word processor, your actual file may be encrypted, but the virtual memory file often remains intact, and a knowledgeable intruder could access it. By turning on the Secure Virtual Memory feature, your Macintosh encrypts all data stored in virtual memory. If you need maximum security, you'll probably want to turn on both Secure Erase and Secure Virtual Memory.

Turning On FileVault

When FileVault is turned on, it works invisibly in the background. However, your Macintosh may run slower since it needs to encrypt and decrypt files as you're using your computer. If you need speed and responsiveness more than security, you probably don't want to turn on FileVault. If you need security and don't mind a slower computer, then turn on FileVault.

Here's how to turn on FileVault:

1. Click the Apple menu and select **System Preferences**. A System Preferences window appears.
2. Click the **Security** icon under the Personal category. The Security window appears.
3. Click the **FileVault** tab (see Figure 53-1).
4. Click **Turn On FileVault**. A dialog appears, asking for your account password.
5. Type your account password and click **OK**. Another dialog appears, asking if you want to use Secure Erase and Secure Virtual Memory, as shown in Figure 53-3.

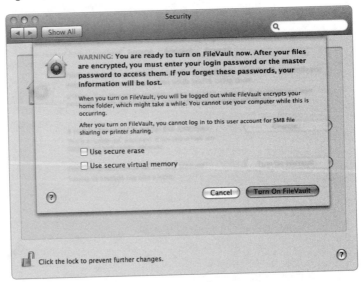

FIGURE 53-3: For added security, FileVault offers Secure Erase and Secure Virtual Memory features to prevent others from peeking at your data.

6. (Optional) Select the **Use secure erase** and **Use secure virtual memory** checkboxes.

7. Click **Turn On FileVault**. The encryption process can take time, depending on the amount of data stored on your hard disk, so be patient.

∗ *NOTE:* **FileVault encrypts only files stored in your home folder. If you store files outside of your home folder, such as on an external hard disk, FileVault won't encrypt those files.**

Turning Off FileVault

You can turn FileVault off at any time. Here's how to turn off FileVault:

1. Click the Apple menu and select **System Preferences**. A System Preferences window appears.

2. Click the **Security** icon under the Personal category. The Security window appears.

3. Click the **FileVault** tab (see Figure 53-1).

4. Click **Turn Off FileVault**. A dialog appears, asking for your account password.

5. Type your account password and click **OK**. Another dialog appears, giving you one last chance to change your mind.

6. Click **Turn Off FileVault**.

7. Click the close button of the Security window. Your Macintosh may need time to decrypt your data, so be patient.

Additional Ideas for Encrypting Your Data

If you use a laptop Macintosh, encrypting your data can protect it in case someone steals your computer. With encryption turned on, a thief won't be able to read any files stored in your home folder. If you use a desktop Macintosh, it's less likely that someone will steal your computer, so encryption is more useful for protecting against others peeking at your files, such as your supervisor, co-workers, or even family members.

By itself, encryption can protect your data, but if your data is truly important, consider storing it on a removable device, such as an external hard disk or USB flash drive that you can disconnect and take with you. By storing crucial data off your hard disk, you won't have to worry about anyone accessing your Macintosh without your knowledge. (Then you'll just have to worry about losing your external hard drive or USB flash drive.)

54 Configuring the Firewall

In the old days if someone wanted to sneak into your computer, they would have to physically break into your home or office and use your computer without your knowledge. Stopping these types of intruders was as easy as locking your Macintosh in a sealed room.

However, the latest danger is that someone can access your computer remotely through the Internet. You could even be using your computer and not know that someone else is quietly sneaking into your Macintosh and stealing data right in front of you.

To stop intruders from accessing your computer through the Internet, you need to use a program called a *firewall*. The main idea behind a firewall is that it blocks suspicious or invalid data while letting in the data that you need or want.

Think of a firewall as an intelligent doorman who tries his best to open the door to your Macintosh only to authorized data and slam it shut against malicious data.

Project goal: Learn how to protect your Macintosh with a firewall.

What You'll Be Using

To learn how to use the built-in Macintosh firewall, you'll be using:

▶   The System Preferences program

▶   The Security window

Turning the Firewall On (or Off)

If you plan on connecting your Macintosh to the Internet, or even to a local area network, you need a firewall. Just as you would never leave your car door unlocked in a dangerous neighborhood, you should never leave your Macintosh unprotected when it's connected to the Internet.

The only time you might want to turn off your firewall is to install a different firewall instead. Computers only need one firewall. If you try to run two or more firewalls, each firewall will interfere with the other one. So the lesson is simple. Always have a firewall and only use one firewall at a time. For most people, the one firewall they'll use is the built-in firewall that comes with every Macintosh.

To turn the built-in firewall on or off, do this:

1. Click the Apple menu and choose **System Preferences**. The System Preferences window appears.
2. Click the **Security** icon under the Personal category. The Security window appears.
3. Click the **Firewall** tab, as shown in Figure 54-1.

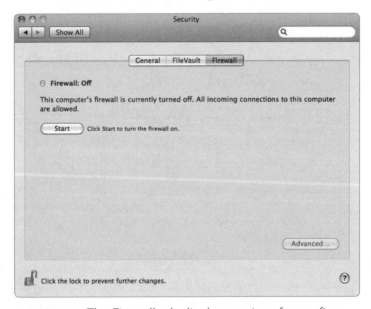

FIGURE 54-1: *The Firewall tab displays options for configuring your firewall.*

4. Click the lock icon in the bottom-left corner of the Security window. The lock must be open for you to make changes. (Skip this step if the lock icon already appears as an open lock.) When a dialog appears, type your password and click **OK**.

5. Click the **Start** button to turn the firewall on. (If you only see a Stop button, that means your firewall is already turned on. If you click the **Stop** button, you will turn the firewall off.)

Configuring the Firewall

When you turn the firewall on, it does its best to block suspicious data trying to get into your Macintosh. However, you might want to take some time to customize the firewall. Three options for strengthening your firewall include:

▸ **Block all incoming connections**   This option blocks all connections except those basic services required to use the Internet. This provides greater protection, but at the possible expense of preventing your Macintosh from doing certain things on the Internet, such as video conferencing.

▸ **Automatically allow signed software to receive incoming connections** This provides greater protection, but at the expense of blocking legitimate software if it doesn't contain a certificate.

▸ **Enable stealth mode**   This helps make your Macintosh invisible over the Internet so hackers can't find your computer, let alone break into it.

To configure your firewall, do this:

1. Click the Apple menu and choose **System Preferences**. The System Preferences window appears.

2. Click the **Security** icon under the Personal category. The Security window appears.

3. Click the **Firewall** tab (see Figure 54-1).

4. Click the lock icon in the bottom-left corner of the Security window. The lock must be open for you to make changes. (Skip this step if the lock icon already appears as an open lock.) When a dialog appears, type your password and click **OK**.

5. Click the **Advanced** button in the lower-right corner of the Security window. Another dialog appears, as shown in Figure 54-2. (If the Advanced button appears dimmed, that means you haven't turned your firewall on yet.)

6. (Optional) Select (or clear) the **Block all incoming connections** checkbox.

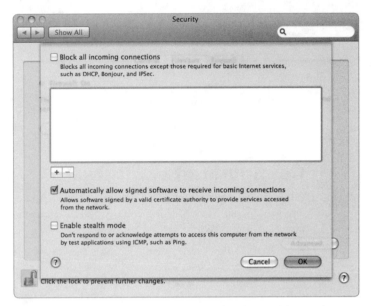

FIGURE 54-2: *The Advanced button displays additional options for strengthening the firewall.*

7. (Optional) Click the plus sign icon to display a list of programs installed on your Macintosh. Then click a program name that you want the firewall to let through. This displays a list of available programs with a pop-up menu, as shown in Figure 54-3. Choose **Allow incoming connections** or **Block incoming connections**.

8. (Optional) Select (or clear) the **Automatically allow signed software to receive incoming connections** checkbox. Any programs (even legitimate ones) that don't have a signed certificate won't be able to access the Internet from your Macintosh.

9. (Optional) Select (or clear) the **Enable stealth mode** checkbox.

10. Click **OK**.

11. Click the close button of the Security window.

Additional Ideas for Using the Firewall

If you use the Internet, make sure you've turned on your firewall. For greater security, enable stealth mode, which essentially makes your Macintosh invisible over the Internet. The idea behind stealth mode is that hackers can't attack your computer if they can't find it.

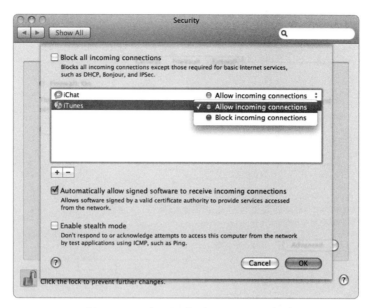

FIGURE 54-3: *You can selectively determine which programs to block or allow to connect to the Internet.*

The other configuration features of the firewall can provide greater security by blocking every program from accessing the Internet except for the handful that you approve. By blocking access to the Internet, the firewall can keep spyware programs from stealing your password or credit card data and sending it across the Internet to a malicious hacker.

A firewall by itself can't guarantee your computer's protection, but it can keep your Macintosh safe from random, unskilled hackers (often called *newbies*) and the growing, but so far unrealized, threat of spyware on the Macintosh.

The Macintosh may not suffer as many virus and worm outbreaks as other types of operating systems, but that doesn't mean it will stay this way forever. The more people there are using a Macintosh, the more tempting a target the Macintosh will become for malicious hackers.

For maximum protection, download software only from reputable sites (such as Apple or Microsoft), never accept file attachments from unknown people, and always back up your data to make sure it's safe, just in case something does manage to get on your computer and wipe everything out. A firewall is your first line of defense, but a little bit of common sense and caution will ensure that your Macintosh stays safe and secure.

The Next Step

This book can't teach you everything there is to know about your Macintosh. Instead, it can give you a solid foundation on which you can learn to use your Macintosh to do actual work. After you get comfortable using your Macintosh on a regular basis, then you can graduate to other books and learn about more advanced features.

Then again, you don't have to learn everything about your Macintosh, because the point of getting a Macintosh is that it helps you get your work done as simply and easily as possible. Once you've accomplished that, learning anything more about your Macintosh may be nice, but it is ultimately irrelevant. You want to spend your time constructively.

Your Macintosh is truly a personal computer because it's flexible enough to meet the needs of rocket scientists and housewives, microbiologists and plumbers, accountants and students, and practically everyone in between. You may never use the features that a computer scientist might need, but your Macintosh will always have those features if you ever need them.

Think of this book as training wheels that give you a gentle push in the right direction—now it's time for you to take off on your own. Don't be afraid of making mistakes. (Remember, you can often undo your last command/mistake by pressing the ⌘-Z keystroke combination.) What makes the Macintosh different from any other computer is that learning how to use it can actually be fun.

Your Macintosh is only a tool. Just as you don't have to learn automotive engineering to drive a car, you shouldn't feel compelled to become a computer expert just to use your Macintosh. As long as you're having fun and being productive in your life, it doesn't really matter how much or how little you know about computers, anyway. All you really need is something that will help you reach your goals, and for most people, that something will always be their Macintosh computer.

INDEX

More No-Nonsense Books from **No Starch Press**

MY NEW™ iPHONE

52 Simple Projects to Get You Started

by WALLACE WANG

This simple, project-oriented book will have you using the best features of your iPhone or iPod Touch in no time. Rather than drag you through some boring manual, *My New iPhone* focuses on individual, fun projects, like configuring multiple email accounts, transferring your music, and syncing your computer with your iPhone.

JULY 2009, 464 PP., $29.95 ($37.95 CDN)
ISBN 978-1-59327-195-4

STEAL THIS™ COMPUTER BOOK 4.0

What They Won't Tell You About the Internet

by WALLACE WANG

This offbeat, non-technical book examines what hackers do, how they do it, and how readers can protect themselves. Informative, irreverent, and entertaining, the completely revised fourth edition of *Steal This Computer Book* contains new chapters that discuss the hacker mentality, lock picking, exploiting P2P filesharing networks, and how people manipulate search engines and pop-up ads. Includes a CD with hundreds of megabytes of hacking and security-related programs that tie in with each chapter of the book.

MAY 2006, 384 PP., $29.95 ($38.95 CDN)
ISBN 978-1-59327-105-3

APPLE CONFIDENTIAL 2.0

The Definitive History of the World's Most Colorful Company

by OWEN W. LINZMAYER

The second edition of this bestseller examines the tumultuous history of America's best-known Silicon Valley start-up, from its legendary founding, through a series of disastrous executive decisions, to its return to profitability, including Apple's move into the music business. This updated and expanded edition is full of juicy quotes, timelines, charts, and photos.

JANUARY 2004, 344 PP., $22.95 ($24.95 CDN)
ISBN 978-1-59327-010-0

THE CULT OF MAC

by LEANDER KAHNEY

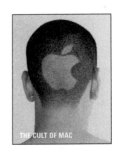

No product on the planet enjoys the devotion of a Macintosh computer. Famously dedicated to their machines, many Mac fans eat, sleep, and breathe Macintosh. In *The Cult of Mac*, *Wired News* managing editor Leander Kahney takes an in-depth look at Mac users and their unique, creative, and often very funny culture. From people who get Mac tattoos and haircuts to those who furnish their apartments out of empty Mac boxes, this book details Mac fandom in all of its forms.

NOVEMBER 2006, 280 PP.
$24.95 (30.95 CDN) ISBN 978-1-886411-83-8 *paperback*
$39.95 (55.95 CDN) ISBN 978-1-59327-122-0 *hardcover*

THE CULT OF iPOD

by LEANDER KAHNEY

The Cult of iPod includes the exclusive backstory of the iPod's development; looks at the many ways iPod users pay homage to their devices; and investigates the quirkier aspects of iPod culture, such as iPod-jacking as well as the growing legions of MP3Js.

NOVEMBER 2005, 160 PP., $24.95 ($33.95 CDN)
ISBN 978-1-59327-066-7

PHONE:
800.420.7240 OR
415.863.9900
MONDAY THROUGH FRIDAY,
9 AM TO 5 PM (PST)

FAX:
415.863.9950
24 HOURS A DAY,
7 DAYS A WEEK

EMAIL:
SALES@NOSTARCH.COM

WEB:
WWW.NOSTARCH.COM

MAIL:
NO STARCH PRESS
555 DE HARO ST, SUITE 250
SAN FRANCISCO, CA 94107
USA

Updates

Visit *http://www.nostarch.com/newmac_leopard.htm* for updates, errata, and other information.

My New Mac, Snow Leopard Edition is set in Avenir. The book was printed and bound at Malloy Incorporated in Ann Arbor, Michigan. The paper is Glatfelter Spring Forge 60# Smooth Eggshell, which is certified by the Sustainable Forestry Initiative (SFI). The book uses a RepKover binding, which allows it to lay flat when open.

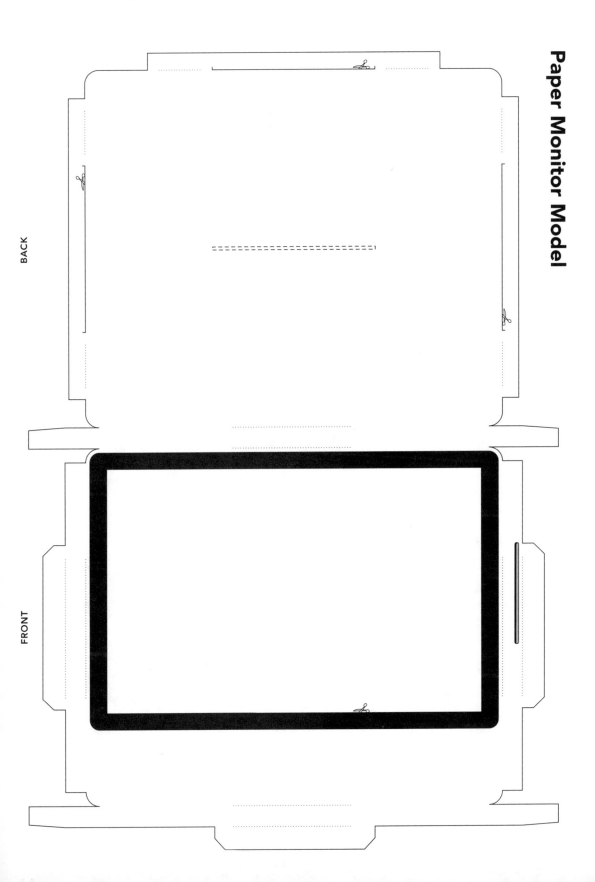

Paper Monitor Model

BACK

FRONT

Monitor Model Instructions

1.   Cut out monitor model.

2.   Cut slits along lines marked with ✀.

3.   Cut slot out of back of monitor (indicated by a dashed line).

4.   Cut out screen.

5.   Fold model on dotted lines.

6.   Build paper base before assembling.

Paper Base Instructions

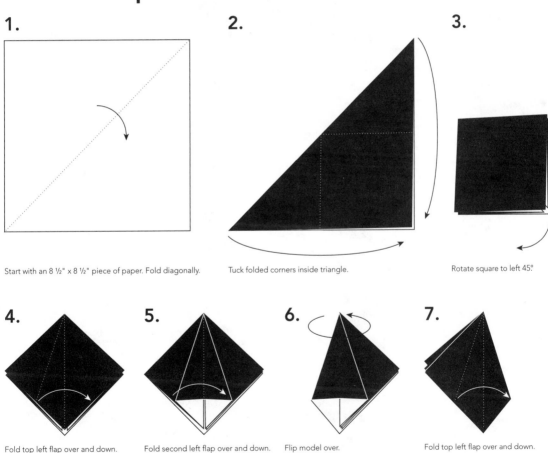

1.

Start with an 8 ½" x 8 ½" piece of paper. Fold diagonally.

2.

Tuck folded corners inside triangle.

3.

Rotate square to left 45°.

4.

Fold top left flap over and down.

5.

Fold second left flap over and down.

6.

Flip model over.

7.

Fold top left flap over and down.

8.

Rotate square. Fold left flap over and down.

9.

There should be four flaps on each side of the model. Fold flaps 4 and 8 toward center.

10.

Fold flap 3 over to the right.

11.

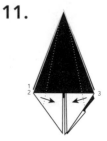

Fold flaps 2 and 3 toward center.

12.

Fold top left flap over to the right.

13.

Flip model over.

14.

Fold flaps 1 and 7 toward center.

15.

Fold flap 6 over to the right.

16.

Fold flaps 5 and 6 toward center.

17.

Fold top right flap over to the left.

18.

Divide model into three sections. Fold top and bottom sections toward each other.

19.

Fold and tuck tip of base underneath bottom.

20.

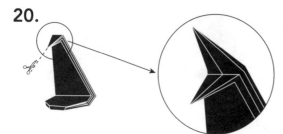

Cut tip horizontally between folds.

Final Assembly Instructions

1.

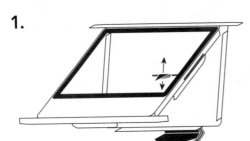

Insert both tips of base into back of monitor model. Fold top tip up and bottom tip down to hold monitor onto base.

2.

Insert screen face into monitor. (Use the face below or create your own design.)

3.

Fold over sides of monitor front. Insert tabs on sides and bottom of front into slits in back of monitor.

4.

Say hello to your paper Mac!

Screen Face

Size: 4 ¼" (W) x 3 ⅝" (H)